UNLIKELY WARRIOR

In my dress uniform in Vienna before departing for Russia.

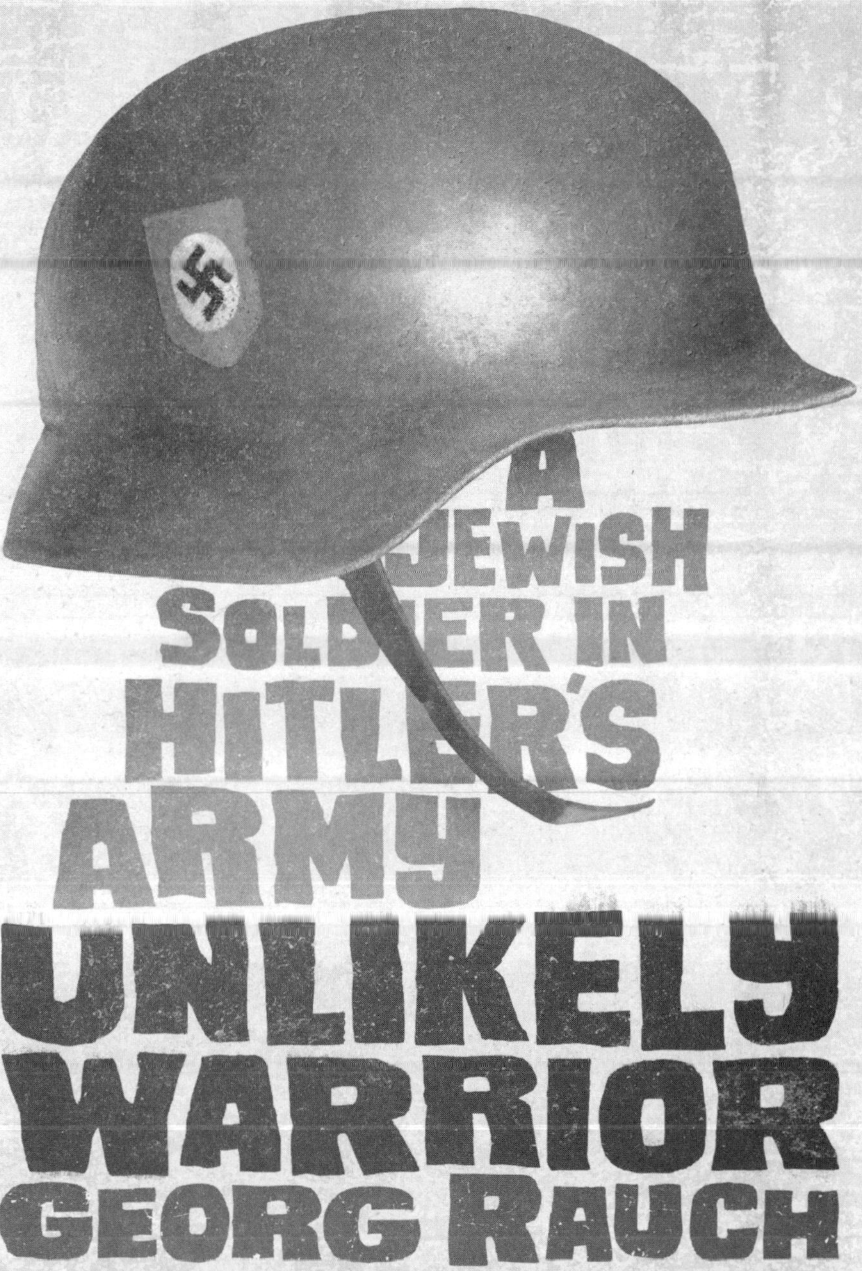

A Jewish Soldier in Hitler's Army

Unlikely Warrior

Georg Rauch

Translated from the German by Phyllis Rauch

* * * * * * * * * * * Farrar Straus Giroux * New York

Farrar Straus Giroux Books for Young Readers
175 Fifth Avenue, New York 10010

First published under the title *The Jew with the Iron Cross: A Record of Survival in WWII Russia*, 2006
Printed in the United States of America
Designed by Andrew Arnold
Revised edition, 2015
3 5 7 9 10 8 6 4 2

macteenbooks.com

Library of Congress Cataloging-in-Publication Data

Rauch, Georg, 1924–2006, author.
Unlikely warrior : a Jewish soldier in Hitler's army / Georg Rauch ; translated from the German by Phyllis Rauch. — Revised edition.
pages cm
Previously published as The Jew with the Iron Cross : a record of survival in WWII Russia. New York : iUniverse, 2006.
ISBN 978-0-374-30142-2 (hardback)
ISBN 978-0-374-30277-1 (trade paperback)
ISBN 978-0-374-30143-9 (e-book)
1. Rauch, Georg, 1924–2006. 2. Jewish soldiers—Austria—Vienna—Juvenile literature. 3. World War, 1939–1945—Prisoners and prisons, Soviet—Juvenile literature. 4. World War, 1939–1945—Personal narratives, Jewish—Juvenile literature. 5. World War, 1939–1945—Participation, Jewish—Juvenile literature. 6. Jewish soldiers—Austria—Vienna. 7. World War, 1939–1945—Prisoners and prisons, Soviet. 8. World War, 1939–1945—Personal narratives, Jewish. 9. World War, 1939–1945—Participation, Jewish. I. Title.

DS135.A93R388 2015
940.54'1343092—dc23

2014041184

Farrar Straus Giroux Books for Young Readers may be purchased for business or promotional use. For information on bulk purchases please contact Macmillan Corporate and Premium Sales Department at (800) 221-7945 x5442 or by email at specialmarkets@macmillan.com.

To Phyllis

For steering me away from mediocrity
and sharing forty years of dreams

CONTENTS

Part One

Part Two

Part Three

LIST OF ILLUSTRATIONS

All drawings by the author are from his wartime letters, unless otherwise noted.

FOREWORD

In 1984, exactly forty years after my husband's Russian experience, he began writing this memoir. A chance event led to Georg's opening the letters that he had written to his mother all those years before. Soon thereafter, Georg left his art studio (a rare event) and began to write. He wrote seven days a week, by hand on yellow legal pads, and read each day's pages to me as we sat on the terrace of our home in Mexico, overlooking Lake Chapala, every afternoon. The next day I translated them into English.

Georg was a total extrovert who loved to laugh and joke. He was a tireless raconteur and easily the center of attention at most social gatherings. Some of his war experiences also figured in his dinner party stories. I had heard the tale related in the early chapter "The Hardest Thing" a number of times before. But the afternoon he read this part of the book aloud to me on the terrace, he began to sob. It may have been the only time I ever saw him cry.

Obviously, the ten years he spent after the war creating expressionist paintings featuring sad men, clowns, and harlequins had not quite achieved the cathartic results he had believed. There were still memories as well as feelings of grief, shame, guilt, and despair to be confronted and dealt with—this time not on a canvas, but in words. Only in retrospect do I understand that Georg's intense days of writing were not just another example of his disciplined nature. He had to get it out. And he had to get it over with.

Had I understood this more fully, I might not have chafed so much under his constant demands to see the English translation. Although I am fluent in German, I purchased two fat German dictionaries in order to deal with a completely new vocabulary, words about battles and weapons, uniforms and ranks. It was slogging, intense work, and sometimes we quarreled when he told me I wasn't translating fast enough. Now, more than thirty years later, I understand much better what was fueling his demands.

Georg sometimes gave an additional explanation for why he wrote the book. Many of his art collectors were Jewish. When we met these people, conversations often led to Georg's history. He sensed that some people were perplexed, or worse, when they heard that he had been in Hitler's army. He said he hoped by writing the book, he could set the record straight. Georg identified as Jewish. He knew and often quoted the fact that Jews adhere to the maternal line—which in his case was unbroken. His family members were treated as second-class citizens, and it was only the fact of his Aryan father's prior war service that kept him and his mother out of the camps.

The book in manuscript form was passed on to scores of friends and visitors to our B&B in Mexico. Many told us that Georg's story needed telling more widely. We finally agreed, and in July of 2006, twenty-two years after he wrote the manuscript, we self-published a first edition of it ourselves. Georg lived another four months, until November.

Seven years later, on the exact date of his passing, I was lighting the candles on my Mexican Day of the Dead altar, when the phone rang. It was my amazing, indefatigable literary agent, Emmanuelle Morgen. I heard her voice for the first time as she said, "I have some news for you." I replied, "It has to be good." Thus I learned that thanks to Emmanuelle, my thirty-year dream had come true. Our book was on its way to the world and the readership it deserved. My affection for my editor, Wesley Adams, began with his wholehearted (and continuing) enthusiasm for Georg's book. I have come to appreciate his perfectionism, but also his willingness to compromise. He is a true gentleman, but best of all, he makes me smile. Could an author be any luckier?

Georg Rauch believed that as long as you could laugh at something, its power to harm you was reduced. In his letters home from Russia, he often tried to find the funny side of things in what were, in reality, very unfunny situations. He takes the same approach in these pages, and the result is a unique tale of one clever, multitalented nineteen-year-old who rose above his situations, put his many wits to use, and survived to tell it all.

—*Phyllis Rauch*

MAJOR EVENTS ON THE EASTERN FRONT

June 22, 1941	Germans launch three-pronged attack on Russia; more than 3 million soldiers and 3,300 tanks cross Russian border; Luftwaffe (German air force) destroys more than 2,000 Russian air force planes.
June 1941	Germans take Minsk and Smolensk (on direct route to Moscow).
September 1941	Kiev falls to the Germans; 650,000 Russian soldiers captured.
November–December 1941	Germans push toward Moscow, come to within 32 kilometers of city before being delayed by order from Hitler.
January 1942	Russians retake Kiev.
May 1942	240,000 Russians captured at Kharkov, in the eastern Ukraine.
August 1942–February 1943	Battle of Stalingrad; bloodiest battle in history, with more than 1.5 million casualties; tide turns in the war.

July 1943 — Largest tank battle in history at Kursk, with about 2,700 German and 4,000 Russian tanks in action; Russians mount counteroffensive, driving German armies back toward their border.

December 1943–July 1944 — Battles for control of the Ukraine intensify.

- *Georg Rauch arrives at front in battle near Znamenka, 240 kilometers southeast of Kiev, December 5.*
- *Eight-day battle at Marianovka, south of Kiev, starting December 15.*
- *Rout of Germans at Pervomaysk, on the river Bug, March 22.*
- *River Dniester crossing and return to front lines, followed by period of quiet, April–July.*

June–August 1944 — German Army Group Center and German Army Group South destroyed in the Ukraine.

July 1944 — Siege on Leningrad lifted; German Army Group North cut off in Baltic.

August 1944 — Romania defeated, becomes Russian ally.

- *Georg Rauch receives Iron Cross following attack, mid-August.*
- *Georg Rauch captured following second Russian attack, August 23.*

May 7, 1945 — Germany surrenders.

Rostock
Gdansk
Szczecin
POLAND
BERLIN
GERMANY
Poznan
Warsaw
Lódz
Vistula
Elbe River
Radom
Dresden
Wroclaw
Lubli
Prague
Katowice
Kraków
CZECHOSLOVAKIA
Brno
Krumau
Linz
Wels
Enns
Marchegg
Mondsee
Vöcklabruck
Vienna
Salzburg
AUSTRIA
Budapest
Danube River
HUNGARY
ZAGREB
YUGOSLAVIA

CAMPAIGNS AND CAPTIVITY
0
50
100
200
300km
LITHUANIA
Minsk
Berezina River
Dnieper River
Brèst
Pripyat Marsh
SOVIET UNION
Bug River
KIEV
Zhytomyr
L'viv
Cherkassy
Alexandrovka
Vinnytsya
Panchevo
Znamenka
Mala Vyska
Kirovograd
Dniester River
Southern Bug
Balta
Slobodka
Birsula
Pervomaysk
Marmarossziget
Balti
Prut River
Tiraspol
Mykolayiv
Iasi
Kishinev
Odessa
ROMANIA
Galatz
Braila
Black Sea

PROLOGUE

Our right hands stiffly raised, we repeated the words of the oath as they were pronounced: "And I solemnly swear to defend *Führer*, *Volk*, and *Vaterland* . . ."

The morning of February 26, 1943, was bitter cold. Individual ice crystals dropped silently from the leaden, low-lying sky. It was too cold to snow.

On a large barracks parade ground just outside Vienna, six hundred teenagers stood at attention, three abreast in a long column. We must have looked like oversized tin soldiers placed there for some child's fantasy. Our boot heels were squeezed together; left palms were pressed to the seams of our trousers; chests were puffed out, stomachs sucked in, eyes staring straight ahead. We were smartly outfitted in the parade uniforms of the German Wehrmacht.

The German soldier, Prussia's pride and invention, was expected to be "tough as leather, hard as Krupp steel, and fleet as a greyhound," but after only three weeks of basic training, we weren't exactly the perfect prototypes.

I can imagine that had he been there, Hitler wouldn't have been very gratified to catch sight of me, since I definitely didn't conform to his ideal type. I measured only five feet ten inches tall, and my hair was a wild tangle of black curls. My eyes looked green or gray, depending upon the light, and the rest of my features were decidedly non-Aryan. My physique boasted no broad shoulders or other impressive details, though I was slim and well-built for my size.

On this particular day my large and curving nose was also red and runny, and my head was aching under the unaccustomed weight of the heavy iron helmet. My thoughts were no less heavy either. It wasn't one of the happier moments of my young life.

The small group of German officers administering the oath stood facing us on the snow-covered ground. Oberstleutnant Kraus, the commanding officer of the communications training section, had just completed his speech, raving about the inevitable victory of the German forces over capitalism and communism.

We were all aware that Stalingrad had fallen and that Allied bombers were making cocky daylight raids on major German cities. I don't believe any of us expected the outcome of the war could be changed by a miracle such as the Wunderwaffe, Hitler's long-promised mystery missile that would ensure Germany's victory. Inevitably, the ever more powerful Allied forces would finally bring Germany to its knees.

Oberstleutnant Kraus, evidently having refused to recognize these facts, reminded us of our duty and described in glowing terms how thrilling it would be when we finally got the chance to split a Russian skull with our spades.

The military band played "Deutschland, Deutschland über Alles," and small clouds of steam from the musical instruments drifted skyward. A review company presented arms. As we were repeating the last words of the oath ("to defend

Führer, Volk, and Vaterland, unto the death") I noticed that two of the soldiers ahead of me had the index and middle fingers of their left hands crossed, just the way I did. I hoped that none of the officers were patrolling behind us, recording for future punishment the names of those taking refuge in that ancient childhood trick. We were adolescents, still playing at the game of war, but after just a few more months of training we would be expected to perform as men, to take the lives of strangers, on command, unquestioningly.

PART 1

Marching to battle

SECRETS IN THE ATTIC

I shined my boots to a mirror finish and polished my belt buckle. Then I rubbed gasoline on a tiny grease spot I had noticed on my uniform jacket. I was nervous. The other soldiers in the room had no idea of what I intended, why I was making such a fuss over my appearance when we were only scheduled to attend rifle practice on the shooting range.

My heart thumping faster than usual, I left the barracks at five minutes before nine and marched across the enormous exercise grounds toward one of the administration buildings. The November fog hung in the leafless chestnut trees; a bell in one of the neighboring churches began to toll the hour.

I had an appointment with the division commander, Oberstleutnant Poppinger, a man distinguished by his red nose swollen from French cognac and the gleaming Iron Cross that always hung around his fat neck. Considering what a tiny cog I represented in the gears of the huge German military machine, my request to see Poppinger was somewhat similar to demanding an audience with God himself.

At 9:00 a.m. on November 10, 1943, I stood in front of Poppinger's desk, facing both him and the large portrait of Adolf Hitler that hung on the wall at his back. My boot heels clicked smartly together, my right hand snapped a lightning salute to the edge of my cap, and, in the overloud voice decreed by the German army, I yelled at Poppinger, "Funker Rauch reporting, sir!"

"At ease. And what does he have on his mind?" Poppinger lounged behind his desk, regarding me with an expression that could almost be described as benevolent.

Thereupon I bellowed the sentence that I had been framing in my mind for weeks. "Funker Rauch wishes to be permitted to report that he cannot be an officer in the German Wehrmacht."

With an astonished, almost idiotic expression on his face, the lieutenant colonel sputtered, "Are you crazy? Did I hear you correctly?"

"*Jawohl, Herr Oberstleutnant!*"

Poppinger, who was almost a head taller than I, stood up. His face was becoming crimson. He came around the desk to stand directly in front of me and snarled, "We decide who will be an officer in the German Wehrmacht. Whoever refuses to serve his fatherland as an officer, once we have deemed him acceptable, is a traitor."

Turning toward the door where the orderly was standing, he said, as though seeking support, "The man isn't in his right mind. Denial of his abilities to serve his country as an officer—that's high treason!"

By this time, his voice had risen almost to a screech. With a visible attempt to regain control of himself, he returned to his chair, sat down, took a drink of water, and continued in a more factual tone, "I demand an explanation."

Again I clicked my heels together. As though charged by an electric shock, I pressed my hands flat against my thighs and shouted once again, "I don't feel able to become an officer in the German army because I have Jewish blood."

Poppinger sprang up, his face almost purple, and blurted out, "What did he say?"

"I have a Jewish grandmother."

"*Mensch*, how did you get here in the first place? Jewish grandmother! You must be completely mad."

He motioned the orderly to his side and, after a few whispered sentences, turned again to me and said simply, "Dismissed."

The orderly took me to his office, where I explained in a considerably calmer atmosphere that I had included the fact of my having a Jewish ancestor in the personal data I had submitted when I was drafted. He dismissed me then, and I returned to my barracks.

When I reentered my room, it was empty. The bunk beds were all perfectly spread. The straw mattresses had been shaken; on each bed two gray blankets were folded as though with a measuring tape and carefully laid over the rough, tightly stretched sheets, and all pillows were positioned in exactly the correct spot at the exact specified angle. The smell of Lysol was pervasive.

I had no idea what would happen next as a result of my interview with Poppinger; nonetheless, I felt relieved. I climbed up to my bunk and stretched out, deciding to enjoy the unexpected bonus of a few free hours to myself until the rest of my bunkmates returned from exercises.

Lying there, I reviewed the events of my military existence up until now. How utterly hopeless I had felt the day that a draft notice finally appeared in our mailbox! Though I was used to enjoying the deep, dreamless sleep of the young, that night I lay awake for long hours thinking of where I could hide myself so I would not have to become a German soldier.

I knew it was hopeless. Hadn't I already gnawed at the problem for a whole year while pedaling my bicycle hundreds of kilometers through the Austrian Alps? That perfect place where I could be taken in, fed, and kept warm and safe while all of Europe tried to annihilate itself did not, unfortunately, exist.

On one of those summer trips in the Austrian Alps, still hoping to find a way to evade the draft.

Regardless of where I might turn up in my civilian clothes, as an obviously healthy young man I would immediately be asked for my papers. Men between the ages of eighteen and sixty and out of uniform were practically nonexistent. World War II had snatched up every man who might possibly be able to carry a weapon.

On the day I reported for duty to the *Kaserne* (barracks) in Vienna, I filled out all the forms, listing my education in a technical school as well as six years of instruction in French and my hobbies, such as radio building. I also indicated my familiarity with Morse code, at that time the only means of wireless communication.

As a result, the Germans permitted me to choose the branch of service I preferred. I chose the infantry, thereby proving my complete idiocy as far as my friends and family members were concerned. After all, most other branches of the service were cleaner and more comfortable: the air force, the navy, and even the tank corps.

Although I was well aware that soldiers in the infantry had to endure great hardships, my instinctive decision was based on one essential fact: in an all-out war such as this one, I didn't want to be caught sitting helplessly in any kind of iron box, expecting it to explode from a grenade, torpedo, or mine hit. The ground, where a fellow could run or hide, seemed a lot more secure to me. If I could dig fast enough and deep enough, I still might have a chance, if worse came to worst.

The camp on the outskirts of Vienna where I received my basic training as a telegraphist, or *Funker*, was an ugly complex of three-storied gray buildings that looked as though they hadn't been painted or renovated since the days of the monarchy. We sweated through most of our first weeks on the parade ground, mastering the fine art of Prussian drilling from dawn to sunset.

Soon we were so well-trained that we carried out most commands more or less automatically, and we began to spend more time on our specialization: the installation and use of shortwave sets and telephones. The training came easily to me, as I enjoyed anything having to do with electrical apparatus.

My transition from playful adolescent to disciplined soldier was far from simple, though. The offspring of doctors and architects, I had grown up with the assurance that my opinion would always be heard and at least considered. I found it particularly difficult, therefore, to follow orders that often seemed illogical, serving only to produce a completely submissive subject who could be depended upon to obey without the slightest objection. One of our training officer's favorite sayings was "Leave the thinking to the horses. They have larger heads."

On three separate occasions I was locked up for minor offenses: failure to salute an officer, unauthorized absence from the barracks, and going back to bed while the others were out huffing and puffing on the drill grounds. But something a little more serious occurred during one of our weekly field exercises.

That lovely May morning, two companies from my camp took the red and white Viennese streetcars to a small mountain north of the city, the Bisamberg. Carrying our spades and rifles, bedecked with all the other equipment and gadgets, and wearing our gas masks, we were hounded, sweating and panting, up one side of the mountain. On the summit, without even having had a chance to catch our breath, those of us in Company Red were ordered to begin fighting Company Blue, which came rushing at us from the opposite side.

Through beautiful spring meadows filled with tender flowers and grasses reaching to our hips, we stormed the other company's position, fell back, and attacked again. Back and forth we went, bullied by constant shouts of "Hit the dirt! Get up! Crawl! Attack!" until noon, when we flopped down, exhausted, to wait for the next assault command.

We lay there in the high grass, spaced about thirty feet apart. The powder smoke from the last blank cartridges had drifted away and was slowly being replaced by the heady aromas of the flowers and the damp spring earth. The pause lengthened, and still the order didn't come, so I decided to make myself a little more comfortable.

Detaching a few pieces of equipment and placing them to one side, I opened my shirt and let the sun dry my perspiration. I gulped thirstily from my canteen, chewed a piece of bread. Honeybees buzzed among the flowers. Ladybugs crept to the ends of the blades of grass and jumped into flight. I sank back into the meadow and, breathing in the soothing springtime smells, promptly fell asleep.

The *rat-tat-tat* of machine-gun fire and a painful jab in the ribs jolted me awake.

"*Mensch*, what are you doing here?" yelled an angry voice. "Didn't you hear the command to attack? Do you need a personal written order to get your lazy ass into motion?"

Through my sleep-fuzzed eyes I could see a black boot in the process of aiming a second, more vigorous blow to my side. The angry face above it belonged to the officer in charge of the entire maneuver.

The shots and shouts of the attackers rang out quite clearly but were already some distance away. Here I lay on my back in the warm sun; under the circumstances, I would have been expected to spring to my feet and begin attempting to justify my most awkward situation.

Defying all the rules, still flat on my back, I cracked my heels together, threw my hand to my forehead in salute, and yelled up to the oberleutnant, "Funker Rauch died for Führer, Folk, and Fatherland!"

Where there's a war, there have to be dead bodies, I reasoned, but I watched carefully and with considerable unease the face looming above me. Suddenly I had visions of being sent to prison, drilling until I fell over dead, or, at the very least, peeling potatoes into eternity.

Heaven only knows what thoughts must have passed through that Prussian brain during the endless seconds, until I spied a barely perceptible twitch in the left corner of his mouth, and he said, "When the troops pass this way again shortly, would you be so kind as to rise from the dead and fall in once more as a full, able-bodied soldier?"

"*Jawohl!*" I shouted up from my still supine position.

A few weeks later, at the beginning of our fourth month of training, Oberstleutnant Kraus, the officer in charge of the camp, put in an unexpected appearance when we fell in for the morning roll call. He exchanged a few words with our captain, handed him a piece of paper, and then left the parade ground.

The captain turned to address us. "The following soldiers are to take two steps forward as I call out their names." He began to shout, "Funker Sperling, Funker Magdeburger, Funker Zoellner, Funker Rauch . . ."

I stepped forward as commanded, wondering which of the many rules I had broken now. As the list of names grew longer, I comforted myself with the rationalization that all of these soldiers couldn't have done something wrong. There was a total of forty names.

With other recruits at training camp in Austria. I am at far right.

"Those whose names I have called are to return immediately to their barracks, pack up, and report to Barracks

Number 28. You are hereby assigned to the course for communications officers and raised to the status of officer candidate. Dismissed."

After all my misdeeds, how was it possible that I was now supposed to become an officer? The news was a complete surprise, and my feelings were mixed, to say the least. At any rate, this change would entail continued months of training in the hinterland, away from any front. I even entertained a faint hope that the war might be over before I could be sent into action. Best of all, I would still be close to home and could call almost every day.

My great awakening came a few months later, in August of 1943. Halfway through the officers' course, 80 percent of us received the order to report immediately to Brno, Czechoslovakia, some 150 kilometers north of Vienna. We were being removed from our communications course and transferred to one for training regular infantry officers.

The reason for this was straightforward. The losses of men and matériel in the battle for Russia were proving to be enormous. More than one and a half million Germans had already been killed, wounded, or listed as missing. Infantry officers were needed desperately, and now I was to become one—supposedly capable of ordering hundreds of men to attack and of screaming with conviction those commands that would send them to their deaths.

After two brief days with my parents, I found myself on the train to Brno. Although it had gradually seeped into my consciousness during the preceding months that I was actually a soldier in the German army, until now somehow I hadn't taken the whole thing seriously. Those training months had been spent in Vienna, the city of my childhood; I had still been at home, in a manner of speaking.

This trip in an express train, however, was carrying me away from my familiar territory. My youth was slipping away along with the city that was disappearing on the opposite side of the Danube. I was on the verge of being swallowed by this monster of a senseless war.

When I had been drafted at nineteen, I had been very naive. I had adopted a negative attitude toward Hitler's war and dictatorship from my parents, without any particular soul-searching on my part. All men were expected to become soldiers, and I had observed that the majority of them submitted to the inevitable and did what they were ordered to do just well enough so as not to give offense.

But to be an officer, that was something else again. Now they would expect me to be responsible for many others, to use my brain for receiving and passing on orders intended to win a war that, in my opinion, should be lost as soon as possible so that the survivors could go home again. It was illogical and idiotic that I, a quarter-Jew and therefore a citizen with limited rights, should have been selected for this "honor."

I was slow to recognize the possibility that I might be able to put in a veto. The closer I came to the Czech city where the officers' training course was to take place, the more determined I became. *Somehow*, I would get out of that training camp, and I would not become an infantry officer!

By the time of my meeting with Poppinger, the weeks in the camp at Brno had turned into months, and still I hadn't managed to convince those in charge of my unsuitability. First, I had tried to act dull, but nobody bought that. Then

I simulated illnesses and physical weakness, but the strenuous training had turned my young body into a healthy bundle of pure muscle. Now, almost at the end of the course, I had made my appointment with Poppinger.

The day following that meeting I learned the consequences. Not surprisingly, I had been dropped from the officers' course and was ordered to frontline duty as a simple foot soldier, albeit with special training as a telegraphist.

On November 11, my mother came to the train station in the small medieval town of Krumau on the Austrian-Czechoslovakian border to say goodbye. Central Europe isn't famous for its sunshine at any season, but November is the grayest month of all. The trees have dropped their last remaining leaves, it rains most of the time, and a damp fog draws the sky down almost to the ground.

During a warmer season in better times, the ancient walled city, with its gabled houses and lovely churches, would have been a pleasant destination for a Sunday outing. But on this damp, cold morning, in the fifth year of a merciless war, Krumau was only a gray silhouette behind the freight depot, the perfect somber background for possibly the last words that a son and mother would ever exchange.

Beatrix Rauch, or *Mutti* (Mother), as I called her, was a strong woman in every sense of the word. She was of medium height and slim, but sturdy and wiry, thanks to a great amount of hard work. Her face was slightly asymmetrical because a case of meningitis had paralyzed a few of the muscles around her right eye, but both eyes shone with warmth and a sensitive intelligence. She always smelled faintly of lavender because of the dried blossoms lying in crocheted bits of wool among her clothing in the dresser drawers.

Although my mother came into the world in Vienna in 1889 with the privileges of an aristocrat and spent her first twenty-five years in all the luxury that the nobility enjoyed at that time, her personality was actually formed during the following decades by the events taking place around her. World War I and the resultant fall of the Austro-Hungarian Empire took away her title and her wealth. As a Red Cross volunteer, she obtained firsthand experience of war and of the suffering and death of soldiers.

During the inflation and depression years of the twenties and thirties, she was a young married woman with two children. She spent most of her time trying to refashion our rags into presentable clothing and helping my father with the countless jobs and activities he pursued in an effort to earn enough money for our survival.

At the end of the depression Hitler entered Austria, and with him came new suffering and desperation for those, such as my mother, who were opposed to his regime. Considering the general atmosphere of evil and suppression, it must have been a most difficult time to raise a child, but my mother was untiring in teaching my sister and me the delicate values of true culture versus materialism and brutality.

During these years, diversions were rare. There was no thought of travel to foreign lands or even trips to the other end of our own small country. Once in a great while, we managed to scrape together something extra for a theater or concert ticket, but most music or other entertainment was provided by a small radio. We did go on outings in the Vienna Woods, carrying a thermos of tea and some slices of brown bread spread with lard. There in the woods and meadows surrounding Vienna, as well as in the city's many free museums and in our own home, we learned from her, directly and by example, what it means to be a decent human being.

I learned another lesson on the streets of Vienna. In the year I turned fourteen, cheering multitudes had welcomed the Germans when they came marching into Austria, and shortly thereafter the streets had begun sprouting National Socialist propaganda.

My mother, Baroness Beatrix von Wieser, at seventeen.

Mutti and me, Christmas of 1933.

One day my mother and I were walking down a Viennese avenue spanned by enormous banners bearing Nazi slogans. She stopped in front of one of these, where letters five feet high proclaimed, "Might comes before Right!" Glancing up and down the almost empty street, she turned to me and said, "Do you understand what those words mean?"

"No," I answered, feeling somehow guilty and a little frightened.

Her expression of suppressed anger and disgust had become more and more familiar of late. "That banner means that he who has the power is automatically in the right. Our current rulers intend to determine what that 'right' is. Do you understand that no civilized or humane person can accept such a philosophy?"

At the time I had but a vague understanding of what she was trying to tell me, realizing only that it was an idea very important to her. In the intervening years, however, she had made her point of view—her complete opposition to Hitler and all he represented—very clear.

That last morning, at the train station in Krumau, my mother and I walked back and forth for half an hour on the platform. None of the hundreds of soldiers sitting on straw in the cattle cars waiting to depart had any idea where the trip would end or whether they would ever return. It must have been obvious to most of them that their chances were slim at best. All one had to do was count up how many friends and relatives had been reported killed or missing in action during the past four years—that is, if they hadn't returned home as cripples.

I was very impressed by two of the things my mother said to me that morning. I thought the first seemed easy enough to understand. She said, "Please remember something in the days to come. In case you don't return, I won't go completely to pieces. I will continue to live a full life, no matter what."

To some this might sound strange, even cold, but with her words I could feel a great burden lifted from my shoulders, the burden of having to survive out there for my mother's sake.

I wasn't to understand her second remark until much later. She said, just as the train slowly started to move and I leaned down to give her a last kiss, "And remember, what doesn't kill you makes you stronger."

The train picked up speed steadily. By sticking my head out the sliding door of the boxcar, I could still see my mother, a slight, pale figure in a threadbare winter coat standing alone next to the tracks, her arm held motionless in the air.

Finally, she disappeared in the chilly morning fog. I knew that soon she would be on her way back to the town square, walking with that typical hurried step. She would be rushing to catch the next bus back to Vienna, for after all, the Jews hidden in the attic had to be fed and cared for, and life must go on.

THE JOURNEY EAST

The train rumbled through the night. We had taken two days to cross Czechoslovakia and Poland, with innumerable stops along the way. By now it had become all too clear that we were not heading for sunny Italy or a quiet duty in Scandinavia. No, our destination obviously had to be the most gruesome and life-consuming front of all—the Russian trenches.

In Czechoslovakia the train had passed through tidy little villages and towns. An occasional castle or fortress was perched on a hillside; country roads wandered here and there. We crossed a chain of mountains, and the landscape became flatter and increasingly dismal. Now we were traveling through western Russia on our way east.

Thirty men of all ages, dressed in the gray German infantry uniform, lay on the straw-covered floor of each of the boxcars. Most of them were either asleep or simply lying and thinking about what lay ahead. Each had his own story to tell, why and for the how-many-eth time he was on his way to the front. I doubted that many, if any, of my companions were eager to arrive at our destination, but perhaps some of them still cherished some sort of patriotic convictions? Well, I certainly didn't share any of them.

I missed my training buddies of the past months and wondered whether I had anything in common with these strangers. So far, there had been no such indication. I spent most of my time in the corner, thinking over some of the unusual events of the past years and preferring to ignore the future.

The house where I grew up wasn't one of the typical Viennese four- or five-story apartment buildings. My family lived on the top floor of a small *Stadtpalais*. It was one of a series of elegant mid-nineteenth-century buildings originally constructed to house individual families of the nobility. In our home, three large rooms had been constructed as an afterthought beneath the baroque copper roof. These rooms were fitted in among the attic storage areas, which were also generously proportioned but very irregularly shaped.

My *Tante* (aunt) Herta, who owned the building together with her daughter, son-in-law, and three grandsons, inhabited the floors below. We were all distantly related through my Jewish grandmother, Melanie Wieser, who had died before I was born, but no one in the house was a practicing Jew.

I had never had any reason to be particularly interested in my forefathers until a day shortly after the German takeover in Austria, when I came home from school and announced, "Tomorrow I have to take birth certificates and baptismal records of my four grandparents to school."

"What for?" my mother wanted to know.

"Oh, it's just something they have to check before accepting us into the Hitler Youth. They are going to give us all uniforms and special knives, and we're going to go camping in the woods on the weekends."

My mother stood there looking at me for a few moments. Then she went into the other room and returned holding a photo album.

Baron Moses von Hönigsberg (1787–1875). Son of Israel von Hönigsberg, who was the first Austrian Jew to be knighted, by Kaiser Josef II in 1789.

Luise Tauber (1824–1894), born Baroness von Hönigsberg. She was Moses's daughter and my great-grandmother.

Luise Tauber and Josef Samuel Tauber.

Melanie Tauber with her two sisters, Luise and Henriette, at Professor Eisenmanger's art school in Vienna.

My grandmother Melanie Amalie Tauber (1854–1908) at sixteen, in Vienna.

Melanie Tauber Wieser with my mother, Beatrix Wieser, in 1891.

"Come and sit down next to me," she said. "I want to explain something to you."

She opened the album and pointed to a small photo of an oil portrait. "This man was Baron Moses von Hönigsberg. His father was knighted by Kaiser Josef II in 1789. This is Moses's daughter, Luise Tauber, born Baroness von Hönigsberg. She was your great-grandmother."

There were many other pictures, all of extremely distinguished-looking persons, many of whom were in fancy uniforms. My mother told me about the positions of influence they had held during the monarchy and for what special deeds and services the Kaiser had raised them to the ranks of the nobility.

"All these I have shown you were your ancestors, and they were Jews. You have every right to be proud of them, and I hope you will never forget that. The reason you were asked to bring those official papers to school tomorrow is because they want to know whether you are a pure Aryan. That is, they want you to prove you have no Jewish blood. As you have just seen, you will be unable to do that."

My thoughts were in a muddle. I was impressed with what she had shown me but also upset at the thought of becoming an outcast at fourteen.

"Well, what am I then?" I asked her.

"According to the traditions of our Jewish ancestors, you are a Jew, because your maternal grandmother was Jewish. In Hitler's rulebook, though, a Jew who marries a non-Jew produces half-Jews. Since my father and your father's family are Aryan, that makes you one-quarter Jewish, according to the Führer. Hitler has even coined a special word for people such as ourselves. One-half and one-quarter Jews are now called *Mischlinge.* I hope this isn't going to make too many problems for you, but it's something you'll just have to get used to."

During the following months it wasn't all that easy for me to come to terms with my new status, or lack of one. I noticed that a number of my schoolmates began turning their backs on me, and even two or three of my teachers effectively ignored me. More and more of the boys my age were wearing the black corduroy shorts and brown shirts of the Hitler Youth and filling their free time with marching and practicing premilitary exercises. They appeared by the thousands at sports events and were also a common sight in the streets, their collection cans emblazoned with the letters *WHW*, which stood for *Winterhilfswerk*. No one was apt to challenge this claim of "winter help for the needy" or to ask where the large amounts of money collected actually went.

In one strange respect, my family turned out to have an advantage over many others. My father, Maximilian Rauch, had served as a captain in World War I and was called up for service again in 1939. Two days later, he was sent back home. The Germans could not permit a man who was married to a half-Jew to be a captain in the German army. Since my father had served honorably, however, they could not demote him to a lower rank. This strange set of bureaucratic circumstances led to the ironic result that he didn't have to go to war at all; instead, he was assigned work as an engineer in a tool factory, Krause and Co.

Papi, 1926.

I had two friends who shared my non-Aryan status, and we often took bicycle trips to the woods and mountains. I also began spending more time alone, tinkering or painting little watercolors. I passed many hours simply dreaming about the fantastic projects I would someday complete. My mind, which I began to visualize as a chest of many drawers filled with unbelievable treasures, became my very best friend of all.

* * *

The eastbound train screeched to a halt, and I shook myself unwillingly from my reverie. Walter Haas, the soldier next to me, stood up, opened the sliding door, and looked out. He then announced to all and sundry, "Halt of indefinite period. Probably waiting for approaching train. You can barter for food. Vodka, too."

With that he jumped down onto the embankment, where a dozen Russian women were standing next to a ramshackle signalman's hut. Various-sized baskets filled with food hung over their arms, and they peered at us appraisingly from under their drab knitted shawls.

Private First Class Haas, who had spent the previous days sitting next to me either snoring or drinking vodka, was already inspecting the wares being offered. He was a pro and knew all the prices. It was his third trip to the front in as many years. Until now we had exchanged only a few words with each other, but he impressed me as one familiar with all the tricks of making war and, more important, of survival.

As I came up beside him he began extolling the goods of the Russian women, just like an experienced carnival barker: "Step right up! Here we have eggs, potatoes, bacon, hard bread, dried cherries, and bottles of booze!"

I wandered over to watch a soldier unloading his old wristwatch on a Russian train official. Then I heard Haas calling, "Hey, Rauch. Come back over here for a minute."

One of the women was holding up a fat goose. "Are you in the mood for roast goose?" Haas asked, rubbing his stomach suggestively. "Maybe we can bargain her down together."

He nudged the woman with his elbow and looked at her questioningly. She traced the number 30 with the toe of her boot in the damp earth.

"You're crazy." He laughed and turned to walk away. She reached out to grab hold of his sleeve and scratched a 25 in the dirt.

"Still too much," Haas replied.

Without letting go of his sleeve, she pointed at my colorful neck scarf.

"Hmmm, that would be a good bargain, if you're willing to part with it. If it doesn't have any sentimental value for you, 'farewell from my girl in Vienna,' and all that." He grinned and added, "I'll buy the next goose."

It was a very fat bird. We roasted it in pieces on the heavily smoking iron stove that was bolted to the floor in our boxcar and stuffed ourselves for two days, washing down the grease with the vodka that Haas had managed to barter for just as the train pulled out.

In the process, we became closer. We had greasy hands, faces blackened from the coal smoke, and dirty, fat-smeared uniforms, but the depressing atmosphere of the trip had diminished considerably.

On the second day of our new friendship, after a last satisfying burp, Haas asked, "Are you worried about all the crap that's waiting for us at the end of the line?"

I shrugged and answered, "Nobody's ever shot at me before."

"Well, take a look at me." With that he rolled up a shirt-sleeve. "I've already been three years with the firm"—his word for the German army—"always right up at the front where things are the hairiest. They must have shot a good six tons of gunpowder at me, and that's all they've managed to achieve so far."

He pointed to a three-inch scar on his forearm. "Not every bullet finds a target," he said, clapping me good-naturedly on the shoulder.

Haas was a broadly built and very sturdy fellow. His face was round and congenial but also filled with peasant cleverness and with the lines etched by the past three years of cold, heat, hunger, and proximity to the dead and dying. Even the most hard-bitten Nazi couldn't have held it against him when he declared at every opportunity, with the charm of a first-class comedian, that the firm, for reasons known only to him, was on the verge of bankruptcy. That's why he had already sold off all his stocks and bonds.

One evening, when the rain had been hammering away for hours on the top of our car, I asked him, "Are there any Germans who cross over to the Russians—who defect?"

"I don't know of any," he answered, gazing into my eyes a few seconds longer than necessary. "In a few days, when you are lying in a hole in the ground and they come toward you in their filthy overcoats, their Mongolian eyes filled with hate, yelling that horrible '*hurrreee*' at the top of their lungs, then you'll understand why no one has any particular desire to go over to them. There aren't any representatives of the International Red Cross with rest homes in the mountains on their side. They want just one thing: to squash us into a pulp, because we have occupied their country."

When I listened to Haas talking like this, I felt as though I were being instructed by a member of the older generation, but actually he was barely three years older than I was. His descriptions of what lay ahead weren't pleasant, but there was now no turning back, so I began trying to accustom myself to the situation.

It's difficult at nineteen to stay depressed and frightened for long periods, especially when the future is such an unknown quantity. Back home I had become familiar with the dangers of Nazi Austria and learned how to avoid them. Probably it wouldn't be long before I became as clever as Haas in dealing with whatever Russia had to offer.

My concerns about my mother weren't so easy to shake off, though. I wondered how much longer she would be able to continue her underground activities without being detected. Even now I couldn't quite understand how she had become so deeply involved.

During the first three years of the war, the German military victories and Hitler's successful economic policies had enraptured legions of Austrians. Those positive developments had assuredly helped blind them to the fact that the Gestapo's grip was also becoming stronger. More and more of the Jewish population began disappearing to faraway work camps, and nothing further was heard from them.

In January 1940, my aunt Dora Breuer jumped from her fifth-story window in the Doroteergasse when the Gestapo came to pick her up. During that same month, at two o'clock one morning, my mother's best friend, Herta Dressler, appeared at our door and asked if she could hide in our attic. She had just managed to slip out of the Gestapo's grasp by climbing over a neighbor's balcony and sliding down a shed roof. She arrived with only the clothes on her back.

I didn't see her until the next morning, when she came through the attic door and disappeared into the bathroom.

"What's Haday [as we called her] doing in our attic?" I asked my mother, who was preparing breakfast.

Calling my older sister, Vroni, from her room, my mother explained to both of us, "The Gestapo is looking for Haday, and we must hide her in the attic for the time being."

"Why did she come here?" I wanted to know.

"We are the only friends with whom she feels completely safe. No one must know she is here, not the others in the house, not our friends, no one! If anybody else finds out about her presence here, we will all be picked up."

I liked Haday. She was a pleasant-looking woman, about forty years of age, with dark, curly hair and a pale, very Jewish-looking face. During the past couple of years she had come often to our house as a Latin tutor for my sister.

I was sixteen at the time, and I accepted this change in our household without thinking much about it. There were so many exciting or upsetting things happening every day, what with the constant reports from the fronts, the news that one acquaintance or another had been killed or wounded, the rationing of everything down to the simplest consumer articles. Above everything else, there was the constant mental bombardment of Reichsminister Goebbels's propaganda spurring the population on to even greater enthusiasm and achievements in the factories.

My father repaired the broken glass in the small attic window, and in one corner I helped him construct a makeshift bed from three-piece horsehair mattresses to accommodate our new guest. We also installed a light with an old yellowed lampshade and covered the small window with black paper. That was about the extent of his active involvement. It seemed to me that, for the most part, my father simply put up with the new situation.

My eighteen-year-old sister was quite occupied at the time with her fiancé, who, just to make things a bit more complicated, happened to be a lieutenant in the German army and was often a guest in our apartment.

As it turned out, Haday's hasty arrival was just the beginning. In the following weeks and months an older couple arrived, followed by a Jewish carpenter and others. I remember the carpenter the most vividly, because it was he who built the complicated false walls into the attic behind which our guests could disappear whenever it was necessary.

The old couple had owned a jewelry store and brought a number of valuable pieces with them. For the Jews already hidden and those who were to follow, it became customary to place their possessions into my mother's hands for management. She then took up the task of feeding and clothing everyone.

I had mixed feelings about one task that fell to me, that of taking some of the money that my mother received for selling our secret guests' valuables and exchanging it for food coupons on the black market. The chance always existed that others involved in this illegal activity could be doing undercover work for the Gestapo. But my mother ordered me to do this, and there was no discussion. It was a time of parental authority, and the thought of refusing to do something because it was unpleasant or even dangerous simply wasn't considered.

I had come to understand that although I was a citizen with limited rights, for the full Jews it was a much harder time. With that, the question was settled, as far as I was concerned. It even seemed rather romantic to me when I discovered that my mother sometimes slipped out of the house after midnight with one or another of our visitors to rendezvous with unsavory characters who promised, for high prices, to smuggle the Jews through Hungary to Yugoslavia or Bulgaria. From there they hoped to make it into neutral Turkey and then to London or the United States.

I helped my mother prepare miniature travel kits, which included a small collapsible Sterno stove, a cup, a spoon, needles, some thread, paper and pencil, and a large traced map of the area through which the refugees would be traveling.

It was also during my seventeenth year that I began building complicated alarm systems throughout the apartment as a safety device against the sudden arrival of unexpected official visitors. The materials for these came from the basement laboratory of Tante Herta Jaeger's husband, a well-known physicist and professor at the University of Vienna, who had died three or four years previously. Since none of his own children or grandchildren had shown any interest in the piles of equipment and electrical apparatus that he left behind, I had been given permission to use whatever I wished.

During the months following this windfall, I taught myself to put simple radios together. At first it was very difficult, but as my knowledge and technical abilities increased, the quality of the radios improved and I even taught myself to build a shortwave receiver. I was so excited the first time I heard the station signal for the British shortwave program in the German language that I proudly turned the volume up as high as possible to let my whole family know of my success. Big Ben rang out loudly over the entire third floor. At that my father came tearing into the room, yanked the cord out of the wall, and hissed, "Are you out of your mind? Don't you know that it is absolutely forbidden to listen to foreign radio transmissions? They'll come and take us all away!"

My spirits were dampened for a while, but shortly afterward we arranged for a particular hour, once a day, when all the attic guests could assemble in my room in order to listen to the latest bulletins from London. Whenever these dealt with Allied advances, their hopes began to rise.

For my next project I laid a wire connection to my cousin Kurt's room on the floor below. Equipped with small beep devices, earphones, and the elegant walnut keys discovered in one of my uncle's treasure chests, we began sending Morse code to each other.

At first we made slow progress, our mistakes far outnumbering the accurate letters transmitted, but with practice we began to master our new craft. Often we would lie in our respective beds, sending Morse messages until late into the night. Our parents, of course, suspected nothing.

We began copying wireless messages from the shortwave

radio. Once in a while we were lucky and came across a message that was uncoded, in German, and slow enough to decipher with our limited skills. Translating these messages made us feel more important and grown-up, even though we were vaguely aware of intruding into a world that wasn't intended for us.

But it wasn't until I constructed real, if still imperfect, transmitters and receivers and we began sending our messages by wireless that our activities were brought to a sudden and frightening conclusion. One afternoon Tante Herta came up to our apartment, accompanied by two men from the SS. "These gentlemen from the Wireless Intercepting Service are convinced that there is an illegal shortwave sender in this house, and they are going to conduct a search. Do you know anything about this?"

My mother and I turned pale, thinking of the hidden Jews. Then somehow I managed to stutter, "My . . . my cousin and I have been learning the Morse alphabet and sending messages to each other on homemade sets. Just for fun . . ."

My aunt jumped in. "Oh yes, my late husband was a physics professor, and I gave my nephew some of his equipment a few months ago."

One of the SS men interrupted brusquely, "Where are the sets?"

I led them to my room and pointed to the corner.

"These sets are hereby confiscated and a report will be filed." With that the two began dismantling and carrying everything away.

It wasn't until some time after they had left that our hearts began beating normally once again. My mother looked at me and then finally just shook her head, saying, "That could have turned out so much worse."

I had lost track by now of how many Jews altogether had passed through our attic, most staying for only short periods. All of the family was involved in one way or another, but it was my mother who took the greatest risks, and both my parents could have been shot as traitors if the Jews had been discovered.

I must have fallen asleep. When I awoke I had the feeling that the train had already been standing still for some time. The tired rays of the November sun shone through the open sliding door, where the other soldiers sat dangling their legs.

I stood up and went over to join them, laying my hand on Haas's shoulder.

"All slept out?" he asked, turning his head toward me.

Others were standing below us on the railway embankment, and when I stuck my head farther out the door, I could see large numbers of soldiers sitting next to the train or walking up and down beside the track.

"What's happening?" I asked.

An older man from Augsburg named Bolder answered, "The approaching train ran over a land mine. The Pioniere [Army Corps of Engineers] are pushing the locomotive and six of the cars over the slope. We'll be cooling our heels for half the day here until they get everything organized again."

Then he added, "There were dead and wounded, too, over a hundred, I think."

"We don't want to hear anything about that," Haas snapped. "There are always dead and wounded in a war. You're just scared silly that we won't make it to the front, either."

"We're all scared," said Bolder. "That isn't going to stop until it's all over and we're home again—until this stupid war is finally lost."

"Ah, but if you're too scared," said Haas, "then you can't really function, and if you're not functioning, you don't have your wits about you. If you don't have your wits about you, then comes that critical moment when you're not on your guard and zap! It gets you."

"You have an answer for everything, Haas," grumbled Bolder. "There are some like you who sail through the war, have incredible luck, and come to depend on it, believing they are untouchable. Then there are the others, afraid or not, who just happen to be ten centimeters too far to the left at the wrong second and they get it through the head."

A messenger ran past calling out, "Three men from every car to the rear to pick up rations."

I volunteered and went back with two others to the last cars, where the ammunition and cold rations were transported. We waited until the number of our car was called, then went up to receive the sacks containing half a loaf of bread and a tin of sardines per man. When we returned we were greeted with calls of "Here comes Santa Claus" or "Not fried chicken and potato pancakes again!"

Meanwhile, someone had placed on our stove a big pot

filled with so-called *Kaffee*. In reality, this was not coffee but a mixture of roasted barley, cubes of dried figs, and chicory, cooked up without the slightest hint of sweetener. Some of the men maintained that it also contained bromide to lessen our sexual needs. I poured myself a cup and sat down in my corner, where Haas was already busily eating. Since my sardine tin had no key, I opened it with my bayonet and ended up pouring half the oil all over my pants.

Haas looked at me with a sympathetic smile. "Your table manners could stand some improvement," he joked.

"Ha, when it comes to manners, I'll bet I could put you to shame," I replied. "I had to learn them the hard way."

"What do you mean?"

"For example, when my sister and I were little, we had to eat with a piece of paper stuck under each arm. If one of the pieces fell down, there was no dessert."

Haas raised an eyebrow. "Hmmm, why don't you tell me more about that to make the time go by a little faster?"

During the following hours, until the train finally started up again and slowly chugged its way past makeshift repairs on the explosion damage, I told Haas where and how I had grown up, making no secret of my Jewish blood. It didn't seem to impress him one way or the other. Of course, I didn't mention the hidden Jews.

Haas described to me his life growing up on the outskirts of Stuttgart. His house was connected to a butcher shop, where he had worked with his father since he was sixteen. He painted colorful images of the yearly carnival and of the various girlfriends that he had never quite gotten around to marrying and of his membership in the Hitler Youth. All the uniforms, flags, parades, and political propaganda hadn't impressed him very much. After a couple of months he had found it boring and reduced his participation to a minimum, just enough so as not to attract negative attention. I admired the way he had maneuvered through all that, simply by using his instincts and good common sense.

These hours with Haas were good for me. Telling him about my prior life somehow seemed to balance the books. I felt almost ready now for whatever was to come.

The eastbound train rolled on. During the next day, the sixth since our departure, we passed more and more burned-out railroad cars next to the tracks. Trenches, riddled army vehicles, exploded tanks, and small knolls topped with primitive crosses and rusty helmets became more constant features of the landscape. It was on that evening that I heard for the first time a deep and sinister rumbling that continued without pause.

It was the front.

INTRODUCTION TO THE TRENCHES

The train jolted over an endless net of switches, then stopped. Amid shouted orders of "Faster! Faster!" everyone gathered up his belongings and jumped down onto the dark ground. A cloud-covered sky, faintly illuminated by the distant moon, shed the only light.

A command rang out. "Cars 18, 19, and 20, follow me!" and then, "Hurry up, don't lose contact, and don't leave anything behind!"

I stumbled through the night toward the silhouettes of numerous multistoried buildings. These had formerly housed railroad workers but were now evacuated. We scrambled up the stairs to take any room that was empty and installed ourselves on the bare floors for the night. That distant hum and rumbling never ceased, and I was afraid.

Shortly after dawn the next morning, we all assembled in an area between the house where we had slept and the narrow trenches that served as bomb shelters. An officer arrived, accompanied by a few sergeants. One of them shouted us to attention, and we clicked our heels together wherever we were standing. "At ease," barked the officer. He passed a piece of paper to one sergeant, and the latter began reading off our names in alphabetical order. It was a list of about 120.

When the sergeant had finished reading, the officer addressed us. "You all belong to Division Number 282,

Regiment 158, Second Battalion, First Company. I am your company commander, Oberleutnant von Fritsch."

After also being told the names of the battalion commander and the accompanying noncommissioned (noncom) officers, we were permitted to fall out.

At the noon hour we lined up to draw our rations. At first, my mouth dropped open in disappointed surprise when I received a chunk of raw horsemeat, three large potatoes, and half an onion. I could tell my companions were obviously as surprised as I was. Even though I was skinny, I had always been famous for my enormous appetite. From earliest childhood the kitchen had held a certain fascination for me, and the fact that I was usually there inspecting the pots long before mealtime arrived earned me the name *Haeferlgucker*, or pot-peeker. At home and on my many teenage bicycle tours in the Austrian mountains I had developed a considerable talent for cooking that was to prove most valuable, a lifesaver in more ways than one.

Remembering one of my mother's favorite sayings, "Hunger is the best cook," I began to take stock. Hmmm, wasn't that an old blackened frying pan that I had seen hanging on the wall of the otherwise empty kitchen in the apartment where I had spent the night? What's more, my piece of horsemeat had quite a considerable portion of fat attached to it. In the apartment next to ours, I had happened to notice an old cookstove and some pieces of coal on the floor next to it. There was salt in my bread tin and a lighter, too. My mouth began to water.

While the rest were still standing around looking

perplexed, I was already on my way to find that frying pan. The rest of the undertaking was child's play. Not more than ten minutes had elapsed before I was standing in front of the stove, skillet in hand, while the luscious aroma of frying meat, onions, and potatoes filled the room.

From my third-floor kitchen I had a perfect view of the train station where we had arrived and the town of Znamenka, which lay a little farther off. These were surrounded by flat, untilled fields and then by the black earth of a plain that stretched away into the distance.

I kept turning the meat and potatoes with the tip of my bayonet, and the smell became more and more tantalizing. *Just about five minutes more, and it will be ready,* I was thinking, when suddenly the air-raid siren on the roof of the adjoining building began to howl. Soon other sirens joined it, and I could hear shouted commands down on the ground below.

Little clouds of smoke from antiaircraft guns began appearing above the town, looking as though a painter's brush had swiftly stippled them there, one after the other. Then I heard the droning of airplanes, increasing steadily in volume, accompanied by the explosions from antiaircraft guns and four-gun turrets.

What to do? *If I run down to the shelter now, I'll have to eat my food half-raw, because the coal will be all burned out by the time this is over. What a shame for this lovely food!* I decided to wait a little longer. Just a few more minutes.

Now I saw the airplanes, at first just specks on the horizon but rapidly turning into streaks that seemed to be heading right in my direction. Then it dawned on me. The train station. An important target. Of course, that was why there were so many bomb craters all around. These planes weren't coming for the first time.

One of the planes dived, trailing smoke as it crashed, and was followed by a second. Now I discovered smaller fighter planes carrying on dogfights in the midst of the larger bombers, all of them approaching rapidly.

"Just one minute more," I pleaded silently. I leaned out the window for a second and saw that there wasn't a soul in front of the house, but the trenches were full of helmeted heads, little steel spheres pressed tightly together.

It finally sank in that I was acting like a total idiot. At that same moment the droning noise became terribly loud and the floor under my feet began to shake. All at once, in the wall in front of me, a crack opened up from ceiling to floor, and a spray of mortar sailed through the air. I crammed my helmet onto my head and took off down the stairs, holding the frying pan handle with both hands.

I heard an enormous crash, and either from air pressure or movement of the house, I was thrown against the stair railing and showered with mortar and cement. I could see daylight through the cracks that were appearing everywhere in the walls.

Staggering drunkenly down the remaining stairs and out to the trenches, I managed to jump in just as the last of the planes roared over us and disappeared.

When I arrived the other soldiers, still holding their mess kits with the raw meat and potatoes, were just beginning to stretch their heads up out of the ground with relief. They laughed at me, pointing and saying what a hilarious sight I had made as I appeared out of a cloud of dust and powder, covered with mortar and wielding my steaming skillet.

I was their comic relief, but I also had the last laugh. Crawling back out of the trench, I sat down on a pile of artillery ammunition, where I scraped my pan clean—not at all bothered by the pieces of mortar.

It rained all that night, and the next morning we pulled out. Since we would be walking through heavy mud, we were ordered to lighten our gear. I didn't know whether to feel dismayed or relieved as we handed in our extra pair of shoes, our change of underwear, our food (all canned), and one of the two packs of emergency rations. In those early days of winter the Ukraine was a broad, forsaken land, sprinkled only occasionally with a few houses or trees. The untilled fields of black dirt were often partially flooded, reflecting the overcast sky. Here and there we passed a small village in ruins.

I noted that no field kitchen accompanied us, and there were no trucks with additional weapons or ammunition. A few of the stronger men carried machine guns instead of rifles, and others hauled heavy iron boxes with the belts of ammunition.

We slogged along to the slow rhythm of a smacking sound each time a boot was pulled out of the mud. In spite of the cold wind blowing into our faces, we were soon dripping with perspiration. The heavy leather straps that supported our belts and gear cut into my shoulders, and the thought of cattle on their lumbering way to the slaughterhouse passed through my mind.

Sometimes we were met by small groups of wounded soldiers, smeared with blood and muck, supporting themselves on each other. Now and then a fast-moving vehicle full of the wounded would speed past, spraying the mud wide on both sides.

Suddenly a call rang out: "Low flyers!"

Up front where the ragged ribbon of a road disappeared on the horizon, two fire-spitting dots were speeding our way. I followed the example of the men in front of me, who dropped almost everything and threw themselves to the left and right in the softened dirt of puddles at the sides of the road. A few seconds later the plane roared over us, blazing fire from every gun.

The men rose up slowly, their formerly clean uniforms, faces, hands, now all a mess of muck and mire. I wiped my face as best I could, gathered my things together, and continued walking onward toward the east.

That night we rested for a few hours in the ruins of a house that was still burning. At dawn, just before we continued our march, I wrote my first letter home.

Somewhere in Russia, December 4, 1943

Dear Mutti,

I still haven't arrived at our destination. Until now the other lively fellows and I have been messing around on the train, in burned-out houses, etc. It's already pretty warlike here. The front isn't far away. Everything is stuck in the mud. We often wade in it up to our ankles and feel after four kilometers as though we've covered forty. I don't have a field post number yet, but it won't take much longer. I am in tip-top shape physically, mentally, and spiritually. You get used to everything, to the mud, too. I don't have one dry thread left on my body. Everything is saturated with mud, but it dries up and falls off again. When the mail is working better, I'll write you in more detail. You should receive this letter by way of one of the guys who is going on furlough. I wish all of you a happy Christmas. Be well and don't worry about me. Weeds don't perish that easily. Many kisses,

Your Georg

Thanks to the chilly rain and the conditions of the so-called road, we were barely recognizable by the time we reached the front. My feet were covered with new blisters, and having caught only snatches of sleep, I felt primarily relief that we finally had reached our destination.

It was already dark as we reinforcements were assigned places within a long stretch of a zigzag-running trench, where we joined the likewise weary, wet, and filthy soldiers already there. I jumped down into the ditch, which measured just the width of my shoulders.

The older, unshaven soldier inside said simply, "Good that you're finally here," and showed me the space where I could stash my things. It was a horizontal hole dug into the side wall of the trench, about the length of a man and relatively dry, at least compared to the bottom of the trench.

It seemed incredible that now only a few meters lay between me and those over there. It was so dark that I couldn't distinguish any details, such as how far away they were or whether perhaps one of them was right now raising his arm to fling a hand grenade in my direction. I felt painfully aware of my inexperience, without a clue from where or when an unknown quantity of them might come sneaking or storming up. I also doubted that my rifle—a ridiculous affair that had to be reloaded after every shot—would be of much value in repulsing an attack. Perhaps I had made a terrible mistake after all in choosing the infantry.

Nevertheless, here I was, in the foremost lines of a front in a war I never wanted, understood, or was able to justify. From now on I was expected to shoot at people I didn't know and for whom I hadn't the slightest feeling of enmity.

The black of the night sky and the yet deeper black of the earth beneath, together with the faint sound of the ever-continuing rain and the hopelessness of my situation, brought me close to tears, but I hadn't even a clean finger for wiping my eyes.

Another day passed with the old veteran and me changing places every two hours. The temperature dropped far below freezing. Every now and then an officer came by, pressing himself past us in the trench, usually with a few encouraging words. It struck me that the coarse, loud tones of the drill ground weren't to be heard here at all. All of that standing at attention and the other obedience-building chicanery had disappeared. Here the attitude seemed to be "We're all in the same soup together."

About midnight some soldiers came dragging heavy iron containers from which they filled our mess kits with an almost-cold stew of sorts. Half a loaf of *Kommissbrot* (rye bread), a finger-thick slice of sausage, and a piece of hard artificial honey completed the day's rations.

Russia, December 7, 1943

Dear Mutti,

And so it's come to this. I have been standing in the front trench for forty-eight hours. It's a very strange feeling to know that thousands before me have already stood in such a trench, and probably just as many will come after. Here we sit, day and night, ready to ward off the attacking Russians. Only here can one first claim to be a soldier, for he who hasn't heard the bullets whistling isn't yet one.

Twenty-four hours ago I couldn't have said I was in such a good mood. In fact I was pretty unhappy, because I have been placed here as an infantry soldier, even though I was ordered to headquarters as a telegraphist. It has struck me here that I really don't completely understand such concepts as bravery and cowardice. For example, I can't reconcile military courage and bravery with the drive for self-preservation that I feel so strongly here in the bottom of my trench.

There is already a little snow. The ground is frozen and the sky cloudy. Overnight it has become bitter cold. I'm wearing no less than two pairs of long underwear, a pair of sweatpants, and my uniform pants. In addition, I have on two shirts, a military pullover, my own pullover, a stomach band, uniform jacket, overcoat, and a blanket. On my head two scarves, earmuffs, and a cap pulled down over my ears. All that and I'm still freezing! But we've been promised quilted suits in a few days. Your mittens are splendid. They have proven themselves wonderfully. I don't want to take them off at all.

I have very little left of the things I brought with me from home, but it doesn't matter. I have the most necessary things with me, and the rest is just a great burden. I haven't washed for almost two weeks, which isn't exactly pleasant, but there has been no opportunity. I don't have lice yet.

In spite of everything, I'm actually in quite a good mood. I look at everything from a certain distance with a kind of superiority, and I really don't know where this comes from. I only notice that it has quite a refreshing and calming effect on the others who, in part, are pretty run-down—spirits as well as nerves.

Of course I won't be celebrating Christmas this year. There's no tree, no friends, no presents. I'll just be happy if I'm not too hungry on that day. With that in mind, I've been saving a piece of bacon and some sugar. But it doesn't matter. I'm not so fussy in this respect. Who knows, perhaps for all this the Christmases to come will be that much better.

You mustn't be surprised at my writing and spelling. It's 7 a.m., my fingers are pretty stiff and dirty, and the trench is just as wide as I am. Besides, one's heart does beat a little faster, after all. I don't know when I'll be able to write again, but it could be a while, since there isn't always a chance.

Be well and don't worry. Nothing will happen to me. Besides, I have faith in your religious attitude, and that simplifies things considerably. Warmest greetings to all who care about me, and tell them I'm fine. Many loving kisses from…

Your Georg

After nightfall on our fourth day in the trenches, a lieutenant came and announced, "The companies will be pulling back at 7:00 p.m., and a small group will remain behind as rear guard until 11:00 p.m. Both of you are detailed to this group."

Our task was to keep walking the trench in one direction until we met the next soldier, a distance of three to four hundred yards, and then do the same in the opposite direction. At the same time we were to fire off a shot now and then to simulate the continuing presence of the entire company.

The withdrawal of the majority took place very quietly, and we began marking off the trench. It was quite still. I could hear only the far-off rumbling of the artillery and an occasional rifle shot.

I worked my way toward the contact on my right, returned to the left, and then went back again. Two hours must have passed in this fashion when, as I was once more walking the trench toward my right, probably more or less absentmindedly, it suddenly occurred to me that I had walked much farther than before without meeting the other man. I stopped and debated whether to keep going or to wait until he came back in my direction. It was very dark and very still, one of those black and cloudy new-moon nights.

As I stood there undecided, I thought I heard something—just a smattering of strange sounds. I glanced toward the dark mass that formed the slope across the way, and there, along the faint contour of the hill outlined against the night sky, I thought I detected some moving spots. The harder I strained to see, the more certain I became; those were people moving up there. Then I also saw some indistinct, even darker spots on the slope but closer to me, and again that low, unfamiliar murmuring.

The longer I stared, the more easily I could distinguish shapes, closer and closer to me and moving silently forward. A chill ran down my spine, and the artery in my neck began to throb as I realized that one of the shapes was crouched not more than a few meters in front of me. Then more of those sounds, whispered scraps of Russian words, but behind me!

"They're in back of us," I thought. "They're already over the trench. They must have killed the other man, and that's why I didn't meet him."

At this moment I discovered what fear is. It became all too clear to me that those creatures crawling toward me through the mud in the middle of the night were there for the sole purpose of killing me. With that they became, whether I wished it or not, "the enemy."

I made myself as small as possible and began creeping back very slowly the way I had come, hoping just not to make a sound, just not to bump into anything, expecting at any minute that a Russian would jump down on top of me or a flare would light up the sky and I would be surrounded by shooting Russians.

I wormed my way along the trench for an eternity. Eventually I started coming to places that seemed familiar: a bunker, a bomb crater. Finally someone growled in German, "Password?" and I gave the response with enormous relief. It was my old veteran.

After I had described the situation in whispers, we went seeking the noncom in charge of the rear guard. Shortly afterward we were all out of the trenches and on our way to the rear, but I soon noted that the noncom seemed to be having some difficulties finding the right way. More and more often the group received the signal to halt while he studied the map with a carefully shielded flashlight. It had begun snowing and the flakes were coming down thicker and thicker.

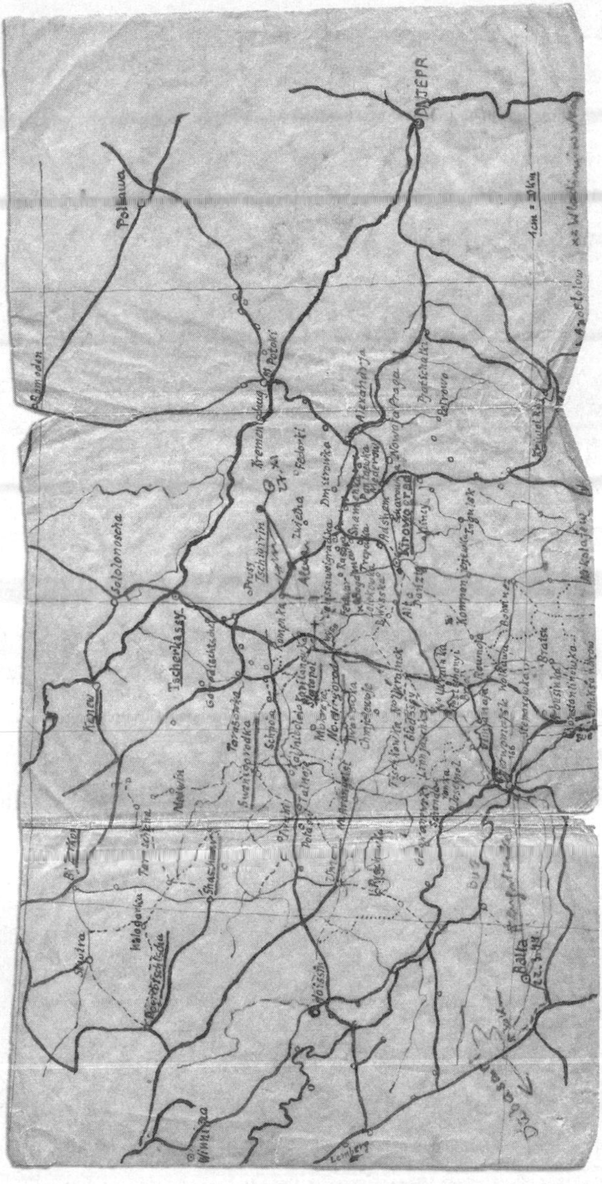

Map my father drew in an attempt to follow my whereabouts in the Ukraine.

I chewed on my last piece of bread and asked myself how long it would take for us to run into our company.

Soon the ground became completely white, and a dismal silence lay over everything. Then the wind began blowing. Before long a heavy blizzard was hurling the snow into our eyes, making it difficult not to lose the blurred shape of the man in front of me. Two hours had already elapsed since our flight from the trenches, and I was becoming very tired, what with all the equipment I had to carry. The pace of the group was slowing down considerably.

Suddenly the silhouette of a house appeared through the snowstorm, and behind it, another. They were the first houses of a village. We searched them, and when they proved to be deserted, the officer ordered us to sleep inside until daybreak. Guards were posted outside, and I found a dry corner where I fell asleep immediately.

I thought at first I must be dreaming when someone shook my arm and whispered, "Wake up, quick! The Russians are on the other side of the street. Just grab your rifle and ammunition and get out the back as quickly as possible. Leave everything else."

It was still snowing. The ground was soft and swallowed up our footsteps as we crept down a small depression, expecting flares and bursts of fire at any moment. After crossing a small stream that plunged us knee-deep into icy water, we disappeared among the bare fruit trees on the opposite side.

Two more days passed before that incompetent nincompoop of an officer finally led us back to our company. Our rations during this period consisted of cooked corn kernels.

When we finally reached the others, no joyous reunions took place among these men who had been fighting next to each other for months. That surprised me. I still hadn't learned how dulled soldiers become, how superficial relationships remain when the dead are constantly being replaced by new faces, these likewise destined to disappear in a short time.

An hour after our return I was in the front lines again, once more in a trench, this time one filled with snow. But a day later my situation took a definite turn for the better.

Russia, December 13, 1943

Dear Mutti,

Today I am in the happy position of writing you a letter full of satisfaction. Half an hour ago, completely filthy, lousy, and dog-tired, I climbed out of a hole in the ground that lay just 300 meters across from the Russians. They hadn't anything better to do all afternoon than to keep trying to place a direct hit in my hole. It was pretty close a few times, but I got out with my bones intact after all.

This evening I said farewell to the trench, and in the future I'll be working as a telegraphist. That pleases me very much, especially since it isn't very nice having to shoot at Russians. The last few days weren't nice at all. But enough of that. I have no idea how the future looks for me since it hasn't yet been determined where I will be assigned as telegraphist. For certain it will be better in many respects, as I am now a member of the regimental headquarters staff.

I have overcome the 100 percent aversion to being here; or rather I had to overcome it.

A merry Christmas and a Happy New Year to you and Papi.

Your Georg

THE HARDEST THING

I was assigned to a battalion headquarters that was situated in a village about three kilometers to the rear. Plodding through heavy snow, I arrived there on December 13. It was late, and I found a space to sleep on the floor of one of the houses.

The next morning I tottered out, stiff-limbed and still half-asleep, to wash off my face with snow. Somebody suddenly grabbed me from behind in a big bear hug and said, "Well, who would have believed it? Rauch has managed to survive his first ten days without suffering any depreciation!"

With that, Haas released me from his clinch and pulled my cap over my eyes.

"Hey, where are you detailed?" I asked him, grinning.

"Same firm, same team. Even the same hut."

I was very happy to see him again. The realization that he was going to be nearby seemed to make the entire situation a lot friendlier.

Russia, December 14, 1943

Dear Folks,

Now I've become a human being again. A short time ago I arrived here at battalion headquarters, where I will be engaged as a telegraphist from now on. I like it tremendously! There are twelve of us telegraphists and phone operators living together in one hut, all very nice guys. The atmosphere is so friendly here, a relief from up front, where there is only yelling and complaining. What's more, I have washed myself from head to toe and brushed my teeth. Yes, now the unpleasant part is all behind me. I can even hope to celebrate a halfway happy Christmas. Today, also, for the first time in a long while, I had a good laugh. That's why I'm in a fantastic mood.

The food is excellent, because the Headquarters Company is feeding us. Schnitzel for lunch, schnitzel for supper, and sausage for breakfast. Meat in large quantities. The cook thinks to himself, whether we eat the pigs and calves today or the Russians eat them when we move on tomorrow, it is all the same. (Of course, it is not all the same to us.)

I feel like Adam, standing here naked, without possessions. The Russians have everything. I'll just have to organize something. At any rate, I don't have to worry much about the loading of my luggage when we are on the march. I feel particularly unburdened.

Outside it's finally becoming bitter cold. *Pfirt Euch Gott* [May God watch over you] and go happy into the New Year. Many loving greetings,

Your Georg

Russia, December 21, 1943

Dear Mutti,

First of all, my best regards from Russia. Nothing has changed here for the last eight days. The daily monotony: up at six, Madka puts the potato soup with chicken on the table, it becomes light. One begins the first lice hunt. In every piece of clothing, twenty to thirty lice. Then the joint gets cleaned up. One man always sits at the switchboard and makes the connections. I am already pretty good at that. Mornings there's nothing else to do.

At twelve-thirty we receive our warm lunch from the field kitchen and right after that they hand out the cold rations: sausage, butter, bread, and coffee. At two it starts to get dark, and you have to hurry up with another delousing or they'll eat you alive.

In the afternoon I blow on the harmonica or write a letter. At five or six there's chicken again. I can hardly bear to look at another chicken since, in addition to our military rations, which are plentiful and good, each of us eats approximately one chicken per day, and they are pretty fat in this part of the world.

Yesterday we also butchered a hundred-kilo pig. Meat, meat, and more meat. On that point we certainly can't complain, but now and then you do miss something that tastes a little different from meat, potatoes, and bread.

At six we usually go to bed (which consists of a pile

of straw and two blankets on the floor of the hut). But I've become used to it. At night each of us has two hours' duty on the switchboard, but one doesn't mind. First of all you aren't very sleepy, and second the lice are biting like mad. Sometimes you think you will truly go crazy, and there's not a thing you can do about it. And so one day passes like another.

Into the bargain, of course, one hears the eternal howling of the mortars, hits from bombs, bullets, and everything else that bangs and bursts around here. The main battle line is three kilometers away. Sometimes the Russians break through and come critically close. Then we also grab our guns and run out in counterattack to push them back. These occurrences are usually pretty bloody.

Except for food, the supply situation is pretty bad, because we're sitting in a pocket that the Russians close up from time to time. In these cases, we have to exert ourselves to open it up again. For that reason not much is getting in. Incoming mail has begun functioning recently. I still haven't heard anything from you, but I also have my third field post number. This one is the final one, however.

I have a couple of wishes that you might fulfill: three number-two pencils, some matches, four safety pins, a lighter and flint if possible, a map enlargement of the section with Alexandrovka and twenty-five kilometers west, a 1944 calendar diary, envelopes and paper, a paintbrush, and a mouth organ in C, since mine is broken or not working very well. These are all things I'm lacking.

I got back part of my luggage, mostly underwear. That's why today is a holiday for me—I have on clean underwear with no lice! Please write me how much mail is getting through and when you receive it.

Many kisses from your Georg

The twenty-first of December was Stalin's birthday, and all day long we could hear the drunken Russians shouting and shooting off their pistols. On the twenty-second and twenty-third they shot at us all day long with mortars and succeeded in wounding and killing quite a few. Haas convinced me that it was better to go without a helmet, because the German version was so heavy and came down so far over the ears that it made hearing almost impossible. And hearing well was vital. There was that sound of a soft blip that came from the Russian positions, the discharge from the mortars that one had to learn to take seriously. Approximately twenty seconds following that sound the hit landed, and it was much better to be prepared.

Russia, December 24, 1943

Dear Mutti,

Christmas in Russia, a rather strange feeling, especially when one is used to celebrating this holiday the way we do. But there is nothing to be done about that here. Nobody has the head for it. The Russians lie one hundred meters away, dug fast into the ground, and any minute they could come our way in great multitudes. Then there's always uproar, shooting, wounded, dead, and afterward everyone sinks down somewhere or other and sleeps a couple of hours to recover. Who could still have the head for a Christmas celebration with presents, etc.? The soldiers are happy about the extra pack of cigarettes and bottle of schnapps that everyone gets. Some have received a package from home in time. Even just a greeting from home helps to a few peaceful thoughts.

Yesterday I went organizing here in the village. That is to say, one goes from hut to hut, pushing open the door, gun in hand. Then you rummage through the whole house without even tossing a glance at the inhabitants who are standing around and wailing, and you take whatever is worth taking. At first I didn't have the heart for this, but in time you learn that, too. Thus I found eggs, butter, sugar, flour, and milk with which I baked a first-rate cake. Together with a little schnapps, it was a real treat. Afterward a few loving thoughts of you and Christmas 1943 was over. Well, one time like that for a change. Otherwise I'm doing great.

Your Georg

As delighted as I was to get out of the trenches, and especially out of the front fighting lines, being quartered a few hundred meters farther back, in a Russian house, was a mixed pleasure.

Very seldom did we encounter the solitary dwellings that one often sees in the Austrian countryside. The Russian houses were almost always grouped closely together in villages, each with its own vegetable garden and often a few fruit trees nearby. Usually the dwellings were uninhabited, evacuated, and at the soldiers' disposal, but sometimes we shared the huts with very old people who hadn't wanted or been able to evacuate, and even people with small babies.

The main building materials were sun-dried mud bricks to which a little chopped straw had been added. The ceilings consisted of thick, often sagging, smoke-blackened beams, over which boards were nailed. Outside the roofs were covered with straw and very steeply pitched so that the blankets of winter snow could slide off easily. The straw roofs, as well as the unbaked bricks, provided the perfect insulation against the harsh winters.

The wooden doors were so low that we average-sized Western Europeans always had to duck our heads upon entering. Windows were sparse and very small, but this aspect and the low ceilings were well thought out for keeping the houses pleasantly warm with only a minimum of heating materials, even during the bitterest of Russian winters.

Most of the huts had almost identical room arrangements. One entered a small vestibule through a door facing the square or street. Doors on the left and right of this hall led to the

Russian village hut interior.

two main rooms. One of these served as living room/kitchen, with the large heating stove occupying one-quarter of the room space. The second, usually unheated room, which contained beds and a chest of drawers, was also used for storing clothing, tools, and seeds for the next planting season.

A ladder or very steep set of stairs rose from the entryway up to the attic, which often provided winter shelter for the chickens. A back door opened to the courtyard behind the house, where the horses, cows, pigs, and goats were quartered. The courtyard usually contained a deep well with a long rope and wooden bucket, a corncrib built on stilts to protect it from mice and dampness, and artfully piled stacks of straw and hay. Towering mounds of dried sunflower stems and cornstalks served as the only source of heating and cooking fuel, since neither wood nor coal was available in the immediate area.

At the back of the courtyard lay the vegetable garden, fenced in to protect it from the chickens and other thieves. Beyond this the fields stretched off onto the endless Ukrainian plain.

The spacious four-by-five-meter main room and the giant stove were the hub of the house, especially in winter. A bed, a few wooden trunks, a large rustic wooden table flanked by simple benches, and a number of low stools for accommodating tired feet or little children made up the humble furnishings.

The brick stove was very complicated and a wonder of heating and cooking technology. It jutted out from the walls by about two and a half meters on each side and had a main platform about sixty centimeters above the floor. Concentric, removable iron rings for the cooking pots and tea kettle lay on this surface, toward the center of the room, and iron bars formed a grill on some of the models. Sufficient platform space was still left over near the walls for sitting and warming one's frozen bones after coming in from the cold on a wintry day.

A separate, higher masonry sleeping platform, back in the farthest corner of the stove against the wall and bedecked with feather coverlets, served as a bed for grandparents or whoever in the family might be ill. An iron door at floor level opened for the removal of ashes. Another door, slightly higher up, received the foot-long pieces of sunflower stalks used as fuel. A door to the bake-oven was the largest of all.

One or two massive columns rose up through ceiling and roof, ending outside as squat chimneys. An extremely complicated labyrinth of draft channels manipulated the smoke, taking advantage of and conserving the last little bit of warmth. Finally this radiating giant performed as a clothes dryer. Diapers, wet coats, and shoes were hung to dry on strings and poles running between the stove and the carved posts that supported the sagging roof beams.

The floor, of either tamped dirt or wooden planks, was covered with straw. The mud we brought in on our shoes could be swept out with the old straw and the floor freshly strewn, but though clean, the straw also provided the perfect breeding ground for fleas.

Small, heavily smoking oil lamps that illuminated poorly and blackened the faces of all present provided the only evening light. Nonetheless, it was easy to imagine how cozy such a room might have been in its original state, sheltering a small family group.

In wartime, however, these buildings with their rising chimney smoke were perfect targets for the Russian mortars. When you considered the shelling, the vermin, the rank smell of six or more dirty soldiers cooped up for days, plus the wailing of old folks and babies, a well-furnished bunker was often much to be preferred.

At night, when the firing was particularly heavy, we descended to the damp earthen cellars in the courtyards. There, in spite of rats and the pungent smell of sour beets and pickles, we felt less vulnerable and sleep came more easily.

Russia, December 29, 1943

Dear Mutti,

Outside everything is white, deep white. When I look outside I see nothing but white. Besides that, it is freezing cold. Such an icy wind roars through the region and hurls ice crystals into our faces. The breath of the men and horses looks as though it were coming from a steam engine.

We are completely outfitted now, and we look like snowmen. When we go outside, we put on over our regular uniform a kind of ski jacket, snow white.

When you turn it inside out it is camouflage material with padding in between. The pants are just as white and warm all the way down, just like long ski pants, and tied at the bottoms. In addition, a pair of felt boots, mittens, everything white on white. The whole thing serves as combination camouflage and protection from the cold.

Meanwhile I have become a skilled telephone operator. I take my turn at the switchboard, go out fixing breaks in the lines, repair telephones. I'm not on the wireless because there's no available equipment. There are constant breaks in the phone lines, though, either from artillery hits, from mortars, or torn up by some vehicle or other. We at the switchboard have to make a line check every half hour—that is, all the participants call in to make certain everything is still functioning.

But sometimes it happens, especially at night, that the guy at the command post falls asleep instead of standing watch. He doesn't hear the phone when we call, and then a repair crew has to tramp the two or three kilometers through the snow to check things out.

That's not always so easy, as it is usually terribly dark, often foggy besides, and since there are no orientation points in this godforsaken countryside, all of a sudden you are lost! There you stand, knowing neither the hour nor the direction, surrounded by snow, snow, and more snow, freezing and thinking of your happy youth.

That's just exactly what happened to me on the twenty-fifth of December. It must have been about 3:00 a.m. There were two of us, each armed only with a pistol, and as we stood there, not knowing where or what, suddenly a group of people came out of the nothingness. We yelled, "Hello, password?" and were answered with an icy stillness, filled only by the whistling of the wind. We were standing about fifteen meters across from each other, and then we heard some Russian word!

At that we made an about-face and took off like a flash in the opposite direction for about thirty meters. A few shots rang out. Voices shouting. We threw ourselves down in the snow, rolled around a bit, and waited. I think we were invisible in our camouflage suits, for they—it must have been a Russian patrol—passed by quite closely and in some agitation.

We stuck to the same spot, walking back and forth until dawn, not daring to stray from there for fear of landing behind the Russian lines. When it became light, it wasn't hard at all to find our way back.

And so you keep having new experiences here. Each time a little excitement, and in a few moments it's all over. You laugh about it and tell it to the others in the accents of a hero.

Right now I'm stuffed so full that nothing else could tempt me. Perhaps a good apple, but nothing else. The Christmas rations were fantastic. Then we all shared in the contents of the many packages from home. In addition, there are special packages, such as the "major battle day" packages, packages from the "comrades stationed in Paris," from the members of the National Socialist Party in Silesia (I'm in a Silesian division) or parcels "from girls to unknown soldiers."

I've received about five of these packages, each one a bit different but none too exciting. One package, from a girl I don't know in Karlsruhe, included a nice letter and was put together with a lot of loving care—some cake and cookies, writing paper, razor blades, an apple, some safety pins, and a few cigarettes, each thing packed and tied up with ribbon—very sweet.

In this way a lot of the soldiers begin exchanges of letters, and it can happen that these fellows receive eight to ten letters or packages from as many different girls in one day. Then when they go on furlough, they check the girls out one by one. I don't think that's my sort of thing. (Daughters of butchers or delicatessen store owners are especially popular.)

Otherwise things haven't changed much. The daily life—eating, sleeping, grenades. I still haven't received any mail from you, but I think something has to arrive pretty soon. If you are able to find something anywhere that works against lice or scabies, please send it to me, as I'm suffering quite a bit from these. They don't give us anything here.

Don't think unhealthy thoughts. Everything's great. Greetings to all and tell them I'm fine. 100,000 kisses from your Georg

On January 1, we were sent to search a nearby woods and the adjacent village for partisans. The village had been evacuated sometime previously. We found nothing in the woods, and then we were ordered to search each house in the village thoroughly. I checked each one assigned to me, going first into the room on the left, then the one on the right, and finally the attic.

In the fourth house I found a young man, about seventeen years old, in civilian clothing and cowering in a corner of the attic. I gave him a sign to come out and follow me, which he did without hesitation. A few officers were standing outside in the square. I brought the man to Hauptmann Winter, the battalion commander, and reported. Then I received the order I shall never forget.

"Go with the man over there and shoot him. He is a partisan."

I stood paralyzed.

"Well, what are you waiting for? Carry out my order. Dismissed."

I was nineteen years old, three weeks on the front, and now I was supposed to shoot a young, unarmed person. I had already studied his face. It was handsome and filled with fear, the features still almost those of a child. Maybe he simply hadn't wanted to go to war, just like me, and had hidden himself when it came time to be a soldier. Or maybe he had still been too young.

I marched away with him, not knowing where I was going or what I should do. I knew I couldn't just shoot him. But was I certain of that? If I didn't do it, what would happen? Refusal to obey a direct order meant court-martial, with an automatic sentence of death. Those were the rules farther to the rear.

Here in the front lines, perhaps it would depend on the mood of the officer. He could have me shot immediately to set an example or have me ordered to a minesweeping unit. I knew from hearsay that this was also a death sentence. The young man would be shot either way, whether I did it or someone else did. On that point nothing could be changed.

Haas came around the corner. He must have sensed my dilemma. Desperate, I turned to him for advice. He already knew me well enough to see right off that mine wasn't one of those smaller problems, something that one just wasn't in the mood for doing. I must have been very pale.

Haas was certainly not a bad person, but thanks to his years at the front he was hardened, rational. He said, "I'll do it for you."

He led the boy away. In all of the war, there was never again a shot more painful for me than the one that shortly rang out over the quiet village. I will hear it the rest of my life.

This was one of the stories that I didn't write home to my mother. In fact, I had made up my mind at the beginning to write only reassuring letters, but I soon found out that it wasn't possible. She wouldn't have believed me, anyway, because of something that I didn't know at the time. She was taking my letters to her sister-in-law, Rhoda Wieser, one of the most highly respected graphologists in Germany. Together the two women regularly analyzed my handwriting in order to ascertain my true mental and emotional state.

The East, January 5, 1944

Dear Mutti,

Today I am more or less on my feet again. For the last five days I've had a fever that was constantly between thirty-eight and forty. In addition I had terrible headaches and was vomiting all the time. I was completely wiped out. At sick bay they took my temperature and then informed me that they couldn't do anything for me. "Everybody has that sometime." Not even an aspirin. Today I have no more fever, but I can hardly stand up. My mood is below zero; that's why I'll write when it's better again. I still haven't caught sight of any mail. I hope at least that you are receiving my letters, since they usually leave with soldiers going on furlough to Germany. Till next time, kisses,

Your Georg

MARIANOVKA—THE FIRST BATTLE

A surprise command to pull out of the village came shortly after nightfall on January 7. In the middle of a snowstorm, given the brief time we were allotted, it was utterly impossible to roll in all the telephone cable we had laid out. What's more, way too few wagons or horses were available for loading. A great deal of equipment had to be left behind.

Heavily burdened with arms, ammunition, and, for those of us in the signal squad, the wireless and telephone equipment, we struggled that whole night against the storm, wearily placing one foot ahead of the other in the deep powder snow.

We continued thus for a week, marching through nights of bitter cold and doing our best to repulse the pursuing Russians by day. Finally we arrived at Marianovka, a small town surrounded by snow-covered hills. Marianovka itself was not of any great importance, but it happened to lie at the narrow opening of an enormous pocket of land, from which an entire German division was attempting to escape to avoid encirclement. We learned the Führer had given a direct order: "The village must be defended to the last man!"

The signal squad was assigned to a dirt cellar, and from there we laid cables out to the last houses on the southern perimeter of the town. The rest of the troops kept busy digging trenches and dragging crates of ammunition.

That afternoon, as I was returning to the cellar for another roll of cable, Haas turned up with two mess kits full of a steaming goulash. Handing one of them to me, he said, "Best wishes from the firm. Keep up the good work! When you get hungry again, the kitchen is four huts down the street."

He pointed toward the south. "There happen to be tons of Russians sitting behind those hills, in case you're interested." Then he added, as though just in passing, "Oh, I almost forgot. These just arrived for you." And he pulled two letters from his inside jacket pocket.

Russia, January 15, 1944

My dear Mutti,

I'm in a most unpleasant position, which we've been commanded to hold "by order of the Führer," but in spite of that, everything is beautiful for the moment because today I received my very first mail from you! Both of your letters were like new, in perfect condition, and they made me so happy. I had felt so forsaken.

For the rest, be well and don't worry. Every bullet doesn't find its mark, and I have a very secure feeling. A Viennese doesn't go under so easily!

Many loving kisses for you both, good old begetters of,

Your Boy

The next morning the Russians began bombarding Marianovka with mortar fire. For several hours we sat in our cellar counting up to one hundred hits per minute. They kept raining down, even during the night, evidently in an attempt to keep us from sleeping and to stretch our already taut nerves to their limits.

We took turns going out to repair the shot-up cables and connections. After two days, barely any snow remained in the village. It had either turned black from the powder or been blown away by the force of the shelling. Many of the houses were burning; the kitchen had received a direct hit.

The first Russian infantry attack began in the early morning hours. I happened to be in one of the foremost houses, replacing a telephone that had been shot to pieces. The Russians, hundreds of black dots on the surrounding hills, stormed down the slopes, roaring fiercely as they ran. The German machine guns fired among the masses, and I could see them falling. Enemy artillery continued to cover the entire village with heavy fire, and new waves of Russian infantry poured down the hills.

When the attack finally halted, the ground was spread with dead and wounded Russians. Soon thereafter they put their antitank guns into action. These fast and low-shooting weapons could draw a bead on each separate man, on every house, on every hole with a German inside. This knowledge had a horrible psychological effect on our troops. The Russian guns produced very high casualties.

All day long new waves of Russians rained down the hill.

The Germans drove them back, but each time it was more difficult, and they were coming closer.

The next day began with a bombardment of heavy artillery, after which not a single house remained intact. One of our team, out fixing a cable, was killed. A hit blasted the wooden door to the cellar, where we sat huddled around the switchboard.

Then, incredibly, the waves of Russians began streaming down again. It was a bloodbath, and our ammunition was becoming scarce. The wounded stumbled or were dragged, bleeding, to the rear. At noon the Russians took the front lines and the first row of ruins. This time we in the communications squad were also called on for the counterattack. Once more we succeeded in driving them back, but with very heavy losses. We began hearing reports of self-inflicted wounds. Others were trying to desert, but there was no way out. There was that order from the Führer—"to the last man"—and he meant it. A row of MPs armed with pistols stood at the rear of the village and stopped everyone. It was either back to the front or be shot on the spot.

The Germans rushed in more men, but our lines were becoming visibly sparse and ragged. The Russians kept coming all day. Morale had sunk to the lowest possible point, and all were close to exhaustion. In our cellar, I couldn't stop shivering, and it wasn't from the cold.

We had to make test calls to the front line every ten minutes so that the officers back at the command posts could keep tabs on how well the lines were holding. The situation became more critical by the hour. Obermaier was wounded and carried away; Haas was ordered right into the first line as a machine gunner. Five of us plus the sergeant remained in the cellar.

A telephone line running across the main square was interrupted. Kramer scrambled out with pliers and electri cal tape. He didn't return, and the connection was still down.

An indignant officer called in from the rear, "Why haven't you lazy pigs repaired the line yet?"

Glatz went out next. Sergeant Burghart and I crept up the stairs from where we watched him jumping from cover to cover, always following the wire. The break must have been on the far side of the square, for he squatted down there, but before he could even fit the two ends together, he simply fell forward on his face.

"Who's next?" the sergeant asked.

Neumann glanced around at us helplessly and climbed slowly out. He didn't even make it to the square before he fell. The sergeant's cool and distant manner was starting to crumble as he realized that only he, seventeen-year-old Baby Schmidt, and I were left. Suddenly it became very clear to me that my own life was about to end very soon if I didn't think of something fast.

I sketched a map of the area, including the ruins, the lines, and the point where everyone was being shot down. The sergeant accepted my plan of laying a completely new line, and we went out together with a roll of wire. We used every possible pile of rubble as cover. By laying lots of wire and running in zigzags, we finally reached our goal to find—*nothing!*

There was only an enormous crater surrounded by rubble. No man. No telephone.

Bent over double, we ran back to our cellar, where Baby Schmidt was reporting apathetically into the mike, "Appleblossom doesn't answer. Pancake doesn't answer either."

An officer roared down from above, "Every man out on the double for the counterattack!"

We ran through the gathering dusk toward the front. I jumped in a hole where a corpse already lay and began shooting. The Russians came at us, and automatically I kept shooting. Load, aim, fire. Load, aim, fire. I could see their faces. The bayonet on my rifle was fixed and ready for them.

All of a sudden, long rows of tracer fire flew from directly behind us and over our heads. Three four-gun turrets from the German antiaircraft forces had been driven into position and were shooting into the haystacks sheltering the enemy, into the masses of Russians. What was taking place in front of my eyes was incredible, and it had a terrible beauty all its own—the last light of dusk, the blazing piles of straw, and the innumerable burning points of unending tracer fire. I lowered my trembling hands, which had been primed for the man-to-man battle, and watched as the Russians whirled around and fled back up the slope.

The attack had collapsed, but for half the night we dragged the wounded and dead. Finally we staggered, a little pile of broken survivors, past the replacement tank platoon that had come to relieve us.

Two socks, two holes. The result of innumerable night marches.

The East, January 24, 1944

Dear Mutti,

Finally I have some peace and quiet again in which to write you a more detailed letter. Well, I am out of the really thick fighting. These were eight very unpleasant days. When you take up your position with about 250 men in your battalion and witness how all but twenty-one are killed or wounded, especially when you are at the switchboard continually hearing the commanders using expressions like "to the last drop of blood" or "not one meter without blood," it's difficult not to wonder when your turn will come.

I was one of the few who got away without the slightest injury, except for tiny splinters. Thanks to a kind of bulletproof vest that I procured from a dead Russian, I found only two splinters that had managed to penetrate my outer clothing and get caught in my shirt. The quilted vest is made of very hard, thick felt and holds off almost everything, but it is very stiff.

My canteen, hanging on my rear end, also took a hit, and the water ran out. My cap too has a hole from a splinter. I have a blue bump on my temple received when the beam in the cellar fell from a mortar hit.

When a mobile tank unit came to relieve us it was certainly a wonderful feeling. In a hut two villages away the mother immediately had to cook two chickens for four of us. And then, four blissful hours of sleep, without a shot, in a warm room.

We were able to look at our faces in a mirror there. They were completely black. Each face was covered with a thick soot from the smoke and dirt, except for two white lines running from the eyes, over the cheeks, and down to the mouth, the result of the tears brought on by the soot. I suspect that a few private tears may have followed the same path.

In the morning three weeks' worth of beard had to go. Then it was off to the new positions. I have been placed here with my buddy as telegraphist at the artillery advanced-observation post. We are situated in a bunker one hundred meters behind the foremost trenches and are sending back firing orders. The Russians are relatively quiet, and the bunker is pretty safe. A little cold, but otherwise okay. I have time to put myself in order mentally, since barely a shot is fired. In addition we have tanks and artillery again to support us. That's very reassuring.

I read with horror in your last letter that you've decided, on Papi's advice, not to send anything baked, but that is exactly what we all desire the most: a few cookies or the like, baked by Mutti, that one can nibble on and think of home.

It is already dark. Excuse the terrible writing, but my pencil is only four centimeters long, the support for my paper is the lid of my wireless, and it's also very cold.

Many good and loving kisses from your Georg, who thinks of you so much.

Thinking back over the experience of Marianovka, I realized that the tank unit that had arrived to relieve us at the last moment was a unit of the Waffen-SS, an elite troop fitted with the best weapons and training. All of the men were blond and measured at least six feet tall. Hitler's darlings, at the final German victory they were destined to be matched up with equally blond and perfect girls to produce masses of Europe's future ruling race. That village must have been important indeed for such a unit to be sent to save us. The SS had the reputation of being cavalry to the rescue among us simple, earthworm soldiers.

I was reminded of a school day back in Vienna when I was seventeen. The teachers had dismissed all the boys from the two highest grades and sent us to an assembly in the darkened gymnasium. We sat on the floor, squeezed closely together, wondering to what we owed our good fortune on this occasion.

A few times in the previous couple of years, the entire school had been marched over to the Ringstrasse, two blocks away, to provide Hitler with appropriately cheering throngs as he approached the Imperial Hotel on one of his periodic visits to Vienna. On these occasions the students' enthusiasm had been decidedly lukewarm. One just did as ordered and enjoyed being released from classes for the day.

But years earlier, when Hitler's soldiers marched into Austria, the skies had been filled with hundreds of droning airplanes. We children had been permitted to crawl over the tanks and cannons that suddenly appeared in the streets and squares. Now, that had been exciting! I could still remember the music, the flags and uniforms, and how much they had impressed me.

At the gym meeting, three SS officers in black uniforms now marched up to the improvised podium. They cracked their heels together, raised their right arms simultaneously, and yelled the obligatory "Heil Hitler!" Then the highest ranking of the three began to speak.

"We're going to show you a series of slides that will give

you some idea about the different branches, training, wartime assignments, and recreational activities of the Waffen-SS. You are all seventeen or more years of age. If you have the required minimum height, you may volunteer at the close of the presentation to be accepted by one of our branches. You require no special permission from your parents. You will receive this year's report card ahead of time, and in a few days, we will summon you to one of our training camps."

Thereupon followed a half hour of slides that depicted SS soldiers waving from tank turrets, presenting arms on parade as they goose-stepped past the Führer, zooming down a Parisian boulevard on snazzy motorcycles, and handling heavy machine guns in action at the front. The last slide showed a fellow with a black cap bearing a skull and crossbones jauntily perched on his straw-blond hair. He was holding an equally blond and very pretty uniformed girl in his arms, and they were singing in front of a campfire.

After the slideshow, many of the unsuspecting students enlisted in the SS, primarily because they were bored with school or because they were fascinated by the German victories and wanted to take part in them. I am certain that none of the boys had any idea then what sort of orders they would later have to carry out, bound to that oath they had sworn.

Following the battle at Marianovka, our quiet time in the bunker wasn't to last for long. One day after lunch Haas was lying outside observing the slope across from us through a pair of binoculars. Since no one else was available at the moment, we were also in charge of directing artillery fire, should it be necessary.

Haas called down into the bunker, "Rauch, come here fast!"

He pressed the binoculars into my hand, pointed in the direction of the distant hill, and said, "Can you see what I see, over there on the horizon?"

"Russians," I answered, "and lots of them."

"Call up the firm," Haas said. "This is going to be a hot afternoon."

The East, January 27, 1944

Dear Mutti,

For four days I was engaged as telegraphist at the observation posts and felt like an artillerist. It was cold, cramped, and there was almost nothing to eat. The Russians were attacking constantly. I kept yelling firing orders into the microphone, and was able to observe immediately the effect through the telescope. It is horrible to see how stupidly the Russians come running in herds of two to three hundred, and when we let fly, there's hamburger. The losses are enormous.

We were sitting in a tiny bunker one hundred meters behind the first lines, which were very thinly occupied. The Russians kept penetrating our lines, often without either their or our noticing. That's why those of us farther back had to keep a good watch out; otherwise someone could simply have tossed a grenade into the bunker.

Now, since the battalion has been exterminated, my detachment has pulled out. Staff and supplies retreated twenty-five kilometers during the night and I along with them.

Our departure was rather hasty. Ivan hit us with artillery fire as never before, then bombers, tanks in large amounts, and finally masses of infantry. Everyone took to his heels.

The entire supply unit, including fifty vehicles, stormed over a cliff with no cover whatsoever, and the antitank guns were shooting in among us. I really don't know how I got out of all that. End result: the regiment is dissolved for the time being.

For about eight hours now I've been sitting here in absolute peace in a very cozy Russian house. I have washed and shaved, eaten, eaten, eaten, and slept. What happens next, nobody knows. We haven't a clue. By now I'm considered one of the old-timers, one who has chalked up enough days in short-range fighting and assault to qualify for those medals on the chest. Pretty soon I'm to be promoted to private first class. Ho hum. Twenty-five *Pfennige* more per day.

In my section it's rumbling pretty well at the moment. Ivan is trying to break through, and he keeps succeeding for a few hundred meters. The 282nd division has already been hit very hard, but I think we'll be getting replacements pretty soon. In any case, for the moment it is peaceful around me, and that feels good.

A lot seems to be changing in Vienna, with air-raid precautions and so on. Well, I hope it will still be a long time with no bombs in your area. I already know much too well how unpleasant they can be. Bye for now.

Greetings and kisses,
Your Son

Russia, January 29, 1944

Dear Mutti,

Yesterday I was at the first-aid station for a harmless problem with my knee. They gave me an elastic bandage and prescribed four days of rest. It was there I realized how good I have it as a telegraphist. Of all the guys on the train out of Krumau, all that are left are four telegraphists, three telephone operators, and one infantry soldier—and they carried that remaining soldier with a head wound into the first-aid station while I was there. Suddenly I became pretty sick, what with all that blood, plus the realization of how few of us are left.

At any rate, it's the officers and those in the communications squad who survive the longest here at the front. Add to that some humor and a lucky star, and you're on top again.

Last night I slept so marvelously on a bed of straw in a warm hut. Who could wish for more? The whole day long we've nothing to do but wash, shave, hunt lice, eat. The rest of the time we lie on the big stove and scratch since we all have scabies.

There I dream of those things I remember as wonderful and beautiful. I dream of a splendidly white tablecloth and clean dishes, with a big dumpling and a real goulash, cucumber salad, and the good chance of a pudding with raspberry jam for dessert. To go with all that, a clean glass of clear water and a few colorful flowers on the table.

Here you let a day from back home pass in front of your eyes, one like so many that were taken for granted, and you notice for the first time all the things you used to ignore, but that were so marvelous.

For instance, just to be able to sleep in a bed with a clean blanket and pillow, freshly bathed, all by yourself, without having to bump into somebody else right and left or have his snores blown in your face.

Or, when you get up in the morning, the coffee and milk are possibly already waiting in the kitchen, and you can begin to do something that gives you satisfaction and lets you know you've come a little bit further. But not like here, where one doesn't know why or for what, and when evening comes you can only observe the one feeble result: "I'm still alive."

The world and its people are so small and meaningless compared to the universe and to the great and beautiful thoughts some people are able to produce. One shouldn't rack one's brain over such silly, stupid things as wars and weapons. You only become gloomy, probably melancholy, and it is a strain on the nerves. I think good nerves are the most important thing one needs in this godforsaken country.

You write that you're getting along so peacefully at home. That makes me very happy. When I know that things are okay at home it makes everything a lot easier. Who knows, maybe I'll be with you pretty soon. My greetings to the whole gang there in Vienna, and don't worry.

Many loving kisses, Your Boy

ACCORDING TO HAAS

Since the regiment had been disbanded, we survivors were quartered twenty-five kilometers to the rear while we waited for reinforcements.

I, along with Haas and Baby Schmidt, our seventeen-year-old, six-foot-three-inch giant, shared a house with two guys from the infantry. Altogether about 150 soldiers were housed in the village. It consisted of two long rows of houses lining a muddy street that stretched in a gentle curve across a small valley surrounded by hills.

Those January days were unusually warm. A southerly wind was blowing mild air from the Black Sea, and a light rain had washed away the remaining patches of dirty snow. With a little effort I imagined I could almost smell spring, though I knew it was still at least two months away.

Outside our hut the sun was shining. I saw soldiers sitting on the doorsteps in front of the houses, writing letters, looking for lice, or patching their ragged uniforms. Not a shot could be heard, no rattling of machine guns, not even the usual distant rumble of the artillery. The Russian women in our house were carrying out Haas's orders: sweeping the floor, keeping the kettle hot, and washing the clothes. All in all, a pleasant scene, both inside and out.

Russia, January 31, 1944

Dear Mutti,

Today was a good day. Two of us took off first thing in the morning with a cart and two fiery horses to a shut-down sugar factory that the Pioniere have planned to blow up. It was quite an adventure, crawling over all the pipes, distilling barrels, steam engines, and whatever all that stuff is called, and always taking good care to avoid the explosive charges that were already in place.

When we finally got to the door of the storeroom, we simply blew it open with two hand grenades and there, right in front of us, nothing but sugar and more sugar! And even though we took three hundred kilos, we felt as though we were just sampling with a teaspoon.

But we couldn't take any more with us, and what should we do with more? The next time we get stuck in the mud we'd just have to throw away everything that is unimportant anyway. This time too we'll probably eat sweets for two weeks and afterward be dreaming over our bitter coffee about the sugar factory in Mala Vyska.

The sky is blue and the sun is shining down quite pleasantly. I am also in such a good mood today, and I don't even know why. I have always had my worst time between November and February. Add to that, this year we have the winter war. My good humor is probably the sun's fault. All the soldiers are so happy, whistling and singing all over the place, and I think I even heard a yodel coming from somewhere. Actually there isn't any reason for all this. In a few days it's up to the front again. The replacements are already close by.

Love, Georg

Russia, February 2, 1944

Dear Folks,

I'm laughing myself silly. In our digs there are two women, one forty years old, the other seventy-six. In addition the five of us from the detachment and a sergeant who is visiting. Each of us already speaks a little Russian, but the women no German. The old one is incredibly funny. She talks all day long, and every two minutes crosses herself three times. She calls us all by our family names, which she has picked up from listening to our conversations. She scolds when we go outdoors without our caps and praises our "culture" when we blow our noses in our handkerchiefs instead of on the floor. She drinks our sweet tea (*tshey*) and begs our candies off of us, and she also praises our culture when we wash every day, because the Russians don't do that.

At any rate, the old gal is dominating us completely.

When it gets too loud, one of us gets up and says very formally, "Psst, Germansky culture, pssst," and then it becomes quiet. I have been laughing so hard that everything hurts. She has to scratch our backs and wash our clothes so there will be *nix partisan* (no lice) in them.

When one of us tries to creep up to her daughter at the stove, the old one yells, *"Arestant, partisan, satana, ne karascho!"* Always a great uproar and lots of fun.

We are always threatening her, *"Madka, Du nix document, Du partisan, Ich Kommandant, bumbum, Du kaputt, ponimaesch?"*

And then she crosses herself three times and screams, *"Boche moi, boche moi! Gospodi! O! O!"* and the din continues. And all my bones hurt, but I can't describe it in a letter. *"Hei, hei,"* she yells between every sentence. *"Hei, hei."* Oh dear, it's so much fun, you just can't imagine, oh! Bye-bye, until next time, kisses,

Your Son

How wonderful it was finally to have enough sugar, even if only for a short while. In my family the story of a certain physical abnormality had been passed on from one generation to the next: we all had two stomachs. The normal one could be filled to bursting with whatever sort of healthy food, while the sweet belly, which was located right beside the first, was still empty.

Especially in the evenings, a member of the family was often heard to announce, "My sweet belly is empty," whereupon my mother would go out to the kitchen to open up a jar of fruit or concoct a treat out of sugar, butter, egg yolk, and cocoa. My father usually added a few drops of rum to his.

In the past two months at the front I had discovered that regular meals were not something to take for granted. The reasons for this state of affairs were as varied as the official food was monotonous and unreliable: supply problems arose when we were hemmed in by the Russians or when mess trucks were shot up or became stranded in mud. Nevertheless, immense physical strength was necessary for survival, and this required decent rations. It wasn't long before I began dedicating more and more of my off-duty hours to organizing something to eat.

Being a telegraphist who was also called upon to handle many of the duties of the phone operators had some great advantages. Whenever one or two of us were called out to patch an interrupted phone line, the path often led across territory that was being observed or shot at by the enemy. But many times our search for the broken section also took us near villages or single houses that were unoccupied due to their proximity to the front. If these weren't in an area where large numbers of soldiers had already been quartered for a long period, we had a good chance of finding something edible. Even if the house seemed empty at first glance, a soldier with the necessary experience could usually discover something worth the effort.

Once again, Haas proved to be an excellent teacher. "When

the owners of these houses take off, it's for certain they can't take everything along, right? So they hide the rest until the time they can return. You just have to know where the goody goodies are deposited," he explained on one of our trips.

A synopsis of the "Rules According to Haas" ran something like this: "Chickens are either hidden with corn in the attic or left running around free. If outside, they're usually difficult to catch. The best thing is simply to shoot them, being careful, of course, to aim for the head.

"Eggs are usually in containers under the grain, flour, or beans, or sometimes, if the amounts are large, buried in the dirt near the house. Meat, marmalade, lard, and items such as carpets or wine are most likely in the cellar, but the door is often barricaded and well concealed under a mountain of sunflower stems or firewood. A little systematic stabbing around with your bayonet will bring them to light in most cases.

"Sugar and spices are put under loose floorboards or behind a removable brick in the masonry. It's worth checking behind the pictures and wall hangings, too.

"With a little patience, a wagon isn't so difficult to construct, either. When the natives can't take them along, they usually dismantle them and hide the axles and wheels in the attic or the barn or else distribute them in different neighbors' gardens."

Haas wrapped it up with "All this, my lad, is known as plundering, perfectly official at the front."

Once we had scraped together various foodstuffs, the questions of a serviceable container and a fire to cook our booty still remained. Our mess kits usually served well enough for pots, and if we needed something bigger, a steel helmet came in handy. Whenever possible since my first experience with the raw horsemeat, I tried to have a frying pan either on a nearby vehicle or attached to the back of my wireless box.

When we weren't quartered in houses, the cooking fire sometimes presented a bit more of a problem. Even in the bunkers or trenches, we still managed quite well by bringing in an iron stove from the next village or by cutting part of the bottom out of an iron bucket.

But it was during those long marches in rain and snow that the official rations were the worst and our hunger the greatest. On one of our wire-patching tours, Haas showed me an ingenious solution. We were just passing a deserted artillery position where mortar shells lay all around the shot-up cannon. Haas seemed to be looking for something in particular. Shortly, he broke open a crate and showed me the long, round packages lying inside.

"Do you know what's in those rolls?" he asked me.

"Sure," I said, proud to know the answer for once. "Those are the booster charges, gunpowder to make the shells fly faster."

"Right," said Haas, with a mysterious little smile. He pulled the heavy packing paper away from one of the charges, laying free the contents, which looked like black spaghetti. "These little babies burn like the devil."

He filled his tin cup with cold coffee from his canteen and placed it deftly on top of two small, well-spaced rocks. Lighting one of the pieces of gunpowder spaghetti with his lighter, he held it between the two rocks, keeping the hot white flame continually under his cup. The giant sparkler burned for a few seconds, and he immediately lit another. With only three or four, he quickly brought his coffee almost to the boiling point.

After this impressive demonstration, I kept a constant supply of those booster charges in my wireless box. Again and again, on icy night marches or during days of endless rain in the trenches with water up to my ankles, Haas's trick helped me to a hot cup and renewed strength.

Sometimes, when we hadn't even matches or a lighter in working order, we fetched the Russian lighters from the pockets of dead enemy soldiers. These consisted of a large flint, a piece of file, and a little cotton batting. With the first two items, a little practice, and a great deal of huffing and puffing, one could eventually produce sparks strong enough to catch on fire.

But for now, in our village, we were relatively well-off, and the peaceful days continued.

Russia, February 4, 1944

My dear, good old Mutti,

Papi described so vividly in his letter the way you already let him know at the iron steps when there is mail from me that I've made up my mind to write even more often. You'll get very spoiled, though, when I'm in a quiet position. Then, when I cannot manage to write for two or three weeks, you will start having silly ideas right away.

But, on the other hand, I can imagine you so well there at home, wandering around the house, going past the usually empty mailbox from time to time, and then looky there! Suddenly there is something inside, and from whom? From me.

And so, for the next ten minutes you don't have the feeling of being thousands of kilometers away from your obnoxious son, and what's more, you are reassured that I still haven't taken off for the beautiful beyond. But you can be sure I haven't the slightest intention of doing that. After all, I'm only nineteen, and I never was the dumbest!

Soon there will be dry meadows and sunshine for which I already long so much. Nevertheless, I would rather be spending this time in the Vienna Woods or some other lovely place near you. Till next time, many loving kisses,

Your Boy

February 5, 1944

My dear Mui,

I just wrote you yesterday, but all four of my comrades are sitting here so cozily, writing by the light of the sunflower oil lamp, that I was prompted to do the same. To be sure, there isn't much room at the small table, but one can find a tiny edge.

Pretty soon we'll have spent five full days in this village, twenty kilometers behind the front, with absolutely nothing to do but become human beings again. That feels very good, especially since the last weeks have been so exhausting and agitating.

For the moment it is quiet and warm around me; my belly is full, I'm slept out, and that feels good, very good! I hope this situation will keep up for a nice long time. Every day one becomes a little livelier here, but one's thoughts become dumber. There is a little town with a small railroad station two kilometers away, and I hear the trains whistling all the time. Then feelings something like homesickness come over me, especially when so many wounded and furloughers are going home. You write that you want to take my favorite things out of my room in case of bombing. I don't know if that is really worth the bother, since I don't have such valuable things anyway, and what I love most is the room as a whole. The only thing might be a book.

Maybe it won't come to bombing that quickly in Vienna. I still hope that it won't happen at all. It is very calming for me here to think that everything at home is okay. I notice how it is with the fellows from the West, who never know for certain whether their homes are still standing.

My dear Mui, don't have any silly ideas. It's not worth it, and if it's going to happen, it's going to

happen. There is nothing to be done, and as much as I can, I take good care. What's more, it's mostly just wounds, and one can live fine with those.

Many kisses, Your Boy

On our sixth day in the same village, Haas, Baby Schmidt, and I went up to the field kitchen. The menu that day was a particularly unsavory stew. I noticed a young sergeant and a gray-haired older soldier sitting on a horse wagon. From the looks of the shiny rifles, brand-new bread bags, and clean laundry sacks lying next to them, I guessed they must have just arrived straight from Germany.

The sergeant was tall and thin, with a pale, narrow face. I couldn't help noticing his long, tapering fingers that, in comparison to our grubby, grease-encrusted mitts, appeared impeccably clean and manicured. I took him for an intellectual.

As I filled my canteen with coffee substitute and Haas went back to refill his mess kit from the mobile kettle, the young sergeant said to me, "There are supposed to be two or three men left over from the Second Battalion's signal squad. Any idea where I might find them?"

Haas laid his mess kit to one side, planted himself in front of the officer, saluted smartly with an impish smile, and shouted, in exaggerated imitation of the Prussian military style, "Obergefreiter [Lance Corporal] Haas, Funker Rauch, and Baby Schmidt—excuse me—Schütze [Private] Schmidt, Signal Squad, Second Battalion, Division 282 present!"

"At ease," the officer said as he stood up and stretched out his hand with a friendly smile. "I'm Sergeant Konrad, your new superior, it seems. This is Private Moser," he added, pointing to the older man. "He's also a member of the new signal squad that I'm supposed to organize here."

After we had dislodged the two infantrymen from our hut and installed Konrad and Moser in their place, a group with a certain feeling of belonging together began to form. Under Konrad's direction, we cleaned and checked the few pieces of equipment.

Moser became my second man, the one who carried the box of batteries for the wireless. He really wasn't good for much else. In World War I he had suffered a head wound and been reduced to a rather simple and lethargic state. He was about fifty years old but seemed older. In civilian life he had spent his days looking for grasses, roots, and herbs in the Austrian woods and mountains and selling them to special apothecaries.

Sergeant Konrad had a small travel chess set, and the two of us spent many hours deeply engrossed in games that carried us out of our surroundings and into the land of kings, queens, and castles. During these games we also became better acquainted. He was twenty-five and a native of Cologne. Even though he had been "with the firm" since the war's beginning, he had managed to squeeze in a year of study in electrical engineering at the university. He never swore, never even making use of those popular vulgarities that were otherwise so common at the front. Like me, he was bored by team sports and loved long debates. Although never clearly expressed, it was somehow obvious that he wasn't a Nazi.

The East, February 7, 1944

Dear Mutti,

We just received the accompanying airmail stamps. Be thrifty with them. Write just enough to cost a mark.

I'm still here with the detachment and it is quiet. As you can see by the other side of this page, I even feel like drawing again. It's funny the way different feelings that one had forgotten in the trenches, feelings for something good or beautiful, slowly start coming back. Suddenly one is in a much better mood.

This drawing will give you some idea of the room we're housed in (or at least an attempt). There is so much standing around here that I couldn't get it all on the paper. To the left, the stove, which takes up a quarter of the room, the bed, and the chest all are the same in every house here. More tomorrow. Many kisses,

Your Georg

The longer the situation remained so peaceful, the more unsatisfactory the pig slop from the kitchen seemed. I began to hang around the kitchen area, and whenever a cow was slaughtered I would cadge a few bones, a piece of liver, or some brains that nobody else wanted.

I turned the bones into tasty soups, and the liver and brains were delicious breaded or fried with eggs. I began to see old Moser in a new light the day he showed up with a collection of roots, bulbs, and tiny leaves that he had managed to dig up God knows where in that wintry, muddy landscape.

He offered them as spices for my cooking, and they added immeasurably to the taste of various concoctions.

Haas also wanted to share in my meals and popped up from time to time with a chicken, eggs, or flour that he had brought from a neighboring village. He was especially proud of an amphora-like container filled with a delicious black plum puree that he produced toward the beginning of my culinary experiments.

That day the kitchen smells were particularly tantalizing, and Konrad, who thus far hadn't participated in our home cooking, seemed, quite by chance, to find himself somewhat closer to the stove every five minutes.

Finally he said, "What is that you're cooking?"

"Oh, not much, Herr Unteroffizier," I answered, as though I hadn't noticed what he was getting at.

"Hmmm, it smells really wonderful. Looks good, too."

"It's just garbage that the mess sergeant was throwing away—old bones, liver, stuff like that. It'll probably be tough as leather."

"Could I have a taste?" he then asked, looking a little embarrassed. After sampling, he pronounced, "Ummm, but it's really delicious."

He went on a while longer with more compliments until I gave him another taste. Then I let him have a small bowl of the chicken soup with little dumplings.

By the time we got to the last course, everyone was helping in assembly-line fashion, and the entire signal squad finally sat down to ten plum-puree crepes apiece.

I disrespectfully renamed our superior officer Konrad Potpeeker. He admitted to me that he had a stomach ulcer and actually should be receiving a special diet that wasn't, of course, available on the Russian front.

From that day on, whether times were turbulent or quiet, I could always depend on Sergeant Konrad's approval (or command, if I wished to call it that) to repair nonexistent broken phone lines so that I could plunder the houses of the area for our gourmet meals.

Russia, February 9, 1944

Dear Mutti,

I think the peaceful time is past. The replacements are just arriving, and tonight or tomorrow we'll be heading with them toward the front. It won't be much fun, wading for twenty kilometers in deep mud, but the front is somewhat quieter for the time being. Ivan seems to have transferred his strong point to the north.

Here everything seems to be falling asleep. Only food and the most necessary ammunition are making it through to us. We haven't received any mail for twelve days now, and then only airmail.

Yesterday we had a field church service that I found very satisfying. The atmosphere was strange: a little room in a riddled hut, with the sun shining through the roof and the wind blowing through the broken doors and windows. The far-off thunder of the cannons and the serious faces of the soldiers—by all means, a very unusual atmosphere.

I'm in tip-top shape again, rested up. My belly is full, and I'm also in quite a good mood. Today we're having fried chicken and pudding with raspberry sauce as a farewell dinner. Tell Vienna hello for me. Thousand kisses,

Your Boy

A TRUE RUSSIAN WINTER

Russia, February 11, 1944

Dear Mutti,

Oh dear, how my bones are aching. Yesterday we moved twenty-five kilometers closer to the front. Now we are situated five kilometers behind the main fighting line in a burned-out village. No chicken, no cow, just here and there a house still standing. This place is the springboard back into the trenches.

Oh yes, and I was on horseback those twenty-five kilometers, on five different nags! I feel like a seasoned rider now, one who knows all the tricks of the trade. The mud makes walking a torture. First you sink in up to your shins, and then you can't get out again.

And so I, crafty old fox, organized a horse. Without saddle, naturally, just with a pair of narrow cords running somehow past the ears as reins. Of course, I don't know the first thing about horses or riding, and it wasn't until after the first three kilometers that I realized I was riding a pregnant mare who bucked and wouldn't run.

Whereupon, without much ado, I went into a barn in the next village and took a different horse, and that one ran. That beast galloped, stood on its hind legs, and never went in the direction I wanted. But I stayed on him for about ten kilometers, until I spied another that I took to be quieter and more docile.

I changed horses once again and, what do you know, it walked quite peacefully behind the wagons, until an expert told me that it was a young horse, about two months old, and would collapse any moment. So I looked for the next horse and discovered shortly after mounting that it was limping. I finally arrived here with an old horse that had a runny nose, and after a few words of thanks, I took my leave of him with a slap on the rump.

Twice in the course of the day I was thrown, to the general amusement of all. I was rather amazed myself at the way I accomplished the separate stages of riding, from the slowest snail tempo to a full gallop.

All in all, it was a delightful experience: by the light of the moon, with a rifle on my back, just like an old cowboy riding over the endless fields. My thighs are pretty sore today though. When I have to walk, it's with a sort of swagger. But I really slept well. In a few hours we are going up front to a bunker in the open fields. Then we'll look like pigs again. But the front is quiet for the time being. I hope the mail gets through. I'll write you again when circumstances permit. Till then, kisses and greetings to Pop,

Your Boy

On my twentieth birthday, I wrote the following:

Russia, February 14, 1944

Dear Mutti,

Please don't be frightened when you see my writing. On a gear of a cable drum I ripped a hole about a centimeter deep in my right hand, just underneath the index finger. So I'm pretty clumsy, but otherwise I'm fine.

I was supposed to go up front with the company as radioman, but I couldn't be transferred because of the injury. Maybe it is fate or my luck. The front continues very quiet here. Hardly a shot all day long. Those of us on the staff are headquartered in the last houses of the village. Here in Panchevo there is neither chicken nor cow. [Author's note: Sometimes, against the regulations, I smuggled in the name of a town in the middle of a letter, in order to let my parents know where I was.] They were all eaten up by our predecessors. We are getting mail in masses now, every day a sack, but all old letters posted around Christmas or earlier. Writing is pretty difficult because the hole hurts quite a bit when I move my hand. Many loving greetings,

Your Son

Russia, February 18, 1944

Dear Mutti,

I'm not in the position of writing you such a positive letter today as the last ones have been. You mustn't take what I write too tragically, since I'm considerably better off than most. Overnight it has become winter here again; that is, the true Russian winter. The temperature is running between ten and twenty-five below zero. You can barely move against the icy east storm. The ice needles tear your skin to pieces. You can see only three meters ahead.

Yesterday, in this weather, we marched for thirty kilometers. Left at 5 a.m. and reached our destination at about 11:30 p.m. Quite a few collapsed along the way and will be listed as missing. Probably somewhere in these unending fields they have frozen to death. One never knows. A few vehicles also disappeared. All that was left of us arrived here, more or less frozen.

"Here" is a *kolchos*. That is to say an enormous barn without windows or doors. Or rather, there are holes in the walls without wood or glass. Inside the snow is just as high as outside, and the wind howls, too. Way at the back are two rooms with a door, and these can be heated. Our battalion headquarters staff has holed up there.

The rest of the company just kept going forward to the trenches to relieve another unit. Then the night passed. I'm sitting here now in the morning at the switchboard, listening to the awful early reports: in every company some dead, many frozen, some suspected of self-inflicted wounds. Some just got out of the trenches and took off on their own.

Everyone else spent the whole night shoveling just to see the sky, since these two-man holes can fill up with snow in a matter of minutes. There's been nothing to eat since yesterday morning, not even coffee. And so, the poor guys are lying out there day and night, slowly freezing to death. I also threw up four times last night, have diarrhea, and sat up all night on the wet ground near the drafty door. In spite of that, I feel like a plutocrat. Enough for today. Kisses from

Your Georg

February 19, 1944

Dear Folks,

A few hasty shivering words. The east wind howls through all the cracks. Your ninth package arrived today, with quince jam, tea, and cookies. Everything is so much easier when you've had a sign from home. Russia is so gruesome.

Continually, eighteen-year-olds with frozen hands are being sent to the rear. Practically nothing is left of us now. But I'm healthy and all right compared to the others.

A holiday in Russia.

About June or July I can count on leave, if I'm not already back by then. Be well and don't worry. Nothing will happen to me.

10,000 Bussis [Kisses], Your Son

February 21, 1944

Dear Mutti,

I'm still sitting here in my *kolchos*. We've been working day and night for the last few days, trying to get this place halfway stopped up. Now, if we heat all day, it gets nice and warm. We've also found some straw for sleeping. You can't imagine how much that means, when outside the eternal east storm is blowing. At least one can warm a meal, toast some bread, and chase one's hundred thousand lice.

A sign on our door reads, "Wireless Station, No Admittance," but many half-frozen soldiers, passing by for one reason or another, beseech us to let them come in and warm up for a few minutes.

Once inside they sit around the little stove, quite silent and thoughtful, and revel in the great happiness of having warm hands and feet once again.

One thumbed through his notebook and suddenly said, "Did you know that today is Sunday?" Each one then described, almost as if speaking of something holy and long past, what he had done at this time of the week before the war. The others gazed silently into the fire. Perhaps some of them let visions of something beautiful from home pass in front of their eyes and were able thereby to forget for a few minutes their horrible current situation.

Sunday, for most soldiers, is the symbol of good times and relaxation. Maybe I think a little differently, since Sundays for us passed by almost just like all the other days. The big dates that many dream of, the bars, variety shows, and movies, weren't so common for me. Maybe I had things so good that I never learned to appreciate the true value of Sundays? But it doesn't matter.

When the soldiers leave after a half hour or forty-five minutes, they have new courage and the feeling of having experienced a few very special moments. Their eyes are glowing again, and thus they return back up front to the trenches.

It was your seventh package, not the ninth, that I received yesterday. Fantastic, and there's hope of more mail. I sent you 159 marks today. Otherwise I'm doing fine, at least more or less. Many kisses,

Your Georg

P.S. The front is quiet.

Russia, February 26, 1944

Dear Mutti,

Quite late yesterday evening some mail arrived, including the letter you wrote on my birthday. I withdrew to a quiet corner and read. Afterward I noticed that my eyes were quite damp. Perhaps it was written with too much love for the disposition of a presently wild and degenerate fighter.

One becomes pretty hard in every respect here, and there are only a few things that really go all the way to the heart. A protecting wall absorbs most things before they get that far.

But when a mother writes from the distant

homeland of her love for her son, and of the extremely favorable balance of the last twenty years, that goes all the way inside, even during the strongest bombardment. So, afterward one has wet eyes. It could happen to anyone.

Today the sun is shining beautifully; the snow is starting to thaw; the trenches are turning into mud holes again. The wind is blowing through the broken doors and windows. No wood, nothing to eat but "water soup," one loaf of bread for four men, and unsalted sausage. So currently not very rosy, but I don't think we will be here much longer. Kisses,

Your Son

March 2, 1944

Dear Papi,

Yesterday a few others from the staff and I went to a variety show in the village. The so-called Spotted Woodpeckers entertained us wonderfully for an hour and a half. It was a Viennese comedian, magician, and musical group from the army broadcasting station, Gustav, one that travels back and forth putting on shows for the soldiers.

It was very strange for me, here in the middle of cannons and uniforms, to see someone in civilian clothing on an improvised stage. They provided us with a wonderful change, and we certainly didn't regret having trudged five kilometers in the morass to see it!

The Russians attack continuously to the north and south, but it is quiet where we are. In return for that, though, we are in serious danger of being hemmed in again. Very little is left to eat, and that little is no good. Give everyone my best greetings,

Your Georg

At noon on the fourth of March, Sergeant Konrad called me to the switchboard, where he had spent the last hour and a half busily connecting the incoming calls.

"You and Schmidt go immediately back to the repair unit and pick up two radio tubes of this number." He handed me a scrap of paper with some scribbling on it.

"Where is the repair unit?" I asked.

"Exactly twenty kilometers southwest of here, there's a good-sized town. That's where the regimental mess and the bakery are located. The railroad passes through, so probably they have all sorts of other backup supplies, too. You can't miss it."

Taking just our rifles and bread bags, we started off. The day was warm and sunny. The track was torn up and softened knee-deep from the military vehicles, but we discovered firmer ground on the edges.

I found myself hopping to keep up with Baby Schmidt's incredibly long stride. Schmidt hadn't earned his nickname because of his age alone. His eyes were baby blue, and his soft pink cheeks still hadn't felt the scrape of a razor. He reminded me of a giant's baby from one of those fairy tales.

That day I asked him, "Why did they take you so young, anyway?"

"I joined up voluntarily," Baby answered.

"Humph," I grunted. "You must already be sorry about that decision."

His face turned red, and he didn't answer for quite a while. Then he said, "My father fell two years ago in Yugoslavia. Partisans. My stepmother took over our farm in the Black Forest. She and I never hit it off so well, and my brothers had all been drafted already. There wasn't anything more for me at home, so I joined up."

I thought about how different we all were. To me, volunteering to be sent to a front like this was the next closest thing to committing suicide. But I kept my thoughts to myself and concentrated on checking my compass as we tramped on.

We took our time, and by late afternoon we reached a small town where a tank unit was filling up on gas. We also tanked up with monster portions of a good beef stew from the field kitchen and slept that night on a soft bed of grain that filled up half a room in one of the houses.

By noon the following day we reached the place where the repair unit was supposed to be. It was a large village, filled with soldiers from the various supply units. The artillery was on the move, and everybody seemed to be in a hurry.

"It looks as though they are all pulling out," Schmidt commented.

I stopped next to a soldier working under the hood of a heavy truck. "Can you tell me where to find the radio repair unit from Division 282?"

"Sorry, I can't help you."

We asked a few more times, but without success. Even at the command post no one seemed to know. As the day wore on, it became increasingly obvious that everyone was preparing for a hasty departure.

That night we made ourselves comfortable in one of the officers' quarters that had just been vacated. Before turning in, I said to Baby Schmidt, "We might as well head back to the front tomorrow. The unit we're looking for is probably long gone. There's no sense in searching any longer."

The following morning the streets were almost deserted. Most of the units had left the village during the night. As we passed the last houses, I stopped abruptly and listened.

"Do you hear what I hear?"

"*Ja*, heavy artillery and other firecrackers."

"Yeah, that, too," I said. "Nothing else?"

We both stood listening for a moment, then took off in the direction of one of the houses. After stopping once more to listen, we circled the house and there it was: a makeshift wooden box with three chickens and a rooster.

"Looks like someone prepared those for a trip but couldn't fit them into the taxi," Schmidt said with a broad smile.

After a futile search for an old woman, we were obliged to kill, pluck, and boil the chickens ourselves. It took us all morning, but while the last two were cooking, I also discovered two horses. We rode away at noon, minus the radio tubes but carrying mess kits stuffed with chicken pieces and two gas mask containers full of hot soup.

Heavy battle noises drifted from the direction in which we were riding. After only five kilometers we arrived at a rear position held by an array of antitank guns, entrenched soldiers with bazookas, and a few camouflaged tanks.

Just a few minutes later I saw a mass of fleeing soldiers running in our direction. "Let's get out of here," I yelled to Schmidt. We pulled up and galloped back to the village.

By two o'clock we could hear that the Russian attack had come to a halt. Asking around, we managed by evening to find the bloody remains of our unit sitting in a ditch next to the road. I served up the four chickens, saving the tenderest pieces, as usual, for Konrad's ulcer.

A little later a bumpy cart rolled past, and there lay Haas, his face contorted in pain. When I grabbed his hand to shake it, he flashed a wide grin that belied his wound. "A thigh shot. I've made it. The war's over for me."

I stood waving goodbye as the horse pulled the cart away. I wondered if he really had been shot, or whether he had finally put to use what he had explained to me numerous times in all the technical details.

Just a few weeks earlier he had said, "And don't forget, if worse comes to worst you can always shoot yourself in the leg. Do it through a loaf of bread or a folded jacket. That way you don't have to worry about suspicious powder burns."

However it had happened, Haas had received his injury, and he had more than earned his trip home. I hated to see him go, and I felt more forsaken than ever.

I shouldn't have felt quite so forlorn, however. A few days later it became clear to me that Sergeant Konrad had received word of the impending tank attack over the wireless and had purposely sent us to the rear for radio tubes to a unit that didn't even exist. He had wanted to save Baby Schmidt, who was too young to die, and make certain that I, his private cook, was also safe from harm!

Russia, March 17, 1944

Dear Papi,

You simply can't describe some things because the reader wouldn't be able to imagine them: the war here in this most forsaken of all countries; the Russians to the north, northwest, east, south, southeast; the river Bug seventy kilometers away, and us—a few sorry units where the staff is often larger than the number of fighting soldiers—continually struggling as much as possible to build a closed front.

Until two days ago the whole country was like soup where everything gets stuck and threatens to sink. By day we're on the spot; that is to say, we build a front. During the night we wade fifteen to thirty kilometers in muck and goo toward the southwest. It takes us from six in the evening until 9 a.m., at least, just to gain a few kilometers.

Then there's usually shortwave communication and shooting, and that's why I've hardly slept a full hour for the last eight days. There's only cold food, and not much of that. To drink? Ditto. The Russians are always close on our tails. The only hope is to get over the Bug as soon as possible, before Ivan really gives it to us.

If a vehicle gets stuck in the mud, it can't be retrieved, because the Russians already have it. If somebody falls behind for one reason or other, Ivan has him. So we trudge, dead tired, hungry, with the feeling "If I collapse, Ivan's got me." The beards keep getting longer, the mood worse, and our strength less.

Since yesterday there has been an overwhelmingly strong snowstorm with temperatures under minus 20 centigrade. I've never experienced anything like it. This morning someone made a joke, and I wanted to laugh but was only able to produce a strange grimace. That made me very sad. I've always liked so much to laugh, and here I'm completely forgetting how.

Just now the Russians have broken into the left flank and are marching through with two battalions. The counterattack is in progress; the telephone lines are down, so I'll have to get onto the wireless.

Since I've adopted the general point of view "What doesn't kill me doesn't bother me," I can still take it. If I croak, I croak. If I don't, that's good, too. I've just reread this letter and noticed that it is nothing but bellyaching from beginning to end. Don't take it too much to heart. This too will pass. Many loving kisses from,

Your Georg

On one of those nights of long marches, a young soldier who had arrived with the last replacements and been at the front only a short time simply sat down and said, "I can't walk any farther."

The others kept marching past us, and I told him if he remained behind, he would fall into the hands of the Russians, who were gaining on us.

"They'll just shoot you," I said. "They aren't taking any prisoners."

"Let them," he replied dully.

An officer came by and ordered the boy to get up, with no result. The officer pulled out his revolver and shouted, "*Mensch*, get up this minute or I'll shoot you. This is an order!" But the soldier seemed to have gone deaf or at least to be in a different world.

At that moment I did something purely instinctive, without even considering the presence of the superior officer. I took off my wireless box, rifle, and gloves, grabbed the young soldier by his collar, placed myself squarely in front of him, and left, right, slapped him hard across the face. At the same time I roared, "Get up, you idiot!"

Slowly he raised himself, and, almost as if in a dream, he walked on, another soldier carrying his rifle.

During the following days, as we all became more exhausted, the order rang out a few more times, "Slapping squad to the rear!" And with that order, they meant me.

Before dawn on March 22, we dragged ourselves into Pervomaysk, a good-sized town on the river Bug. My regiment and many others were immediately ordered to secure a bridgehead. That entailed building a ring around the city so that each of the many thousands of Germans still within could retreat to the opposite bank of the river. The Russians, of course, were intent on taking Pervomaysk swiftly so that they could capture as many of us as possible.

Konrad and I were situated with the wireless on the ground floor of a two-story building on the eastern edge of the city. We were attempting to keep communications going between several companies and battalion headquarters, located a few houses away. Many of the nearby buildings were on fire, and smoke came through the broken window, making our eyes smart and tear. The city was being fought for street by street, house by house, and we could hear the battle raging in the distance.

By noon the racket sounded much closer. I was just wondering where the Russians had broken through when Konrad yanked out the cable connecting the wireless to the battery box and yelled, "Get out the back! The Russians are in front of the door."

He was already on his way out the window, the battery box in one hand and a submachine gun in the other. I threw the wireless over my shoulder by one of its straps and grabbed my rifle, and the first bursts from the Russian submachine guns thwacked into the room as I vaulted out the window behind Konrad. The blast of a hand grenade blew me through the opening even faster than planned.

I scrambled to my feet and took off after Konrad across the open square. At the sound of heavy machine-gun fire, I glanced back to see that a tank had shoved its way through one of the ruins facing the square and was merrily shooting away at anything that moved. Zigzagging around debris and riddled vehicles, I made it into one of the side streets. Konrad had halted a few houses farther away to check his compass. He waved his arm in the direction ahead of us and we began running once more.

The street was darkened by heavy smoke. Some of the four-story houses on my right were enveloped in flames, and I could feel the blazing heat as I ran past. The noise on all sides was deafening: mortar hits, machine-gun fire, and the crackling and roaring of the flames from the burning houses.

All of a sudden, the wall of the house just to my right began tilting forward. The panic that seized me at that moment must also have endowed me with tremendous strength. In spite of the heavy wireless still hanging over my shoulder, I somehow ran faster.

A giant cloud of fire and dust exploded through the ground-floor window. The wall buckled at the second story, and all the masonry from the top floors, including the flaming roof beams, came tumbling down with a horrible earsplitting crash.

Some of the longest seconds of my life elapsed before my own legs and the monstrous air pressure propelled me just enough so that I was hit by only a few chunks of brick. I was tossed to the ground in a scorching cloud of dust. I staggered to my feet, checked my bones, and continued to run. Finally I overtook Konrad, who had paused in a doorway to catch his breath.

"This morning one of the bridges crossing the river was still intact," he said. "If we can find it, and it's still in one piece, we should be able to make it safely to the other side. The river can't be too far away, maybe just a few blocks. Let's go!"

We soon reached a wider street filled with scores of Germans, all running in the same direction. Without hesitating, we joined the rest. The Russians hadn't penetrated this part of the city yet; nevertheless, all signs pointed to an uncontrolled full-scale flight by the Germans.

We reached the bridge and rejoiced to see it still whole, but it was choked up with soldiers and vehicles, all moving at a maddeningly slow pace toward the west bank. I could see Pioniere attaching explosive charges to the pilings. It had begun to rain.

After finally working our way to the opposite side, we were met by bellowing officers trying to bring some semblance of order or grouping into this milling mass of soldiers. It was a chaotic mixture of everything military: members of the tank corps without tanks, artillery soldiers with no cannons, wounded men on stretchers or still on foot, and officers of every rank. Some of the officers were hastily organizing battle units that they sent marching off in various directions.

"Hey, you two with the wireless, over here," called a colonel to Konrad and me. A sergeant gave us ammunition and directed us to a column of about five hundred men who were already waiting to depart, bazookas and machine guns in hand.

"Column march!" rang out the command, and we were on our way. No one had any idea what our destination was. It was a sorry heap of hungry, battle-weary men who didn't seem to care where they were headed, just as long as there was still someone to give orders and at least an impression that they knew why they were giving them.

The rain poured down steadily as we marched past huge amounts of war matériel, some shot up and some still in good condition. In a few minutes we had passed the last houses and ruins on the outskirts of town and were headed out into the flat, marshy fields.

There thousands of vehicles had been left standing up to their axles in the mire. Stinking horse cadavers with legs pointing stiffly toward the sky lay next to artillery cannons and mountains of ammunition crates that stretched as far as we could see. Bomb craters filled with water were everywhere.

A tremendous battle must have been waged in the section, but the Russians had evidently waived their right to this strip along the west side of the river, at least for now. It was obvious that all this equipment would fall into their hands sooner or later.

The ranks broke for a few minutes when we came up to an overturned truck. Crates full of canned foods lay open on the ground, and the eager soldiers helped themselves at will. Even the officers, as hungry as the rest of us, stooped to filling their pockets and bags. No one could say when circumstances would improve enough so that we could once again have a field kitchen and regular meals.

Back on the march, most of us opened one or two of the tins and gobbled up the contents: cold, greasy meat. At our backs I could hear the noise of continuing battle within the city. The Russians had brought in bombers and heavy artillery by now. No matter where I was headed, I felt very lucky to be walking along this far side of the river.

A series of heavy explosions made me glance back. Great chunks of steel were flying through the air in a huge black cloud—they had blown up the bridge.

Konrad made a face. "Certainly made it out of that one just in time."

I nodded, thinking of Baby Schmidt and Moser, whom I hadn't seen since we entered the city.

The officers urged us to more speed. After another half hour we reached our destination: a soggy airfield containing a few shot-up buildings. A troop carrier with its motors running stood a short distance away. The front portion of our column was ordered into the plane, while the remainder was told to keep ready; another aircraft would come later to pick us up.

Overcome by exhaustion and hopelessness, I stood watching as the plane began moving faster along the bumpy runway, finally leaving the ground to disappear in the rain clouds. I had very little hope of seeing another one.

We stood in the rain and waited. Konrad wandered to another group of soldiers and returned. "They claim the Russians have not only taken the city, but they've also built a larger circle around the entire area, including this airport, or what's left of it. Could be just a rumor, though."

I hadn't expected any good news at this point. When

Konrad didn't get a response from me, he set off again on his search for news.

Looking around, I saw huge piles of crates and suitcases of every size, shape, and style stacked as high as small buildings. I sat down on one of the crates. Some soldiers had begun breaking open a few of the suitcases and were rummaging around in the contents. After listening for a while to amazed shouts, I became curious and shuffled over to see the reason for all the excitement.

What I saw was incredible. The suitcases were stuffed with French perfume and condoms; bottles of the most expensive cognacs and champagnes; elegant clothing for men and women, including tuxedos and French designer dresses; Russian icons of inestimable value; and old books bound in leather and gilt. There was also a thick roll of pure silk cloth and several dozen pairs of silk stockings, still in the original packaging.

We foot soldiers never owned more than the absolute essentials, and usually not even those. But the motorized branches of the service seldom came near the front lines. If the front disintegrated, those soldiers, and especially their officers, always had plenty of time to send their luggage back to the rear. As we now could see, this luggage contained not only priceless booty but also treasures brought from France and elsewhere, enabling the officers to maintain the good life, even on the Russian front.

This time the poor generals had miscalculated. The usual transport system hadn't functioned in Pervomaysk. Everything had happened too quickly, and now those higher-ranking gentlemen's only hope was to bring everything out by air.

I hadn't seen anything civilized for six months. I had just escaped a very close encounter with the Russian bullets, and for weeks previous to this I had been unwashed, unshaven, covered with muck, and wet through to the skin, my tattered socks sticking to legs oozing pus. My surroundings had consisted primarily of blood, filth, and lice.

In such a state of mind and body, what an experience to open a suitcase and be assailed by the aroma of forgotten cleanliness and elegance. I stretched out my mud-encrusted hands to feel the unbelievable softness of pure silk. I reached into a completely different world and, almost without knowing what I was doing, I tore a strip from the roll of silk, wrapped it around a pair of stockings, and stuck the small package in my rear pants pocket.

At the sound of a low hum, I whirled around. A shadow appeared out of the heavy gray skies; a plane was coming in to land. "It's a Ju 52," somebody yelled.

An officer shouted, "Form ranks."

We hurriedly grabbed a few more of the bottles lying around, and I snatched up a large hunk of smoked ham at the last second before running toward the plane.

I was more or less shoved into the aircraft. It was grotesque to see all that the soldiers were trying to carry or drag with them. Loud commands forced the majority to drop most of their loot before being permitted inside:

"No more. Move back. The rest of you will be picked up later."

The motors whined; we bumped and rattled for half a mile and were at last airborne. I had begun the first airplane flight of my life, but whatever fear I might have felt was far outweighed by the wonder of having escaped the deadly situation below.

Russia, March 22, 1944

Dear Papi,

Right now I'm sitting in a warm hut again. I have slept a whole night and eaten my fill. My clothes are still full of mud, but otherwise I'm fine. Seven of us are waiting for the rest of the battalion, which should already have landed here in Balta by plane twelve hours ago. Eight empty bottles are standing on the table in front of me: two bottles French red wine, one bottle Cru Saint-Georges-Montagne, one bottle Weinbrand, one bottle Bordeaux Medoc, one bottle Jamaican rum, one bottle Stock egg cognac, and one bottle gin. We have consumed all of that since yesterday evening!

The days at the bridgehead in Pervomaysk were very hot. I'm not all that impressed by the war events, but you can believe I would rather not have experienced those three days. And then, all of a sudden we were flown to Balta. Here it feels as though the Germans are definitely beginning to lose control. I don't know exactly what is ahead of me. It is still raining day and night.

Communications squad, with Sergeant Konrad and Karl Haas in center of back row and me seated in front in the vakja (sledge).

I had to leave everything behind again. Now I have only my clothes and a few little things in my pockets. I organized a jacket, and in my breast pocket is a pair of silk stockings. I still have my wireless set, too. So now we're waiting to see what the future will bring.

I heard from a pilot that Vienna has been bombed. Please write me more details about this. It is important to me. Otherwise don't worry. The war will be over soon, because it can't go on much longer like this. Then I'll come home again, and everything will be better. Give everyone my love, and please take care that at least everything remains okay at home. Many loving greetings.

Your Georg

The transport plane with the third group never arrived. We sat around for two more days, eating and drinking all the goodies the soldiers had managed to carry away from the Pervomaysk airport. Even Konrad got a little drunk, something I would never have thought possible.

"What regiment are you from?" was a common question. We were a mixture of thirty men from all sorts of branches, and not even half had any frontline experience. The rest were from transport, artillery, staff, engineer corps, and so on. Almost nobody knew anyone else from before, and I considered myself lucky to have Konrad nearby. He was sometimes gone for hours, trying to find out what was going to happen, but without success.

All of a sudden we were ordered to walk to a tiny railroad station, where we boarded a train with only five cars, and off we went. I caught the name of Birsula at one small station through which we passed. The ride finally ended in Slobodka, thirty kilometers farther southwest.

Immediately upon descending from the train, we hiked in groups of fifty men into the falling night. Some had light machine guns; a few others lugged lightweight mortars.

"I don't like it," said Konrad. "I don't see any supply equipment whatsoever."

"And as far as I can tell, you and I have the only wireless," I replied.

It snowed the whole night. The temperature sank lower and lower, and the wind reached blizzard proportions. After the recent springlike temperatures, no one had his padded pants or jacket any longer. It was now the end of March, after all. We froze pitifully.

At daybreak, confronted with the sort of winter landscape we hadn't seen for weeks, we dug ourselves in for the day. Konrad went spying.

When he returned he said, "No one has any idea of where we're going or why. The unit that we were supposed to reinforce doesn't exist, and the Russians seem to be all over the place."

After the following day's hike we reached an evacuated village. It huddled silently in the snow, empty of people and even chickens, but we did find some coverings to protect us from the biting cold. When we moved on, we resembled more than anything a group of armed beggars. Some had wrapped themselves up in colorful curtains, others had discovered some of the bright rugs typical of the region, and lucky were the men who had turned up a *pabacha*, a tall sheepskin wool cap. Various rags wrapped around our hands took the place of gloves.

In a letter to my parents I wrote,

> We took eleven days for the stretch from Slobodka to somewhere near Tiraspol on the Dniester, all in night marches. The Russians were continually all around us. At night we kept looking for a hole, for a way out of the sack. In the mornings we were surrounded again. And all the time terrible cold and snowstorms so bad that we often had to lie flat on the ground so as not to be blown away. And absolutely nothing to eat.

I thought, *I wish the powers that be could see their German soldiers now, wrapped in old carpets, muffled up in rags, unshaven, not having slept for days, on their knees begging the few locals for a piece of corn bread, too weak even to search the huts for food.* As we came through one village, half the group stormed up to a woman who was carrying a pot of milk and fought over it. Very quickly we became fewer, the ammunition ran very low, and the cold became worse.

On our tenth day as a lost group behind the Russian lines, we were reduced to one hundred men. The highest ranking was a sergeant. Then scouts discovered a river ten kilometers to the west that might be our salvation, and we headed off in that direction without even waiting for nightfall.

The sun was already low in the west when I caught sight of an airplane headed in our direction. At almost the same moment the command rang out, "Low flyer, take full cover!" Everyone threw himself into the snow, but a minute later Konrad was up again waving his arms and shouting, "It's a Fieseler Storch, a Storch!"

By the time the German light reconnaissance plane passed over us at a very low altitude, we were all on our feet and waving, full of hope. The plane made a loop and, when it was above us again, the pilot threw down six bags, two containing ammunition and the others filled with emergency rations. Each of us received two packages, neat little cardboard boxes about the size of a large book. The printed inscription read:

EMERGENCY RATIONS—
FRUIT BREAD. IF COOKED WITH A
LITTLE WATER MAKES PUDDING.
WITH MORE WATER SOUP.

On April 3, we climbed up a small hill. Below lay the river Dniester, that goal we had been longing and striving for. It shone, a silver ribbon in the afternoon sun, running through the white winter landscape—a beautiful sight.

Enormous numbers of German vehicles and soldiers were assembled directly below us on the plain. The few available boats were occupied with ferrying some of them across the river.

Considering our appearance, it wasn't surprising that the Germans shot at us until we were able to make ourselves known. Once past our own defense lines, we barely had time to eat a bite before we heard the deep hum of heavy diesel engines—the Russian tanks. They weren't even visible yet, and not a shot had been fired, but everyone took off toward the river without even waiting for a command.

The water was about two kilometers away, and everyone ran, taking only rifles and leaving everything else behind. I still hauled the wireless on my back; Konrad carried the other box, and we ran as well as we could with this burden.

The tanks rolled up behind us, at least thirty of them, painted white and gleaming in the sun. Immediately they began firing into the fleeing masses with everything they had.

"Hopeless," I said. "Nobody's going to make it across that river."

"We swim through," Konrad said.

"Through that icy water? Good luck."

I stopped, took the wireless off my back, removed a hand grenade from my belt, and was making ready to blow up the box when an open Volkswagen pulled up next to us. One of the three officers inside yelled, "You two with the set. Get inside fast!"

I grabbed the wireless; we jumped in and took off, driving wildly through the midst of all the fleeing soldiers and vehicles and the panic-stricken horses and cows that were running desperately in all directions.

Shells hit all around us, but by zigging and zagging around bomb craters and war matériel, we managed to draw closer to the river.

The sun was setting as we arrived at the bank. I asked myself why it happened to be us they had picked up, and what was the use anyway. There were no longer any boats to be seen, only despairing soldiers trying to decide whether to throw themselves into the freezing waters or wait to be finished off by the approaching tanks.

I was on the point of jumping out of the car when the officer at the wheel shouted, "Hold on!" The car rolled down a gentle slope to the river and right into the water. For a few seconds the current pulled us downriver, the car bobbing like a little boat. Suddenly a small propeller in the rear began to hum and, as if by magic, we chugged through house-high water fountains made by the shrapnel exploding around us and landed on the opposite side.

The car continued up the far bank and into the frozen fields and then finally stopped. Still without completely comprehending what had happened, I was waved over by one of the officers.

"Get into this crater. Send this message and wait for

the answer," he said, handing me a piece of paper. It was a request for new orders and position from division headquarters.

Some time later I remembered that back in Vienna I had once inspected an amphibian auto exactly like the one that had just transported us across the river; I hadn't dreamed that such a vehicle would one day play a vital role in my life.

Very few others made it over the river. The majority remained behind.

April 10, 1944

My dear Mutti,

On the third of this month, we made a dramatic crossing of the Dniester, and after one day of rest we were back on the lines. Since then a major battle—tough, ruthless—has been raging for every meter. Each time we retreat, a counterattack follows shortly thereafter. And so it continues, back and forth.

The units are dissolving rapidly. Our division dwindled into a battle group and when that, in turn, became too small to be effective we were attached to another division. And so it continues. I almost never know the name of my commanding officer, since I belong to a different unit every few days.

Many are falling and wounded. The procession of wounded no longer has an end. I see more and more of those little hills with the crosses. The last little bit of humor is also disappearing, because blood is everywhere and everything is in shreds. All are becoming more nervous by the day. Add to that the weather, which is warmer now but melting all the snow and turning the whole country into puree again.

Thus we stand in the mud, day and night, everything wet and dirty. I have twelve boils on my leg, with no bandage because the medics need all the bandages for the wounded. My feet are lumps of mud, and everything—underwear, pants, and stockings—is equally slippery. My boots aren't watertight either.

Yesterday it got to be too much for me, so I went back to the village to the doctor, who treated me and prescribed three days' rest at the supply lines. Since telegraphists are lacking, they exchanged me with the regiment telegraphist. I had barely finished washing up when the Russians took the village. We had to get out in a hurry, so I spent Easter Sunday without a bite to eat, out in the open on a kilometer marker in the middle of the morass. Thank God the sun was shining a little.

In the evening the village came back into our hands by way of a counterattack, and since then it has been quiet. The stove is drying my clothes, and a chicken with potatoes is filling my stomach. What's more, after a lice hunt (300–400) I slept like a baby the entire night.

Today is Easter Monday. The sun is shining gloriously, and everything looks a bit better again. A mail stoppage is in effect. I haven't received any more mail from you since March 18. I'm curious how I'll get rid of this letter. Don't worry. I'll get through somehow. Kisses,

Your Boy

INTO ROMANIA

With the crossing of the river Dniester, we took leave of Russia and entered Romanian territory. Communication became difficult once again, because the Romanians understood neither our German nor our newly acquired Russian.

We weren't permitted to steal any more chickens, because Romania was a friendly country, one whose divisions were fighting on the side of the Germans. We were expected, therefore, to pay for everything in lei, the Romanian currency.

Spring had finally arrived. The soft hills of the Romanian landscape were covered with a multitude of flowers. Grass began sprouting, and the fruit trees were ready to bloom. Everywhere things were beginning to stir, and an endless cackling covered the whole region. Thousands of little chicks, kittens, puppies, piglets, and baby goats were hopping around. It was amazing and reassuring to see how everything had multiplied in spite of the ongoing destruction all over the land.

I enjoyed the luxury of a reasonably clean house on the edge of a middle-sized village, several kilometers behind the front. The sun shone constantly, and the never-ending rumbling of the cannons in the distance didn't concern me now, because the fighting had shifted to the north. I had ten hours of undisturbed sleep every night and spent many hours a day on a blanket in the sun, where the numerous pus-filled sores on my legs finally began to heal.

Everything in this new place was so soothing: the awareness that winter was over, the assurance that we were beyond Russian shooting distance, the abundance of food, milk, and wine, a friendly woman in the house, and a pretty seventeen-year-old girl who seemed to smile at me in a particular way.

Sergeant Konrad, the last of the staff from the second battalion, and I shared a house while waiting to be united with the replacements and leftovers from other units into a new battle group. As far as we were concerned, the longer they took to put it together the better!

This new country was considerably different from the Ukraine. The Romanian people seemed to prefer everything a few degrees neater and cleaner. The walls of the houses were often whitewashed, and sometimes the front gardens even boasted flower beds. The generally higher standard of living enjoyed by the Romanians was obvious in many ways and especially exhibited by the five or six large wine barrels to be found in almost every cellar.

Not surprisingly under the circumstances, the old men of the village were drunk most of the time. When the rumbling sound of the artillery came a little closer, they quickly found their way into the cellars to get even more inebriated. Afterward they staggered around, yelling and laughing, sometimes making life rather difficult for us by becoming too interested in our weapons or equipment.

My duties were minimal. I had the wireless set up under a big walnut tree in the yard, on standby for unexpected circumstances. The other soldiers lived in a house across the street and spent most of their time drinking and playing cards.

I enjoyed being by myself or playing a game of chess with Konrad. I spent most of the time daydreaming, perhaps in an unconscious attempt to get my brain, body, and nerves back into some semblance of normality after the events of the past winter.

One day we were taken to a sauna, where we handed in the remainder of our outfits, mostly in shreds, and were given used but clean uniforms, without a louse in them. It was a tremendous feeling for the few days that it lasted. During my hours of sunbathing I managed to divest myself completely of military clothing, wearing only a pair of bathing trunks sewn from a stolen white curtain.

From dead soldiers at a nearby field hospital, I obtained the few things one needs: pencil, paper, shaving soap, towel, and wash kit. I still had the pair of silk stockings I had found at the Pervomaysk airport. There was probably nothing more useless I could have carried around. Once in a while I took the little package from my pocket, unwrapped it carefully, and pressed it to my nose, savoring the odor of a forgotten world.

The official rations were sparse: watery soup once a day and bread, butter, and sausage every three days. Whatever else we wanted we had to find ourselves, even if it was not officially permitted. I consumed an average of ten eggs a day: two soft-boiled for breakfast, a five-egg omelet around midday, and the rest stirred into milk or hot red wine. A chicken per day stewed or fried and some of the hard, dry bread of the region kept my belly full. When the girl, Ana, wearing a dress much too pretty for a weekday, came bringing fresh flowers to the table and smiling that special smile, I noticed some long-dormant desires beginning to awake.

One day some mail from home arrived, including pudding powder and raisins that were very quickly transformed into a thing of beauty, a bright yellow vanilla pudding, cooked in an old steel helmet and turned out on a board ready to be eaten. Soon it was only a lovely memory, but something else arrived in the same parcel that was to have an unexpected effect. It was a brand-new Hohner C-major mouth organ. I had been without a harmonica for quite some time, having left my last one behind in some hasty retreat.

The sun was already setting when I picked up my new harmonica, walked out through the little vegetable garden into the field, and climbed up on a haystack. There I lay, playing a sonata, looking up into the sky and feeling as though I might be able to make it after all, protected by an entire family of guardian angels.

It wasn't too long before the girl Ana came creeping up to sit next to me. We had communicated before in a sort of Romanian that seemed to come easily to me, thanks to the little bit of Russian I had picked up, my school French, and my native German. On that particular evening we didn't speak. I played the harmonica, she listened. Later we watched the moon come up from the haystack. As so many times before in my young life, the harmonica had proved itself to be a truly good friend.

For a few days, I enjoyed a very intense romance with this dark-haired girl who had such a happy laugh. She seemed to think it would go on forever, but the end came fast. One day while she was in the fields, we received the order to pull out, and thirty minutes later we were on the march to another village some twenty kilometers away. There had been an outbreak of typhoid in Ana's village, something the German army could not curb; better to leave than let it take its toll on the already heavily reduced troops.

May 3, 1944

My dear Mutti,

During some moments one really becomes aware that a war's on. When the bombs are bursting the loudest, one thinks the least about it. I want to describe a wartime scene for you now.

I am sitting in the chimney corner with a giant boil on my buttocks and writing. A construction of brooms and blankets underneath is intended to help me avoid sitting directly on the boil. The scene of the action is a little house in a small village on a side arm of the Dniester. Time, 4 p.m. Outside it is raining, springlike. Practically the entire detachment has gathered here in the kitchen, because of the warming stove. Here one can also light a cigarette, because no one owns a lighter or matches anymore.

A large barrel of wine stands in the entrance hall. In front of a window two men are standing close together. One is eating some bread with a few Portuguese sardines and drinking wine. The other is crushing a louse on top of a politician's face in a

German newspaper and whistling the song "I Dance with You into Heaven."

Two meters away another is whistling just as loudly, and off-key, the "Volga Boat Song," with brief interruptions each time he tosses a sunflower seed into his mouth. A photo of a girl is leaning against the wall in front of him, and he begins to swear because he is here and not at home. The Russians have shot off one of his ears.

Another fellow is lying on a bench, sleeping off his drunk, while a little farther away someone else is just drinking himself into the same state. He keeps filling up his glass from the watering can we use to bring the wine in from the barrel. A child is crying continuously near the stove. This scene being displayed in front of us probably offends him just as much as it does me!

Over in the corner a self-assured Don Juan is flirting with the pert little tenant from house number two. He is just in the act of crossing over from spiritual tenderness to that of a more active variety. In another corner two sedate family men from Baden-Baden are talking about their wives and children and also tipping their glasses regularly. Our youngest is sitting in front of the fire eating scrambled eggs (not less than eleven) from a large frying pan. Now and then he guzzles some of his hot wine. Just now the two whistlers, the louse crusher and the photo viewer, have fallen into such a persistent dissonance that they have suddenly become embarrassed and fallen silent.

Someone just came in and announced loudly, "All furloughs are canceled until further notice."

Another soldier swears loudly.

The conversations change to complaints about this endless war and what a fine state of affairs it is when we aren't even given any furloughs, and everyone has to stay here until he either is wounded or croaks. Everyone is sick to death of it all. It has just stopped raining, and the sun has reappeared. Most of the soldiers go out. One is snoring on the bench. I'm still sitting with my boil by the stove.

Outside everything is blossoming. The countryside is filled with fruit trees, so the bees are already very busy. The region is rocky and hilly, and here and there a little brook like the ones we have at home is flowing. There are also masses of fleas, but we are learning to catch them; it takes a quick hand. Don't worry, because I'm fine. Kisses,

Your Boy

May 5, 1944

Dear Mutti,

One day after the next passes by without any change here. Now and then the Russians attack, but it's no big deal. Three hours a night on the switchboard, and by day I go three houses away to get my rations in my mess kit. One or two hours a day are devoted to procuring eggs, wine, etc. Yesterday at noon, I brought a large watering can full of wine for the eight of us and definitely had the feeling "Will that be enough?"

And it's exactly the same with eggs. When I return from my daily walk and have only ten to twelve eggs in my pocket, I really have to be thrifty until the next day. And in spite of all this, nothing ever tastes quite right. I would a thousand times rather have an egg prepared by you at home, on a clean dish in a proper room, than all these vast quantities. But that can't be changed.

My only fruitful pursuit is the study of the Romanian language. It is often very difficult to figure out the meaning of separate words without a dictionary or grammar, but the pronunciation is easy for me, and I pick up complete idioms quickly since they are so similar to French and Italian.

Yesterday we had to sign papers to the effect that organizing and plundering will be punishable by death. In spite of that, we still have to herd the so-called Allied civilians out of their houses with rifle butts, in order to force them to dig trenches or build defenses.

You needn't count on my having a furlough before August. They are creeping up the list accursedly slowly. But you can see that your son is thriving and even has a few decent thoughts in his head. Bussi bussi,

Your Georg

P.S. If you can discover a Romanian dictionary or something similar I'd be very grateful.

The tenth of May wasn't much different from the days before. Konrad was struggling to bring a newly assigned telegraphist to the point where he could send or receive a message more or less without errors. The seventeen- and eighteen-year-olds who were currently arriving as reinforcements usually had received only a few weeks' training, and accordingly their knowledge left much to be desired.

A few were able to send or receive Morse code in normal, quiet room conditions, but we could imagine all too easily how poorly they would function under fire, in a trench, or when those rushing waves of Russians came into view. Of course, it was exactly under those circumstances that it was most important to be able to transmit commands quickly and perfectly.

I was occupied with putting together a list of Romanian verbs, laboriously obtained from the local inhabitants. The door opened, and Funker Moser, who had been missing for six weeks, entered. With a slightly embarrassed smile, he tossed one of his rubbery salutes in Konrad's direction and said, "Funker Moser reporting for duty."

I filled a tin cup with the wine that was a constant on our table and held it out to Moser. I was happy to see my old herb collector, whom we all had believed lost.

When we were seated, Konrad asked, "What happened to you? The last time I saw you was in Pervomaysk, when you and Baby Schmidt got the order to repair a broken line."

Moser rolled and unrolled his cap between his fingers, picking at the threads on the eagle with the swastika. Then he said, "There were too many Russians in the area. And a tank cut off our way back. So Schmidt and I just ran back to the rear."

"Isn't that what's usually known as deserting?" asked Konrad.

"There were hundreds who were all running to the river."

"And what happened then?"

"*Ja*, I was separated from Schmidt when we crossed the bridge. They ordered me to march off with a newly assembled battle group. Then we were loaded into a troop carrier and flown pretty far north. I was in heavy fighting with the Fifteenth for a long time."

Meanwhile Moser had stood up and was rummaging around in his wash kit. A large onion appeared, and he laid it on the table.

Konrad asked, "And how did you get here?"

A second onion appeared along with two heads of garlic. "I could barely understand the North German accent in that regiment."

"So?"

Moser had pulled out some folded-paper packages and began opening them, one after the other. "I asked to be reassigned to my old division, the 282nd. Two weeks later I got my marching orders."

By now the table was covered with all the new splendors: the onions, garlic, dried marjoram and thyme, fresh parsley, a jute bag with coarse salt, and linden flowers that were still green and yellow.

"I brought those things," said Moser with his shy smile,

"so that the Herr officer could have something decent to eat again."

Konrad could have submitted a report about Moser's disappearance in Pervomaysk that would probably have led to considerable unpleasantness, and Moser knew that.

After a long pause, Konrad finally said, "Welcome back to the Second Battalion's signal squad."

That evening we had parsley potatoes with chicken in herb sauce and red wine. The linden-flower tea we sipped just before going to bed.

The East, May 17, 1944

Dear Papi,

Switchboard duty is the best opportunity for writing, especially at 4 a.m. With all the animals in the barnyard, one hasn't a peaceful minute anymore. On top of everything else, our newest acquisition, a radio, begins playing and then I haven't the quiet for writing a letter.

We have a real working farm in action now. When we arrived here the two women were sitting on the stove, staring into space or singing horrible Oriental songs. The barnyard was in terrible shape, and a half-starving ox and chicken were standing in the stable. The roof of the veranda was also threatening to cave in. The rooms were filthy, and the window was broken.

How that scene has changed! The house is clean and repaired; the women work all day and they seem to enjoy it. Twenty-seven chickens are running around in the barnyard, and they lay about twenty eggs a day. An ox, a cow, our three horses, three sheep, and, most recently, three geese are in the barn.

I also have my own dog, Flocki, a faithful animal that I rescued half starving a week ago and am lovingly nursing back to health, while teaching him his European manners. He is a very young mixture of pinscher, poodle, and dachshund—funny, faithful, and hungry. He loves artificial honey and chases our chickens around the barnyard. For four days we've had a cat that has three kittens in the attic.

I learn a few words of the local language every day, because I sit together with the inhabitants of the surrounding houses and gab with them about this and that. I'm very popular with them; I am often used as interpreter and they all simply call me Georg. Wherever I go I always hear my name. Often someone furtively sticks two or three eggs in my pocket, just to be sure that no other soldier will notice. For the girls of all ages I generally represent something special.

Thanks to my small language talents, I am often ordered out to organize wine or something else. That's very rough then, when I'm sent into a house where I'm well known. In general the prevailing opinion is *Austriako nix zap zarap*—an Austrian doesn't steal.

You could actually call our life here peaceful, were it

not for the trench running from in front of our door to the cellar, which we have to use often when the Russians shoot over here. Now and then wounded are carried past, and then one realizes again that there's a war on. The continuous machine-gun fire is the daily noise in the war, just like the sound of passing cars at home, and we don't hear it at all anymore.

On occasion somebody leaves on furlough, and that means a lot, because everyone knows then that his turn has to come up eventually, too, even if it is still in the distant future. From here I could be in Vienna in four days.

Dear Papschi, everyone is starting to get up. Be well, give everyone my greetings, and enjoy the cigarettes that I have been able to furnish you with. Many loving greetings,

Your Georg

The East, May 25, 1944

Dear Mutti,

I have moved from our last position and am now in a house in the same village but only 800 meters from the foremost line, formed by a river. The Russians are sitting on the other bank and have a very nice overview of us. Now and then they also merrily shoot into our midst. In so doing they almost never wound soldiers but usually civilians, for these tend to run around in the open, unprotected.

Then, when someone is killed, a terrible wailing begins. There is weeping and at the same time the singing of some short, monotonous sounding phrases. First of all, the closest relatives run weeping and singing through the village streets to announce their sorrow. Soon thereafter, all the women of the village come to the body, and each sings a crying prayer or stanza before she disappears again. In this manner they all file past.

The men pay no attention whatsoever but hammer around on a coffin a few meters farther away. Then, in the presence of thirty to forty women, accompanied by intense wailing, the body is washed and buried immediately.

On all this one can see so crassly the differences when somebody dies. Among us soldiers it is so insignificant. When you find out that someone has been killed, you don't say much. Perhaps you tell each other some of the last, striking details from his life; you speculate about who will take over his function, and so the matter is settled. And then, by comparison, all this ceremony.

There is a long, narrow hollow a hundred meters away where we go riding daily. It is fun to gallop along on these lively, small horses and then trot around in circles like circus performers.

Slowly we have acquired a great deal of confidence

with these unsaddled horses. I can't remember a time that I've fallen off recently. My new friend Flocki is very sweet. He drinks wine just as happily as milk, and all of us spoil him a great deal. He gets lots of bones and barks at every stranger. For the rest, I'm fine. The business with the furloughs goes very, very slowly.

Many kisses,
Your Georg

LONG HOT SUMMER ON THE DNIESTER

June 1, 1944

Dear Mutti,

It seems as though it's on purpose, that we're not supposed to feel good even for a minute here at the front. In the winter we freeze, and the lice are always biting. During the summer it's terrifically hot, and now it's the fleas, mosquitoes, and flies biting for a change. These two seasons are separated by the periods of heavy mud and more lice. So the whole year through a soldier never has one moment when he can lie down and really feel contented.

Last night two other men and I were sent up front to company headquarters. My task is to provide wireless connections when the telephone lines to the battalion are interrupted. We lie sixty meters away from the Dniester, which is only a stone's throw wide at this point. Ivan is sitting on the opposite bank. In the evening we can hear the Russians talking quite clearly.

Last night we were busy building bunkers, since they are the only place where one can be halfway secure. What's more, there aren't so many mosquitoes in the bunkers, and it is a few blessed degrees cooler. The heat makes us quite weak, especially since our only drinking liquid is one canteen of coffee per day. We can't gather water from the river, as the Russians would shoot us down immediately. The closest well is three kilometers away. So we sweat all day long doing nothing and then sweat through the nights while we dig.

It is almost impossible to wash oneself here. Very seldom, and then only by chance, do we come upon sufficient water. Thank God they keep relieving me every eight days so I can get back to the battalion.

The surroundings are actually quite pretty: endless groves of fruit-filled trees, meadows, and woods, all completely without a sign of human effort. On the whole it looks as though this is going to be a permanent situation. The Russians are making no further attacks but just keep shooting mortars over the river at us, day and night. Casualties do occur from time to time, but they are minimal.

Usually it's the newcomers who fall. Those who have been here longer know only too well where and when they should move about freely and when to throw themselves in the dirt.

Very little mail or food is getting through. We make soups from wild birds, cook up some thistle spinach, or brew an herb tea. But all this costs us such effort; one becomes so slack and weary here. The only consolation is that I'll be getting furlough in a few weeks. The day before yesterday my former troop leader went on leave. He may call you, if he doesn't forget.

Dear Mui, it is really time for me to get back home again, because I realize that I'm turning into a complete idiot here. I can't even write properly anymore. I have no interest in anything. The degrees of depression, with their accompanying signs, such as becoming filthy and stupid, no longer writing letters, etc., can be seen quite strongly in some of the soldiers. Along with these other symptoms, our cheeks become hollow and our eyes look so empty. Movements are sluggish and indifferent. Mouths never twist themselves into a smile. I hope all that won't happen so quickly with me.

As an antidote, I pose complicated math problems to myself and then exert great effort in trying to solve them. I look for someone with whom I can have an intelligent conversation. Or I try to check out the separate parts of my rifle from an engineering point of view; by that I mean figure out the purpose of each part and its shape. All of this takes great concentration but seems to be the only way to remain halfway fresh. It has a horrible effect, you see, when I observe the stubborn, stupid, sunken faces of the others.

Enough for today. I'll write again soon. My love to Papi, and tell Vroni that I wish her much happiness and success in the coming weeks. [Author's note: My sister was about to give birth.]

Your Georg

(From left) Unidentified soldier, Baby Schmidt, and me, with Konrad kneeling behind.

The East, June 6, 1944

Dear Mutti,

It is so still and peaceful here since the Russians have stopped shooting those mortars. The only shots come now and then from a sharpshooter. Tomorrow night, after eight days' duty with the company, I'll be relieved and head back to the battalion. The food is better there, but more important, the sharpshooters can't shoot that far. Right now a pleasantly cool little breeze is blowing, and that feels so good to all of us. During the day this damp heat really does us in.

Today news of the beginning of the Allied invasion of Normandy came through the radio. A sigh went through the whole front, for everyone hopes that an end will soon be in sight, let it be what it will. Heavy debates and verbal duels are raging everywhere. No one knows anything, but everyone has an opinion and believes his is the correct one. Oh well; it's all the same to me, because I know that the Atlantic wall is impregnable, that the English and American soldiers don't know anything about shooting, that Germany is winning on all fronts for Europe because the wheels are rolling for victory, the thousand-year victory. So I have neither scruples nor doubts, fear neither hell nor the devil, but rather wait for my supper that won't arrive for four and a half hours and will surely consist of an unsalted water soup with four or five potatoes. Right now we are blessed with ration level 4, the minimum for just keeping us alive.

The sun is going down in front of me, and I have been observing that the pink of the sky did not blend at all well with the juicy green of the trees. The effect was quite kitschy.

I have to put the mosquito net over my head because the beasts are starting to become unpleasant. I might report, as a special event, that I found only two lice today. That pleases me very much, for, after all, I haven't been deloused for one and a half months and have had periods since then with a great many lice.

I read in the newspaper of a major bombing attack on Vienna. Please write me where they hit. (Twenty-sixth of May.) A few good kisses from your Georg, whom nothing can hit because he sneaks through, like the ghost of a thread!

My division was part of the Sixth Army and formed the most southerly flank of the front. At this time, Romania and the southern Ukraine were strategically unimportant for the Russians. They put their main forces into action farther north, in the front's midsection, and succeeded in pushing deeply into Poland in battles that involved high casualties on both sides.

Romania had been occupied by the Germans toward the beginning of the war and afterward fought, if unenthusiastically, on their side. The Russians speculated that probably the entire southern flank could be overrun with a minimum of effort. That was why, with the exception of occasional mortar fire and a few locally confined skirmishes, the front remained very tranquil where we were during the spring and summer of 1944.

As the days grew warmer, an abundance of fruit became ripe, and the German soldiers began to recover from the hardships of the preceding months. The fact that mail or rations seldom made it to our position was primarily the fault of the 250,000 partisans who were busily blowing up trains and bridges at the rear.

Following the brief weeks of mild spring, the heat, mosquitoes, and boredom began to do their worst. The lack of water, the bad rations, and the slowly dawning realization that we were sitting in a trap where our connection to the rear could be cut off at any time began to wear us down.

The East, June 18, 1944

Dear Mutti,

Today in the Wehrmacht's report we heard that the new German weapon has been put into use, also news of the bombardment of Vienna. Then I received your letter where you write about your gallbladder attack, etc. All in all, I'm in a pretty bad mood. It really looks as though this war will be fought until the last German croaks. The only consolation is that future historians can write about how the Germans fought to the last drop of blood. Their eternal glory is assured. We all end up heroes here, whether we want to or not.

By now most of my comrades wish they had never heard of Germany, but rather had lived out their eighty years as naked savages under a palm tree. Then perhaps their souls would not have become so black and bloodstained. It is very unpleasant for us to continue fighting in undetermined battle actions, while at home the cities are falling. There's still no end in sight, until one day some German, American, or Englishman will notice that he is the last one in the slaughter field—the victor—but nevertheless unhappy and despairing.

Officer Zimmerman probably won't be coming, since evidently all those who have left on furlough until now are being sent to France. If you absolutely want to send a one-hundred-gram package, then please include sweet things, white thread (no needles), map sections of the French and Italian fronts showing the names of the most important towns, and, if you can dig it up, a lighter. It can be old and unmodern, but it's important that the fluid doesn't evaporate too quickly by itself. Otherwise I don't need anything. I would appreciate if you would include with your letters a few pages from an old math or engineering textbook, beginning with equations, so I could have something sensible to do here.

Dear Mui, try to become strong and healthy again, and don't worry too much. What can happen to me anyway? What's gone is gone.

1,000 Bussis, Your Georg

The East, June 24, 1944

Dear Mui,

The long deliberations and purchases for packages and furlough were all for nothing. The noncom won't be visiting you, and I won't be going on furlough. At least

I now have a very nice substitute here—the fruit—for the packages you wanted to send. Cherries abound, and in the next few days the currants and gooseberries will be ripe. Then the apricots, peaches, and plums will come along. The trees are already bending over.

We are now in a new location out in the open, two kilometers outside a town. Today I spent the whole day in Criulem, obtaining boards, doors, and chairs for our staff bunker. While occupied with this task, I went up into an attic, and a young Romanian of about twenty years fell into my hands. He really has no excuse for being here at the front, because all the civilians have been evacuated, so he had to do whatever I said. I made him climb up a cherry tree in the Russian line of fire to pick two buckets of cherries for me, and afterward I let him go. Then I stewed the cherries, masses of them, in three buckets. Now I'm sitting here with sticky fingers at the door of a cellar, ready to jump down, because Ivan is shooting pretty heavily.

Around eleven tonight a vehicle will come to pick up all the other stuff and me.

Boy, will my buddies lick their chops when they see what a treat I'm bringing. In a few days I'm going forward to the company again, and perhaps I'll stay there longer than eight days, because my relief was killed. It doesn't make that much difference to me where I am. The only disadvantage is that the food is worse up front, and if the Russians come I'll have to run a little faster. The heat and the flies are unbearable. If at least one had the chance to wash all over every day—but that's just not possible.

Dear Mutti, it's so hard to write today—the heat, the full stomach. You know I'm still alive and am doing fine, and with that the purpose of this letter has been accomplished. If you could dig up a few watercolor paints and some glue (Uhu, Sintetikon, but not Pelikanol), I'd be very grateful. I have brushes, etc. Loving greetings to Papi and Vroni.

Your Georg

One day during this very hot, dry period I was sitting listlessly in my bunker on a wobbly stool in front of the wireless. I was bored and surrounded by thousands of flies. There was nothing to read, no one to talk to, and I had already written a letter home.

I pulled a piece of bread out of my sack and spread it with some of the softened artificial honey. A drop of the sugary syrup fell on the top sheet of the tablet of forms for recording incoming messages, and a fly immediately landed next to the drop and began eating. Still bored, I sat and watched as a second fly landed next to the first, and very soon the honey drop was completely surrounded by flies.

With my index finger, I lengthened the drop of honey across half the page. Barely a minute passed before the borders around the finger-thick strip of honey were fully occupied. I counted forty flies, and then I started to wake up and become interested. It was beginning to dawn on me how I might become master of the plague of flies.

I took a fresh page, made ten parallel honey lines with my finger, and then waited. It definitely wasn't more than ten minutes before 800 flies had taken their places in an orderly fashion around each of the lines, just like guests seated around a long banquet table. Slowly I stood up and carefully reached for a large piece of cardboard. Raising it in the air, I took careful aim and, wham, brought it down on the feast. Far surpassing the little tailor in the old folktale, I had slain 800 at one blow. Not a very pretty sight though, to say the least. After I had repeated this procedure two more times, the fly population had sunk so drastically that I had difficulty in my fourth and final attempt even to lure fifteen flies to the paper. With that the plague of flies in our bunker ceased, until there was a change in our diet and a kind of liverwurst was substituted for the artificial honey.

I tried using sugar water as bait for a while, but the results didn't begin to compare with those previous. Evidently the Romanian flies had developed a special fondness for the National Socialistic brand of artificial honey.

The East, June 30, 1944

My dear folks,

I'm up front with the company again. I received quite a bit of mail from you during the past few days and was glad to hear that everything turned out all right with Vroni and baby. Tonight the company chief and I went swimming in the river. It is only fifteen meters wide, with Ivan situated on the opposite bank, but the weather is so unbearably hot and humid.

We had two machine guns set up on the bank, plus five men armed with hand grenades. They shot a little bit at first, and then we dived in. It was simply wonderful! Soon afterward a lovely rain, the first in almost two months, began falling. We all breathed a sigh of relief. When it first warmed up last spring, we used to lie in the sun, but now we avoid every sunbeam. One can become quite stupid and the brain dries up completely in this heat.

There are so many cherries and giant mulberries. Runny bowels are the order of the day. I hear the Wehrmacht's report daily, so I'm always up to date. Thus I know immediately whenever Vienna has been bombed. It takes a long time, though, until you get to hear just what all was destroyed.

Except for that worry, I'm fine. Ivan isn't stirring at all, just a shot now and then. It doesn't upset me at all anymore. It is very funny the way the others are constantly bellyaching if they are lying uncomfortably, or if they haven't had enough sleep, or if the food is bad, or if the Russian artillery sends off a round. That's because 95 percent of those with me now are newly arrived and have never been in Russia.

As for me, if I'm not feeling so great, I just draw upon a memory of a day from last winter by comparison, and immediately I can see how fantastic everything is right now. Last winter did have one advantage. If I should ever be very badly off sometime in the coming years, I now know exactly how to manage with a hunk of bread for half a week and a newspaper for a blanket. I understand now that I don't need a house all year long or regular meals, to say nothing of a bed or other such luxuries. All of this has a very comforting effect, because I'm not convinced that the situation is going to be all that rosy in the years following the war.

Am running out of paper and I have to be thrifty with it. I am waiting longingly for the math book pages. Many loving greetings,

Your Georg

July 2, 1944

Dear Mutti,

The days pass by very monotonously. Always the same activities, the same weather, the same too little to eat (beans, peas, lentils, beans, peas, etc.), and hardly ever any cause for laughter.

I'm working now on the art of being happy and taking delight in very small things. The average person lives here completely without joy. And if there is an occasion for happiness, when it's repeated it has already lost its effect. Thus, everyone rejoices the first time he sits in a tree full of cherries, but the next time such an experience is sullenly taken for granted. Tempers can even flare up if everything isn't exactly the same.

The radio is another case in point. I remember it seemed a miracle after three or four months to hear music again for the first time. Now we have a radio that plays half the day, but everyone is so indifferent, no longer capable of rejoicing.

Recently I've been trying, with increasing success, to submerge myself into even the least important things and thereby to seize great happiness. Thus, with the necessary concentration and love, you can be transported into the heights of rapture simply at the sight of a tiny bug on the lid of your mess kit. Others perhaps might have thrown him away or squashed him, with a bitter twist of the mouth.

With practice, one can so intensify this feeling that afterward the big things such as war, death, hunger seem very tiny and unimportant. So one doesn't necessarily have to have a whole pair of pants or a full butter jar. The disagreeable things that bring the monotony so crassly into consciousness every day become so unimportant that it is truly a pleasure to observe how one can defend oneself against those chapters of life. I think the haiku poets are the masters in this, but I can see that it is not impossible to learn. I don't know whether it also couldn't have something to do even with religion.

Maybe these lines will seem completely unintelligible to you. In that case, I just haven't managed to catch hold of the right words. If you do understand, however, what I mean by all this, then you have every reason to be happy that your son is on the point of learning a way never again to be bored, bad-humored, or sad while sitting in a hole in the ground. In this spirit,

Your Georg

ROMANIAN RESPITE

On one of my returns from the battalion to the company something happened that I couldn't write home about. The details were simply too unsavory, too disgusting.

It was raining when my replacement arrived. I shouldered the wireless, picked up my rifle, and started on my way back. As usual I didn't walk inside the narrow zigzag trenches but rather up top, through the hip-high grass. I didn't enjoy having to maneuver my wireless through those cramped subterranean passageways, and I hoped that the Russians on the other side of the river wouldn't notice me, what with the rain and the falling dusk.

At first all went well, and I was making good time. When I had put approximately three of the six kilometers' distance behind me, a few scattered shots flew in my direction, but not so close that I considered seeking cover. Shortly thereafter, though, a machine gun set its sights on me, and I sprang as fast as I could into an artillery crater.

Because of the heavy wireless on my back, I fell facedown into a horrible stinking mass—a rotting horse cadaver.

At first I couldn't find a hold in the soft mush threaded with bones. The heavy box on my back pushed me down yet deeper, and, seized by an almost hysterical panic, I began flailing and thrashing around like a madman until I managed to right myself.

I worked my way out of the hellhole as best I could, and when finally I made it up over the edge, dragging the wireless behind me, I threw up. But I had to go back down once more to fish out the rifle that I had let fall.

Normal people, in the course of a typical ordered life, never find themselves in the position of having to inhale such a pestilential stench in such overwhelming concentration. I tore off my clothing and rolled around naked in the wet grass, always staying low enough not to attract the attention of that Russian machine gun. I tried to wash my face and hands in a rain puddle and also to rinse off my pants as much as possible.

Long after dark, without shirt or jacket and still stinking something fierce, I finally reached the battalion, where I was given fresh clothing. I spent the next morning cleaning my putrid wireless and rifle, during which process I again vomited. My comrades responded to my plight with malicious and gloating jokes. As long as it hadn't happened to them, it provided them with a great distraction and a much-needed change of scene.

July 8, 1944

Dear Mutti,

The weather is wonderful again today. After the continuous rain of the last few days, the sun is shining beautifully and the temperature is blessedly cooler. The water is standing in the trenches, though, and we still can't think of dry feet for a few days.

It is a few minutes past 6 a.m. The others have just gone to bed and are snoring their best. I can't do that today, because I've been plagued for three days with shingles. These are endless little blisters about ten centimeters wide, beginning at the spine and continuing around the left side at breast height until exactly the middle in front. It is quite painful. I can't lie down, and I also have a fever. What's more, it hurts to breathe, and I don't feel at all well.

The medic here at the company has never seen anything like it and was doubtful whether he should heal it with powder, salves, and bandages or with pills from the inside out. I've decided, therefore, to forgo his cures and walk the two kilometers back to the battalion tonight, so that the doctor there can take a look at me. I don't mind, because the path runs along the top of the west bank of the Dniester. To walk with this bright moon through unharvested cornfields, with a view of the silver band of the river, the village houses glowing white in the moonlight, plus the rocket and parachute flares in different colors and shades, is all very pretty.

Your packages are wonderful. Yesterday I cooked a pudding with vanilla sugar, and that wonderful marmalade was a festival for me. The food is really miserable, and everyone's getting sick from it. The menu for the past few days looked more or less like this:

> Sunday: fried potatoes, beans, meat (warm, canned), cheese, butter, and bread

Monday: bean casserole, canned meat, artificial honey, and bread
Tuesday: pea casserole, cheese, margarine, and bread
Wednesday: bean casserole, canned liverwurst, jam, and bread
Thursday: bean stew, cheese, butter, bread, and stewed cherries
Friday: dried vegetable stew, canned meat, margarine, and bread
Saturday: for sure beans or peas again!

Otherwise I'm fine. The flies and mosquitoes are annoying, but you get used to them. It doesn't matter anymore if five or ten flies are constantly running around on your face. Man is a creature of habit. Hopefully also in relation to the beans. Many kisses,

Your Georg

July 9, 1944

Dear Mutti,

Right now I'm lying at the main dressing station, thirty kilometers behind the front, with a high-grade case of shingles. I'm in a lot of pain and can't lie down, but standing or walking doesn't suit me either, so I don't know what to do. Added to that are the unbearable heat, fever, and the endless flies. I long for my cool bunker at the front and no pain. I'll have to stay here for a few days though.

They try to do everything to make life a little easier for us. We receive excellent light meals, sweet tea, pudding, wine, etc. There are no beds, and one cannot really undress since the sick and wounded lie on blankets on the straw-covered floor. I'm bathed in perspiration. My lungs and heart have been affected somehow also. Breathing is very difficult, and it hurts. My heart is beating very irregularly. But it's not enough to get me into the hospital because, in comparison to the head and belly wounds there, I'm in pretty good shape.

Today I saw four German women for the first time since I left home last November. It was a strange feeling, sitting in the recreation room with a fever while up on the stage, four women, accompanied by a piano, were singing songs from Italian opera, Mozart, etc. All the appropriate costumes and commentary were included. Such a change from the coarse women I have been seeing for the past half year.

They are running a movie the day after tomorrow. That's really great. We receive a portion of our pay in lei, Romanian money, so I can also buy cherries, peaches, milk, and wine here at fairly cheap prices.

Mui, it's such an effort. When I feel better I'll write again. For the time being, my address remains the same. Many kisses,

Your Georg

I spent seven sweltering days at the main dressing station. While I was there, a request that I had filled out months earlier for orthopedic arch supports was approved. When my general condition had improved slightly, I was sent by Red Cross truck to Kishinev, the largest city in the area, to get the arch supports made and to receive additional treatment for my shingles.

Three-quarters of Kishinev was in ruins, but the streetcars were still running. Not a shot could be heard, and I began to feel as though I were on vacation. Kishinev boasted movie houses everywhere, as well as swimming pools, restaurants, and markets. I could see, for the first time, how good the soldiers had it who were stationed just a few extra kilometers away from the front.

I spent the mornings running around to various doctors, but my afternoons and evenings were free. The city street scenes struck me as very strange, sometimes even humorous. The remnants of the population were going about their business through the ruins, some clothed quite properly for the city, others in rags and tatters. Anything could be purchased in the markets or bazaars for lei—rusty watch springs, fruits, trouser buttons, wagon wheels, fabrics, even a sick horse with three legs. The sellers simply spread everything out on a rug in the middle of the street.

Bargaining was loud and fierce. I saw two women giving each other bloody noses, while nearby someone fiddled Oriental tunes on a violin and two drunks clutched each other in a dusty dance. The local costumes and fiery temperament of the people combined to make the setting very colorful.

The dour-faced Germans, exhausted from fighting, provided quite a contrast. Some, like me, admired every little thing as though they were coming from another world, as though they had just escaped from hell. Others looked indifferent or disgusted—repelled, evidently. Finally there were the sick and wounded, who merely observed the entire passing scene as the first station on the lovely trip home.

After a few days it was decided that although the arch supports could be made in Kishinev, there was no place to attend to my shingles, so I was ordered to take a 150-kilometer train ride to Galatz, the next big city, still farther to the rear. My vacation was becoming even longer than expected, and that was certainly fine with me. I enjoyed the train ride and the beautiful summer weather, while I tried to ignore the pain I still had and the pus-saturated bandages around my chest.

In Galatz I discovered a hospital bed but no orthopedic station for the arch supports, so my journey rearward continued for twenty additional kilometers, until I finally reached the beautiful city of Braila on the delta of the Danube.

July 24, 1944

Dear Mutti,

I've been here in Braila now for three days, and I am forgetting the war. Nobody reminds you here. It is a very pretty little city, directly on the Danube, with a large and beautiful harbor, streetcars, parks, movies, variety shows, etc. Everything, everything can be found here.

The most beautiful cars are steered by a variety of males (young and civilian), the type that are dying out at home. Add to those the pretty, well-dressed women and a sense of gaiety that we don't know at all anymore.

In the stores you can get whatever you want: cars, refrigerators, clothing, everything, everything, everything, but only for lei. I managed to exchange a few, so I'm living like a god.

I'm systematically enjoying all the things I've always revered. After eight and a half months, what a delight to partake once again of ice cream, *Cremeschnitten*, movies. I bought a piccolo harmonica for 360 lei (my old one was already battered), a neck scarf, pocketknife, and flashlight.

The men and women are completely different from those at home. Everybody deals in everything, even if his profession doesn't have anything to do with commerce. If you are talking with someone, he will ask you, seemingly offhand, "Do you have anything to sell?" In this way many used items, for high prices or low, end up in the hands of the Romanians. The soldiers like to sell their blankets, shirts, whatever they have, but this is severely punished. Because of Frau Blaschke, I've never done this. [Author's note: See explanation on page 177.]

I also bought a phrase book, and I cause a lot of amusement everywhere with my few scraps of Romanian. Eighty percent of the soldiers don't understand a word. Right away, on my first day here, I managed to find a cute little girlfriend who has a good deal of sympathy for my limited finances. So I'm able to have a good time while acquiring my fruit and ice cream inexpensively.

I'm living at the Recovery Company. Here one is obliged to be in attendance from 4 a.m. until 6 p.m., but by 4:30 p.m. I'm already out of the house (theoretically to have my dressings changed), and I'm not to be seen again until the following morning at 10.

Tomorrow the arch supports will be finished, and so all this splendor will soon be over. Unfortunately. But one mustn't be presumptuous. When I imagine that I might have spent this period in a hole at the front, I'm certain it wouldn't have been so lovely.

They are really giving Vienna a good working over it seems. I hope they don't knock the whole city down. Maybe it will be over soon. But thinking is forbidden.

My movie begins in half an hour. *Ich vertraue Dir meine Frau an*, with Heinz Ruehmann. Write me about the bombs. My post number is still the same and, when I get up to the front again, I'll receive my mail. Pardon the writing, but I'm sitting in the park and writing on my knees. Many good kisses,

Your Georg

When someone tells a Viennese a story that he doesn't believe, one of his answers might be, "You can tell that to Frau Blaschke," thereby referring to a dumb old gal from the Naschmarkt who believes everything, or at least pretends she does, for business reasons.

When I mentioned Frau Blaschke in connection with selling pieces of my uniform, I wanted to let my parents know that yes, I definitely was selling my things, but of course I couldn't write this directly because of possible censoring. After nine months in the cold and filth, in a lost war staged by people who first classified me as a member of an inferior race and then forced me to fight on their side, I had no inhibitions whatsoever about selling my uniform or my rifle to the Romanians.

It was pretty clear to me that these things were being purchased for the partisans. If I had wanted to follow the thought to its logical conclusion, the same rifle I was selling might eventually be used to shoot at me. But after three-quarters of a year on the front lines, I now suddenly found myself for ten days in a peaceful city with elegant inhabitants and full stores where, if you had the money, you could buy whatever your heart desired.

So I sold my uniform jacket to the first one who asked. It was summer, and I knew I could get another. For ten days I had everything: the best food, a girl to take out and to hold on to, whatever I wanted to buy. I went by taxi to concerts, knowing that in a few days I'd be back under fire and that I'd possibly never see a city again.

When they stopped me on the street with their "*Haben Sie*

nichts zum verkaufen?" I gave them first whatever parts of my uniform I could get along without, then my bayonet and my blanket. When I found out how much they were willing to pay for my rifle, I could see the seductive delights of Braila becoming even more affordable and hesitated only for a moment.

The money disappeared quickly from my pockets. No problem. I went to the train station, where hundreds of soldiers were sleeping and waiting for the next train to take them home on leave. Their duffel bags lay next to them on the ground; their rifles leaned against the wall. For a while I sat down and also pretended to sleep; then I got up, automatically taking the rifle next to me as though it were mine, and left. The other guy would probably miss it, but I was sure he wouldn't be needing it on his furlough.

On my last day of wandering through Braila, I stopped in front of a bookstore display and discovered, attached to the inside of the window, a map that aroused my interest. It was one of those beautiful maps published by Freytag & Berndt, and it showed all the countries of southeastern Europe. The mountains were brown, the plains shades of green, lightening in tone as the altitude dropped. The roads, railway lines, rivers, all were drawn in. I was able to pick out the cities I had neared during the retreat and the place where my battalion was probably still holed up.

With my finger I traced a route south from Romania, through Bulgaria, to Greece, all countries occupied by the Germans. Along the very bottom edge snaked the Bosphorus, the channel dividing neutral Turkey from the European continent.

If I could only make it to there, I thought, instinctively looking over my shoulder to see if anyone was observing my traitorish thoughts. Actually, there were masses of people in the streets, but of course no one was paying any attention to me.

I sought the map's scale and gauged the distance from Braila to Greece at nine hundred kilometers. My fantasy was obviously impossible. I would have to cover most of the route by night, steal my food from the fields, and, above all, not get caught. If captured, I would be shot immediately as a deserter. Definitely too risky, I decided, but during a brief pause, when there were no other clients, I entered the store and bought the map.

It felt bulky in my pocket. Just owning a map of this sort seemed to point me out as a traitor. After all, why should a simple soldier, interested only in a German victory over Europe and the rest of the world, have need of such a map? Later I hid it in the bottom of the cloth shoulder bag where I always carried my personal possessions.

THE IRON CROSS

The East, July 31, 1944

Dear Mutti,

I've been back with my old division for a few hours now, after three very beautiful weeks. The return trip was wonderful. First I traveled by ship down the Danube, which was really blue, then 150 kilometers on the roof of a railway car until Kishinev, and from there by truck. I have the arch supports now, and the shingles are also healing slowly. Yesterday they removed my festering left thumbnail with anesthetic. Now I have four days' garrison duty. During this past period my knowledge of Romanian increased considerably.

I'm certain the political events are absorbing you the same as us. For us it is, after all, a question of survival, because our little corner here is quite unpleasant. You needn't worry about me, though. I'll find the right way. Enough for now. In three days I'm heading up front again. Will write more then. Many loving kisses, also for Papi,

Your Georg

August 2, 1944

Dear Mutti,

I just heard something on the radio about "decisive measures for recruiting pensioners and laborers." According to that, things should start getting really crazy in the future. Will this affect Papi also?

We are following the course of the war on the radio with great interest, map at hand. Obviously a lot is happening, but here reigns only a ghostly quiet, with not a shot all day long. Deep trenches give us good protection, and we don't leave them or the bunkers all day long because of possible Russian firing. No one wants to get his at the final hour! A lot of guys are coming down with malaria and spotted fever. I seem to be a type, with my dark skin and hair, who is resistant to that.

Compared to the other German cities, the bombing of Vienna doesn't seem to be so bad. That reassured me, for one does get a funny feeling when the report of a bombardment comes over the radio.

I have a very nice friend, Konrad, with whom I spend most of my time. He is from Cologne, twenty-five years old, and had begun to study engineering before the war. We play chess, follow the news, and talk about everything imaginable that I haven't discussed with anyone since last fall. Please excuse the hieroglyphics, but the light is almost nonexistent here in the bunker. Otherwise I'm fine. Many good kisses,

Your Boy

The contents of the following letter, written a few days later, were not of any great import, but they were to be the last words my parents would receive from me for a long time.

Romania, August 6, 1944

Dear Mutti,

I've just received my first mail in four weeks. So good to hear that everything at home is fine. The medicines won't be necessary anymore. The shingles are okay now, except for a few festering spots. I'm sure there will be a lot of scars, because it festered very heavily. My thumb is also getting better slowly, but I've had diarrhea for three weeks. I can't keep anything down; it just comes right back up undigested. For that reason I've become pretty weak. But nothing can be done about it since the rations consist solely of bread, cheese, beans, and fruit. It will be all right again. Right now I'm fasting; maybe that will help.

There is quite a bit to do here at the battalion. We hardly have time to sleep, plus the heat and the rain. Wednesday I'm going back up front to the company for one or two weeks. There I can recover, for it is quiet all day long. Take good care.

Kisses, Georg

It all happened so fast. I was with Konrad in the company farthest to the north when the attack began. Russian tanks advanced rapidly to our left and right, followed by massive infantry support. Our setting couldn't have been worse: a chain of hills backed by a river. In no time at all we were cut off from the main body of the German troops, from our own regiment.

We were thrown together with some of the frontline soldiers from another unit, but mainly with a host of high-ranking officers, supply and mess units, and medical corpsmen. Konrad was ordered to take a platoon of soldiers from the supply lines and show them how to fight in the trenches.

It was clear that the vise finally had snapped shut—around roughly two thousand men with rifles and a few submachine guns, but almost no heavy weapons. The confusion was awful, but the Russian bombardment was worse.

Then they came to me, the officers with those red stripes up the sides of their pants. They ordered my wireless and me down into a deep, stinking cellar filled with barrels of sour tomatoes, beets, and plenty of rats. Above our heads the mortars were bursting, but the sounds of the battle were muted. The order they gave me was brief: "You are the only telegraphist with a wireless in this whole mess. Make contact immediately with Number 282 and give them our position and situation."

My answer was equally brief: "I can't do it, Herr Oberstleutnant. My data for wavelengths and decoding ran out last midnight, and I haven't received the new information."

They stood there, looking at each other helplessly. One of them snapped, "Then just do something, *Mensch*! That's what you were trained for, after all."

Easy for them to say. In order to send a wireless message, we had to have decoding documents, which were changed periodically. Included in these were all the call signs for various telegraph stations, a list of wavelengths, and, finally, a decoding system based on a set of alphabet graphs that changed every two hours. Lacking these papers, I could run up and down the available scale of possible wavelengths for an eternity and hear nothing in my earphones but groups of five unintelligible letters and numbers in Morse code, with no hope of deciphering them.

And that wasn't all. My set had an ampere meter. When it was turned on and the needle pointed to the right of a little red dot, I could tell that the batteries still had enough juice. The needle pointing left of the dot, however, indicated that the batteries were empty. Right now the needle was pointing just very slightly to the right.

This had been the day I was scheduled to go to the battalion for the new papers and batteries. *That idiot of an officer should try working a miracle himself, if he's so smart,* I thought.

The officers were upset and making no secret of the fact. In spite of all the medals around their necks, they were quaking in their custom-made boots. High officers usually didn't find themselves in such a situation. They weren't used to being confronted with the ideas of capture and death.

And there I sat, feeling pretty sick myself. The shelling would surely continue until all were killed, or, if we were lucky, we might be captured, though no one had any idea of just what that might entail either. As though to justify my existence, I turned the wireless set on from time to time, fiddled with the knobs, and was rewarded with only a meaningless "beep, beep, beep" in my earphones. But then, what else did I expect?

Around noon, while leaning on one elbow and holding part of the earphones to my ear, I turned on the receiver for the fiftieth time. All of a sudden I was jolted to attention. Someone was just beginning a message with the usual abbreviations and call numbers. Nothing out of the ordinary about that. But what had electrified me were the two strange letters on a very special point at the beginning of the message, a *K* and an *H*, two letters which should never have been there because they were strictly forbidden.

Groups of letters like these, which had their own name, *Funkeigenheiten*, consisted usually of the initials of the first and last names of the wireless operators (but in my case were RA). We were accustomed to inserting the initials at a predetermined spot in the message in order to let the man on the receiving end know who was on the wire. The initials saved a great deal of time and effort, letting one know immediately how fast the message could be sent without endless checking back and forth.

These *Funkeigenheiten* were forbidden because, if certain initials repeatedly disappeared and popped up again at different locations on the front, they could possibly aid the Russian interceptors in following the movements of German troops. In spite of those prohibitions, however, the trick was used constantly in the chaos of retreat.

Only one KH existed in my neck of the woods, and that was my old friend from Upper Austria, Karl Hofer, with whom I had completed my basic training in Vienna. Almost automatically I went into action. Without orders, without special permission, and contrary to all the existing rulcs, I broke in on the same wavelength: "RA to KH, RA to KH. Come in, KH."

Hofer interrupted his message, and after a brief pause I heard the priceless signal. "KH to RA, KH to RA, come in, RA." He had heard me, had changed to receiving, and was actually waiting for my message! But I had no coded message, and it was obviously forbidden to send in clear text because of the very active Russian interception.

The dialects of the Austrian provinces are very different from High German. *Wir sind*, for example, would translate in dialect to *Mir san*. Assuming it was most unlikely that a listening Russian would be able to understand Upper Austrian, I began sending the details of our predicament in heaviest dialect, with the fewest number of words possible. Hofer's reply was immediate. "Answer in two hours, same wavelength."

The officers had noticed the sudden activity and moved closer. Others came down from upstairs and wanted an explanation. I said only that a message would possibly be coming through in two hours. I think they wanted to keep me in a good mood, because I wasn't pushed for further explanations or given any orders.

Two nervous hours crept by. Finally, exactly to the second, the message arrived, "KH to RA, nothing new, next contact in two hours." As I acknowledged this message, the needle on the ampere meter moved to the left of the red dot. The batteries were obviously almost dead. According to my experience, receiving might still be possible under very good conditions, but sending was now out of the question.

I explained this to the officers, and they again gazed back at me helplessly. Obviously something would have to occur to me, since no great idea seemed to be forthcoming from anyone else. I racked my brain while the Russian shells kept raining down. I recalled something I had read while building my first radios as a teenager. Hadn't there been a theory about warming up empty batteries to create a certain amount of voltage for a brief period? Would it really work? But how warm, and for how long? I hadn't the foggiest idea, but it was our only hope.

I made a brief search in the house and surroundings for the appropriate materials. Then I lit a few pieces of charcoal, an item that was used for ironing and could be found in almost every house. After improvising a hot plate with a piece of sheet metal and a frying pan, I called for a cup of coffee and couldn't help feeling a perverse satisfaction as it was served to me, the Jewish corporal, by a German general.

I began to act on instinct. Ten minutes before receiving time the coals had heated to the point where the metal was just hot enough not to burn the bottom of the anode battery. I put it on the sheet and waited. Five minutes before receiving time I turned the set on briefly, but the needle still pointed to the left. Two minutes later it had reached the red dot and, right on time, the Morse numbers began coming through, the first signifying a location on the map, the second standing for

5:00 p.m., all very faint and barely audible. I acknowledged the message with the tiny bit of current that I had fabricated so laboriously. Then I relayed the message to my companions in the cellar.

The officers began to recover their normal confident expressions. Now they knew where and when they had to organize the breakthrough. Once more they were in their element. They shouted, gave orders, and shifted all the men and matériel close to the designated area. The breakout would begin at 5:00 p.m., and we could expect strong German support from the other side.

At 4:00 p.m., we heard the racket of an exceedingly heavy German artillery attack coming from a few kilometers north of the agreed-upon point. I went pale. An hour too early and in the wrong place! On account of the weak reception and my overtaxed nerves, I must have mistaken a dot for a dash, or vice versa, and written down two of the numbers incorrectly. Now there wasn't a prayer for bringing the two thousand men out of the sack.

Everyone was in an uproar and at a loss once again. If all were to perish now, it would be my fault alone. I couldn't believe I might have made such a mistake. Under difficult circumstances, I was usually able to receive 90 letters a minute and send up to 120, and a few of those present knew that very well. I packed up the radio set, fished a beet from one of the moldy barrels, and trudged up the stairs, gnawing at it. My function was over. The only thing left was to explode the wireless with a hand grenade so it wouldn't fall into enemy hands.

For a while I sat in a bunker and thought of all the things

I would so much have liked to do with the rest of my life. Then, a few minutes before five, I heard the droning. It was the sound of many swiftly approaching airplanes. I saw the officers raising their binoculars and heard the cry "Stukas!" as they recognized the fast-flying German bombers.

At the point where the breakthrough had been stipulated, the planes tipped from the sky and dropped their bombs, one wave after another. Giant fountains of explosion shot up to the sky, and the German artillery did their part in plowing up the narrow corridor. Shortly thereafter we all marched out of the pocket without firing a shot. The artillery bombardment an hour earlier had been purely a distracting maneuver.

Two days later I was ordered to appear in front of a row of high-ranking officers. One stepped out of the line and walked up to plant himself directly in front of me. He glared at me in silence for a moment, and then he said, "I've had a difficult decision to make. One possibility was that of having you court-martialed for the illegal use of *Funkeigenheiten* and for sending in clear text. The other option, thanks to an accomplishment made possible only through your personal courage, talents, and ability to make rapid decisions, was to decorate you with the Iron Cross, First Class. Corporal Rauch, I have decided upon the latter."

His orderly handed him the medal, and he pinned it to my left breast pocket. We saluted, and I marched away.

Later I removed the medal and stuck it in my jacket pocket along with my other battle ribbons and my good conduct medal. I thought of my mother and wondered whether she still had Jews hidden in our attic. I felt utterly confused, somewhat ashamed, and fairly certain that, according to Hitler's rule book, I probably never should have been permitted to receive that medal.

A few days later Konrad sat shirtless in front of the bunker, following a Russian reconnaissance plane with his binoculars. Then he polished his boots, picked up his jacket, and went to the rear to attend a staff meeting.

One hour later he returned and asked, "Do you still have that map you showed me once, the one you bought in Braila?"

"Sure," I replied.

"I'd like to see it," he said.

When I brought the map, he directed me to a bunker that was half-finished, where nobody could see or hear us. While opening up the map and looking at it he said, "The situation we're in stinks. We are sitting at the far end of a giant pocket, the entire Sixth Army. Russian tank divisions are moving in fast from the north and the south. If we don't run soon, none of us are going to get out in time."

He pointed out the situation on the map and said, "I'm clearing out. Do you want to come along?"

A few other soldiers came into our vicinity. Konrad stood up and walked away. When he turned back to look at me, I nodded.

That same evening he said to another soldier, "Rauch and I are going to the rear tonight to pick up a piece of equipment. You'll take over meanwhile."

"Jawohl, Herr Unteroffizier!"

At midnight we rode back to the kitchen area on the cart that had brought our rations. From there an ammunition truck that was just leaving took us farther to the rear, right up to the main *Rollbahn*, where we encountered plenty of brisk traffic. All manner of vehicles were on the move to the south. Up to this point, Konrad had forged our marching orders. From now on we would be on our own. In the event of a paper check, we had no documents and no plausible excuse for our presence. We were deserters, an ugly word.

A truck that was already carrying about twenty other soldiers picked us up. All were in good spirits, since they were on their way to the rear, going on furlough. Everyone was singing, drinking, and yelling over the roar of the motor about what he was going to do when he got home.

The road was bumpy; the hours passed. Suddenly the truck came to an abrupt halt. In front of us a long column of vehicles was stopped, all with their motors turned off. We heard voices shouting orders; officers and MPs came running by. Would they ask to see our orders or our furlough passes? My temperature went up a few degrees, and Konrad was visibly nervous. Up ahead I could see soldiers jumping down from the trucks and cars, and finally it was our turn. "Everybody out! Come on, get a move on."

The vacationers slowly came to life. "Get out? What for?"

"Hurry up, get going, no exceptions!"

A master sergeant jumped into the truck and bellowed, "That's an order! Can't you hear? Everyone out at once."

Someone stuttered, "But, but I'm going on fur—"

"Not interested. Fall in, three to a row." We jumped down

and lined up into columns consisting of soldiers from every branch of the service and every possible rank.

"Ready . . . march!"

Grumbling, the column began to move. They led us to a point where we were given ammunition, machine-gun belts, and a few bazookas. Then we marched cross-country toward a gently rolling chain of hills. No one knew who his superior officers were or whether anything would be provided to eat. What's more, I couldn't see any heavy weapons anywhere, just a few machine guns and mortars. We were a mixed-up mass of wildly thrown-together soldiers. It was chaotic, and I had a distinctly uneasy feeling in the pit of my stomach.

I swore, giving vent to my frustrations and fear.

Konrad nodded and replied, "At least we're not at the far end of the sack anymore."

"And no longer deserters, either," I added.

THE LAST BATTLE

Dusk was falling as we marched up the slope. Ripe grapes hung from the bushes around us, and fat melons lay on the ground. I could hear artillery fire up ahead. Night fell, but we hadn't yet reached our destination.

Now the racket of machine-gun fire was blending into the din of the artillery. The flashes of the shots and bomb hits became visible. After we crested a final hill, we were ordered to halt. Other columns continued on to our left and right. We were distributed along the top of the ridge, two men every thirty meters or so, and ordered to dig ourselves in.

Konrad and I had just one spade between us. The ground was covered with low grasses, and the dirt was soft. By the light of the night sky and the flashes from the artillery, we took turns digging a deep trench for the two of us. We threw the dirt onto a piece of canvas. The one who wasn't digging dragged the dirt away and scattered it about, making the trench a less visible target.

When we had almost finished, a half-moon crept over the horizon, and we could see grape bushes not far from us. I was sleepy and stretched out on the ground. Konrad disappeared, but after a while he returned with a giant watermelon. That was one of the reasons I had considered our chances good for deserting at this time of year. Everything was ripe: grapes, plums, corn, and melons. The nights were warm. We could have walked during the nights and slept through the days, hidden in a haystack. But now, obviously, all that was out of the question. We ate the melon in silence and then lay down to sleep.

I slept very poorly. The trench was tight and damp, and I had nightmares. Again and again I woke up, climbed out of the ditch, and walked up and down. It was quiet. Once an officer came by but said nothing. Then I remembered what Konrad had talked about back in the camp before we deserted: massive tank concentration. And he had seen where they were located on the map.

Konrad got up and smoked a cigarette. I gestured toward his map pocket and asked, "Is this the area where the large tank concentration was reported?"

He nodded apathetically. It seemed to me as though he had lost his momentum, his confidence. He looked like a man with no hope.

I hated tanks! They made me feel so utterly powerless. What could one man possibly do, faced with a steel colossus? I remembered something that we had been told back in officers' training regarding tank strategy and defense. "Dig a hole as narrow, short, and deep as possible. Make it just large enough to contain one man, so that the tanks can roll over it if necessary."

According to those instructions, our foxhole was obviously too large and too shallow. I picked up the spade and began shoveling again by moonlight, digging another hole, a few meters closer to the grapevines this time. I felt fresher again and wanted to assure myself the best chance of survival.

Working like one faced with his imminent demise, I dragged the dirt away, distributing it carefully. Finally, though sweaty and tired, I was satisfied. The new hole was very tight. *Like a pair of too-tight-fitting pants,* I thought with a rare touch of humor.

When the first streaks of morning light appeared in the east, the Russian artillery began shooting. Gradually the firing became more intense, and the shells hit closer. The explosions, combined with the dawning light of the approaching day, lent an almost theatrical illumination to the surrounding landscape. The stage manager was going all out to provide a worthy setting for this, the final act.

The mortar hits were now uncomfortably close, so I crawled into my hole and placed some extra ammunition within reach. The Russians were doing a fine job of systematically battering down this range of hills. Pressed deep in the bottom of my hole, I let the clods of dirt fly through the air around and on top of me. The din was deafening and frightful. The ground shook; soon my nose was filled with the smells of gunpowder and my own sweat.

I listened to each salvo, praying it would be the last, but yet another would follow, and the dirt kept raining down into my hole. I was afraid that the next would tear me out of my hole and into the air. It was a counting of the minutes, as one might do while waiting for a migraine to subside after taking a strong pill. *What wouldn't I give to be still alive tonight?* I thought.

With increasing daylight the mortar firing intensified, and I could hear quite clearly among the artillery hits the *bloop bloop* of their discharges. Now they were aiming at each individual hole.

I hope mine isn't too close to the front . . . good that I dragged the dirt away . . . I think I dug this one a little farther back than the first . . . you can't think of everything!

Actually, it's a wonder I could think of anything sensible at all under the circumstances. Normally one could count to twenty-two or twenty-three from the moment of discharge until the mortar hit, but now there were too many. The Russians were masters of this weapon. Three or four men could carry the things anywhere they were needed, and they certainly had enough of them.

Another hit came fearfully close, loosening the dirt from the walls of my hole. It was impossible to guess how long the bombardment lasted. After a time, a feeling of lethargy set in, and I submitted to the situation, resolving to go on living again only after the status quo had changed.

Then it became strangely quiet. The only sounds were the cries of the wounded and a distant low rumbling. I stuck my head out of the hole, straining to hear better. The sound was deep and full, and I listened with a sinking heart. It was the faraway thundering of heavy diesel motors, of a great many motors—the motors of tanks.

The human ear is an incredibly sensitive organ. I could discern that these motors were slowly, but oh so steadily, coming closer, heading directly for me. Konrad's head poked out of his hole. His nod in my direction was full of meaning.

Eventually I perceived yet another sound, a cacophony of shrill tones, the sinister squeaking of hundreds of tank chains. Fear began creeping up inside me again. I had known for a long time that eventually I would have to face this assembly of iron monsters. Now that hour had arrived, I knew no one could hold them back.

In my panic, my imagination turned morbid and perverse. First they would shell everything left worth shooting at; then they would pulverize whatever remained with those many-tonned steel bodies. They had the ability to pause on top of each hole, fill it in with a quarter turn, and roll on, leaving a grave behind. *When the first wave is past*, I thought, *the next and the next will come, and only thereafter, the moment for which we were brought here: the hordes of accompanying Russian infantry.*

If I'm still in one piece by then, I might have a chance. If there are still enough of us alive in these holes, and if all of us shoot fast enough and aim well enough, a lot of us might just make it. First, shoot fast and well. And if they are too many, throw hand grenades, and whoever yet comes closer can still be stabbed with our bayonets. Or, as that officer so poetically expressed it the day I took my oath, we can split the Russians' skulls with our spades. Jewish blood in my veins or not, that's exactly what I'll do, because I want to live. *I'm only twenty years old.*

All of this I thought as I stared out of that hole toward the opposite slope. I knew if I were still alive an hour from now, what I had experienced would influence the rest of my life. Either I would be dead, or nothing would ever be able to frighten me again!

Thin black stripes, etched against the sky, rose from behind the hills. They were the slim gun turrets of the creeping tanks, followed by the obscenely fat blobs of their bodies. I couldn't count them; there were too many. The German artillery opened fire. The mortar shells gurgled over my head, followed by the detonations. I dived down in my hole once more. Again the ground trembled and shook in the inferno of explosions. I lay, eyes squeezed shut, pressed to the floor of my hole. My hands were cramped tightly to my rifle, its safety catch released. Eternities passed, endured only by the humble hope of surviving.

I could feel and hear, above the noise of the shrieking chains, the continuous working of the heavy diesel motors. The uproar intensified to an atrocious pitch, and yet I knew the exact moment when one of those motors detached itself from the general orchestration of the attack. I could tell it was heading directly for me.

Squashing myself a few last centimeters deeper into my hole, I felt like some fragile underground animal, crouched and waiting for the hunter's mortal blow. Then he was there. The earth wall to my left pressed down, and my subterranean chamber embraced me even more tightly. One of the tank's chains sprayed the dirt from the edge of the hole over me. The noise was nearly unendurable.

They rolled away over us. It was a span of time that could not be measured with clocks. In their wake they left a plowed-up terrain planted with the dead, the half dead, and the survivors.

An eternity had trickled by, and an entire war machine

continued rolling on to the rear to destroy the German wagon columns, but back on our battlefield, the last act hadn't yet taken place. As the departing tanks faded into the distance, all was quiet. I sat, waiting for the familiar screams of the Russian infantry, but the silence lengthened. No massacre followed. We had been rolled over and forgotten. We were no longer of the least strategic significance for the closing of the giant sack.

Timidly I raised myself. I heard the moans and cries of the wounded. Then I went to Konrad's hole. In the crushed and turned-over sod, it was no longer recognizable. I called out, "Konrad!" and something moved.

Slowly Konrad raised himself up, an ancient, dirt-encrusted troll, like a piece of the earth itself. He shook himself a few times and reeled away in the direction of the grapevines, dragging his rifle behind him by the sling.

I followed, and we sat for a long time under a grapevine, eating with dirty, trembling fingers those wonderful, dark blue grapes, the ones with the whitish shimmer that taste a little like wild strawberries. I looked at Konrad, twisting my mouth into the semblance of a smile that fell just short, and said, "The burial didn't take place after all."

More Germans came into the vineyard. An oberstleutnant staggered past, acting as though he hadn't even seen us. It was a strange situation: no front, no superiors, wounded without help, and no rations. Everyone was left to his own devices.

We studied the map. The river Prut, on whose other side the next German defense line lay, was approximately twenty kilometers away, twenty kilometers of uncertainty. The sun was already high as Konrad and I tramped through the fields over rolling hills toward the west. Many others were on the march, alone or in small groups, but all with the same goal: "To the river."

The landscape was so lovely. It reminded me of the midsummer meadows in the Austrian Alps. I thought of my parents and wondered what they must be doing now. What would I write them today if I had any paper, or any chance of sending a letter?

My dear folks, I would write. *It's now August the twenty-second. I haven't had the chance to write the last few days. So much has been happening. We're on our way somewhere all the time, and the mail isn't functioning. The Russians are attacking very heavily, but I'm still in one piece. Don't worry; nothing will happen to me. You won't get any mail from me for a while because . . . because we are shortening the front right now. I would so much rather be with you. Many kisses, Your Georg.*

Or, *My dear parents. The situation here is miserable. But I promise I will use all my senses, powers, and brains to try to get out of here alive. Just in case I don't succeed, I want to tell you something more. It was so wonderful being your son. I want to thank you for teaching me to have respect for people and ideas and to understand that the most beautiful things in life can't be purchased.*

And thank you, Mutti, for explaining to my father, that time I was lying on the sofa staring into space, that it wasn't laziness but rather a state of "creative inactivity." Thank you for having so much confidence in me, for telling me I could never starve to death and that, as in your story about the Kaiser's place at table, wherever I was would always be "the top" . . .

I didn't get any further in my thoughts, for we suddenly heard shooting not far away. Also, once more, the motors of tanks. We just had time to duck under a large bush before they rolled over the crest. Peeking through the branches, I could see them coming in a row, spaced at intervals, shooting down the fleeing Germans. They were combing the territory for soldiers.

"Just don't run away," I said to Konrad, "or they will shoot us down like rabbits. As long as we stay under our bush and out of sight, they won't shoot at us. At the worst they can roll over us, but we can still throw ourselves to the side at the last minute."

Keeping very low, Konrad crept to the next bush. I watched a tank that seemed to be heading right toward us. I could already see the massive front plates and the links of the chains coming my way and was preparing to jump, when suddenly it changed direction and rolled just barely past us.

In the next instant I was amazed to see Konrad with a bazooka in his hand. He must have found it in the bush, and he stood up aiming it at the retreating tank. The rocket whizzed toward the tank, trailing a tail of fire; then the explosion came, with pieces of metal flying in all directions. Yes, Konrad had made a hit all right, but the monster began moving again. It turned completely about on its axis, the guns swinging in our direction. Konrad had shot off one of its chains, and the tank couldn't move from the spot.

Suddenly Konrad flew toward me and knocked me to the

ground. At the same second the machine-gun fire whooshed around us. If the tank was immobilized, the gun turrets definitely weren't! We lay on our stomachs and waited. Then we began, very slowly, without disturbing a twig, to creep away. Only when we had finally reached a field of high corn did I stand up and ask over my shoulder, "Konrad, you idiot, was that really necessary?" But Konrad wasn't there. I called his name a few more times, cautiously, but no one answered. Was he wounded or dead, or had he lost sight of me and taken another direction? There was no way of knowing, and no way to find him now.

As night fell, I could hear only a faint thundering of distant artillery. One might have taken it for a summer storm. I made myself a den of grass in the middle of the cornfield and gathered together a pile of fruit. The stars and moon bathed everything in a soft light. I drew a few deep breaths and experienced very consciously the awareness of still being alive, if now alone.

At dawn I began to walk. During the next few hours more and more soldiers came into my vicinity, all headed for the river. Since no one attempted to stop us, an optimistic euphoria regarding the future began to take over. Perhaps we would only have to swim the river and then, hurrah, we'd be on the other side, with new clothes, hot food, and decorations, clasped once again to the military bosom of the thousand-year Reich.

I paused from time to time to conserve my energy. The last few days had weakened me considerably. The overgrown hills to my left and right became higher, and I walked through a wide valley. It ended where a small but thick stand of trees formed a sort of barricade. Beyond the little forest stretched an enormous completely flat area of white sand. It was a few kilometers long, not very wide, and looked as though it might be a dry lake.

As I neared the woods, I could see that they were full of Germans. Several hundred already milled about, and more were constantly arriving. I also noticed that the first hundred meters of the sandy plain were scattered with riddled military vehicles and dead horses. One of the earlier arrivals explained the situation.

"This forest is the end of the line. Every truck, every man who tries to cross the plain is fired upon from the hills by machine guns, mortars, and antitank guns. A few have tried, but no one has succeeded."

From the direction I had just come, we could hear once again the distant rumbling of motors. I was looking into the faces of hundreds of desperate men. Hardly anyone considered the possibility of surrendering in the woods to the Russians. The official word had always been that the Russians took no prisoners.

A group of officers passed down an order that all, of course, were expected to obey. In a few minutes a flare would go up. Three minutes later, when the second flare was fired, everyone would begin to run, all at the same time, across the plain. It was the only hope.

But without me, I thought. *I won't let myself be slaughtered like an animal. I'd rather stay here alone in the woods. Or maybe something else will turn up.*

I calculated my life within the given factors. I walked past all those nervous soldiers to the edge of the woods, right to where the white sand began. I waited, gauged distances, and figured. The first three hundred meters were filled with shot-up vehicles. They would provide good cover. I could sense that another of those situations that entailed minimum chances for survival was fast approaching, and I wanted at least to be able to steer these few possibilities. I wanted to decide for myself whether I would rot out there as a dead piece of flesh or continue to live at least a little while longer.

The first flare flew into the sky. I began to count the seconds. In three minutes all of these hundreds of men would start running into the volleys of the Russian machine guns. I counted to sixty. Then I began counting again with one. When I reached sixty, I began to run, all alone and one minute before all the rest. That was my plan.

I ran as never before in my life, with nothing on my head and only my rifle in my hand. I ran among the riddled wagons and cadavers. They shot at me; I don't know from where or how many, but the shots ricocheted against the trucks and tore into the ground around me, spraying the sand into my face. I ran in a wild pattern, always keeping to where the wrecks were thickest.

The hits around me decreased, and I heard mortar fire behind me. The third minute must have elapsed. The great mass of Germans had begun running, and the Russian weapons turned away from me toward them, while I continued to run for my life. I would have to cross the remainder of the flat area swiftly enough to keep the others from gaining on me, keeping my distance from even the fastest runners.

Now I was on the open plain. There was no more cover, but hardly anyone was shooting at me now. My calculations seemed to be working. Until now I had never run such a distance without pausing. The motivation, however—my life—gave me incredible strength to put this stretch behind me, and when I glanced back over my shoulder to see where the others were, I felt an enormous sense of relief, much like what a gazelle must feel upon escaping a panther.

Finally I reached the bushes at the far side. Gasping for breath, I sank to my knees, my body slumping over from exhaustion until my head touched the ground. I didn't count the few who came after me. For certain, some remained behind in the woods. But the majority died. It was one of those situations for which even the best strategists and sandbox theoreticians couldn't have found the solution. My survival was made possible only by the death of the others.

I had to go on. I stumbled over grass-covered clearings, pushed myself between bushes, past trees. Mortars were starting up. A shell hit a few meters away, and I was thrown to the ground by the blast. I got up and kept running. Suddenly, directly in front of me, I saw a man leaning against a tree, supporting with both hands a heavy pistol and pointing it straight at me. He fired twice from not four meters away.

I saw the gun flash, heard the reports. At the same instant I pulled my trigger, reloaded, and fired again. The man crumpled, and I stood, waiting for my senses to fade, expecting also to keel over. I had heard that you often didn't feel anything at first, at the most something like a punch. I stood and waited. It didn't seem possible that he could have missed. I began touching myself, checking my head, stomach, legs—but nothing! No pain, no blood.

The man had no cap, the same as me. He wore only a nondescript, filthy jacket and tattered trousers. As I finally ran on, I knew only that I had shot a man to death, a man who had fired at me because I came running at him with a rifle. Perhaps he had been wounded. I had no idea whether he had been a Russian, a German, or a Romanian partisan. And he would never know who had killed him.

The sun was high and hot when I arrived at the river. I staggered and slid down the embankment, throwing myself into the muddy brown water. Gratefully, I drank it and rubbed it over me. Then I became aware of all the other Germans, hundreds of them up and down the river. One of them told me that the Russians were already on the opposite bank.

With that, the last hope ended. Our weapons had lost their value, and we threw them away, wondering what would happen now.

The afternoon sun had tinted the heavens red when the tanks appeared on the bank behind us and began firing. We threw ourselves back into the water and swam toward the reeds that divided the river in half. Many died before they reached the water; many drowned. The remainder of us made it to the reeds, where we stood in the muck with the water up to our chests. The shots whipped through the thin blades and splashed off the surface of the water.

Darkness fell. I stood there all night, with nothing to lean against and water up to my shoulders, surrounded by the spindly stalks of the reeds. Again and again I began to fall asleep, waking up with a start when my head hit the water. My skin became sodden, and I pulled my boots from my swollen feet. I began to feel sorry for myself and tears came into my eyes. In my mind I formulated a last letter . . .

Dear Mutti, It looks as though it's over. Everything has fallen apart. The situations kept getting more and more difficult. I needed more and more luck just to stay alive. My strength is exhausted. My nerves and senses are also losing their clarity. I wandered alone, against my will, through a country I didn't know, whose language I didn't speak, whose enemy I didn't want to be. They shot at me, and I shot at everyone who stood in my way. I fed myself on stolen food. I ran past the wounded who cried out to me without helping them. I ceased being a human, following the things you had taught me. I can't help myself anymore. And I'm so terribly tired.

Another day dawned, and they shot at us again. A few hours later something came floating slowly toward me through the reeds. As the dark shape approached, I first thought it was a dead soldier, but then I realized it was a two-meter-long piece of wood, a nice, thick portion of a fallen tree. I needed only to reach out my hand in order to grasp it. Gratefully I hung my exhausted upper body over the log and was able to rest. I must have fallen asleep in this position, for when I awoke the firing had stopped. A voice kept calling out in German from the far bank, "Give yourselves up. Come out. You won't be shot."

Slowly I pushed my tree trunk through the reeds into the open water. Carefully I peeked through the last stems that were shielding me. I could see some Russians with submachine guns standing on the other bank. They were searching the pockets of several soaking-wet Germans who had already crawled out of the river. I hesitated a minute longer and then, pushing the trunk in front of me, I swam to the other side.

As I pulled myself onto the bank, a clean young Russian soldier was already standing in front of me, his submachine gun pointed at my chest. Holding my hands in the air, I tottered up the slope and forward into a highly uncertain future.

PART 2

Endless journey

IN RUSSIAN HANDS

As I crawled up onto the bank, I was aware that my situation on this side of the river was going to be very different. I was leaving behind me the German military organization and everything connected with it. From now on I would no longer be expected to execute military orders or devote a large percentage of my time to the care of weapons and equipment. I would no longer have to be always on the alert for the approaching enemy, constantly aware that the slightest slacking off or relaxing of my guard could mean my imminent death.

That prior existence, however unpleasant, had become at least a known quantity. Now, facing the utterly unknown, it seemed almost natural for me to be coming up out of the water like a newborn, not naked, but dressed in the barest sense.

The Russian soldier simply stood there with his finger on the trigger of his submachine gun, waiting until I finally came to stand in front of him. My new master. I could imagine that my rights were few, if any. I was guilty of entering the country as a member of the century's most aggressive army, one whose sole intent was to kill the inhabitants and destroy the government. It obviously wasn't the moment to mention my Jewish blood or the fact that I had never wanted to be part of the German war machine.

Wordlessly, the soldier searched my pockets, made me turn around, and jabbed the barrel of his gun into my spine, pushing me in the direction of some other German prisoners. We were all herded to a nearby farm and locked up in an empty barn. Quite a few others were already inside. They lay on the little bit of straw that barely covered the floor, shivering in their wet clothing and worrying about the uncertainty of their future. The experiences of the past several days were written on their faces; they were hungry, dirty, and very tired. I pulled out my mouth organ, the last of my possessions, and played a few songs. The music seemed to have a calming effect, and many fell asleep.

Around midday, a Russian soldier came in, pointing at me and beckoning me to follow him. He led me to the adjoining farmhouse, where he knocked on a door and then pushed me in ahead of him toward a table where a Russian officer was seated, eating.

The officer interrupted his meal, indicated that I should sit down, and then, with more gestures, his hands waving back and forth in front of his mouth, he called upon me to play. I obeyed, beginning to feel safe for the first time in days. A man who has someone play dinner music for him isn't likely to get up afterward and shoot the musician.

Now and then he hummed a few bars of a song, and if it was one I knew, I played it. At one point he gave his orderly a command, and the latter left the room. He returned shortly with a mess kit full of food and a large piece of bread that he placed, oh wonder, in front of me. Motioning with his spoon and a corresponding movement of his head, the officer told me to eat. It was my first cooked meal in many days, and I ate reverently and slowly, soaking up the final drops with the last little piece of bread.

I was taken back to the barn, where I sat down next to a young infantryman who was dressed in a ragged bloody jacket and had a wet, bloodstained bandage around his neck. Pointing to his neck, I asked, "Is it very bad?"

"It's not so much the pain as the loss of blood that worries me," he answered weakly. By the way he twisted his whole upper body in my direction I could tell that his neck was very stiff. His white-blond hair was also sticky with dried blood. I could read in his eyes the same fear that we all knew so well by now: the fear that a life that hadn't even really begun was about to come to an end.

Fresh blood ran from the wet gauze down his neck and into his jacket. Carefully I began to remove the bandage, exposing a large wound. I could see no splintered bone, however, nor the strong gushing that would have indicated rapid and extreme blood loss. It looked like a flesh wound to one side of the spine, near the shoulder. Some of the other soldiers glanced almost shyly over at us, but no one spoke a word. Bright red blood flowing from an open wound produced a respectful silence.

But then one of the others called softly, "Hey." When I looked in his direction he tossed me an unopened package of gauze. It was soaked with river water and thereby assuredly no longer sterile, but by using it and the old bandage, I was able to apply an improvised pressure dressing.

When I had finished, the young soldier lay down on his side and asked in a heavy Berlin accent, "What did they want with you inside?"

"They wanted me to play the harmonica for the captain while he was eating," I answered, purposely failing to mention what I had received as a reward. I noticed that the wound had stopped bleeding.

The next morning we set out. Russian soldiers, who usually rode on small horses and were never without a submachine gun in their hands, organized our departure. We were completely searched again and again, and everything but family photos and German money was taken away. Most of those who still had boots were also relieved of them. I wore only a lightweight blue jacket and a torn pair of pants.

Only a few hundred of us marched away at first, a column of weary, barefoot men, five to a row, many with wounds of varying degrees that had not been properly bandaged. Russian soldiers rode at both sides of the column, their weapons ready to fire.

Slowly we wound our way along a hot and dusty country road that curved through gentle hills. Another column of a few hundred was added to the first some hours later. In the course of the day, this sad procession of defeated warriors continued to grow until it numbered at least two thousand. The guards, constantly riding up and down the lines, would not tolerate the slightest disorder in our ranks. Whoever stepped out of line was immediately thrust back with a blow from the butt end of a rifle.

The hills in this eastern part of Romania were completely overgrown with corn, grapevines, and trees still laden with fruit. The houses appearing from time to time along the side of the road were surrounded by lush vegetable gardens. When we trudged through the town of Iasi, the people came out to watch. Many spit at us, and some threw stones. I couldn't blame them.

Around noon the guards directed us into a cornfield and permitted us to pull off a few half-ripe ears. We drank water, like cattle, from a muddy pond.

I was limping because my left heel had festered under the thick and hardened skin. The boy with the neck wound was walking next to me. I called him simply Berliner, and he addressed me as Austrian. It was simpler that way. Why should we introduce ourselves with complete names when we probably would lose sight of each other again within a few hours or days?

"Why are you limping, Austrian?" he asked.

"I have an infection under the callus on my heel. Walking on it hurts."

The Berliner pulled a straight pin from his jacket collar and offered it to me. "Pierce the skin and let the pus out. You'll see, it won't hurt so much when the pressure is released."

The hours seemed to drag out longer and longer. From time to time I used the needle to release the pus. Each time I stopped the Berliner stayed with me, and we ended up toward the rear of the column. I could already see the end, consisting mostly of the wounded who couldn't walk any faster.

I happened to look back just as one of them collapsed. He cowered in a curve in the road. Next to him a Russian stood holding his horse by the reins. We had already rounded another curve when I heard the brief burst from a submachine gun. Soon the Russian soldier came galloping to catch up with us.

Prisoners' march. Three hundred kilometers without shoes or proper food.

"So, that will be our fate when we can't go on anymore," I murmured. "I'm taking off."

A minute or two later the Berliner replied, "I'm coming, too."

We studied the landscape, the mounted guard, and the road, which was paved now and was winding and slightly ascending. The slopes, covered with corn and fruit trees, offered good possibilities for cover. The Berliner moved ahead of me into the right-hand row of the column. We saw a deep cement-lined hole next to us on the roadside. Perhaps we could jump down and hide in the thick pipe intended for directing the rainwater to the other side of the road. But the guard was right behind us. We passed by a second such cavity and then another, but the Russian remained in the same location, just to our rear. I kept expecting that each drainage hole would be the last. Up ahead I could see the landscape flattening out.

The next of the cement depressions appeared, and we were just coming up beside it when the Russian soldier galloped past us, yelling loudly to a prisoner who had stepped out of the line. At the same moment we jumped. The Berliner crawled ahead of me into the pipe, which was just slightly wider than our chests. I followed and lay flat with my head in the direction from which we had come. I could hear the soldiers walking overhead and feel the vibrations.

Suddenly a Russian soldier jumped down from the road into the cement cavity, blocking the light at the entrance to the pipe. I closed my eyes and waited for the round of shots, but all I heard was the rattle of a tin can that the guard had picked up and was examining. A moment later he dropped the can and disappeared again.

The end of the column drew near and passed overhead. The noise from thousands of shuffling feet slowly became fainter, and then all was still. We waited a few minutes longer, and then, very carefully, we crawled out of the pipe, peered down the road, and crept away.

That night, the following day, and the next night we spent in the fields near a small creek. We ate fruit and corn and slept in a haystack. I rested with my foot propped up high as much as possible, continuing to puncture the scab from time to time. I had a fever and felt miserable.

The second morning we heard noises—tank motors, many voices, and rifle shots. We moved to the top of a hill covered with trees from which we could see a tightly closed chain of soldiers and tanks spread out over the countryside, heading in our direction. The Russians were systematically combing the territory for remaining German soldiers. Much later I found out that the Romanians had freed themselves at this time from the German grip and gone over to the Russians, enabling them to enclose and capture an entire army. Many thousands of men had already been taken prisoner in this area, but scores were still running around free.

We immediately realized how senseless it would be to run away. In fact, it seemed absolutely imperative that we not flee, since a runaway would be shot at. We inched a little way on our hill to a bare spot with no trees or bushes where we could be seen from a distance, stood up straight with our hands above our heads, and waited for the Russians. Soon we were walking with a small group of prisoners toward the next village and from there, in an ever-increasing column of several thousand, once more headed for our unknown destination.

My limp was becoming noticeably worse. Now I could step only on the ball of my foot, and even that caused severe pain. The fever had also weakened me considerably, and I fell back in the column, where I was overcome by panicky fantasics when I saw the tail of the column once more close at hand.

The end for those who couldn't keep up was now generally known. Also, because of a few incidents, the guards were becoming stricter. One soldier who stepped out of the column simply to pick up a corncob was shot. He lay, bleeding to death, as we passed by. The late August days were indescribably hot, and we walked in a constant cloud of dust. Our only thought or desire was for water. I had always imagined that lack of food was the worst deprivation until I learned on this march what it is to be thirsty.

I dragged myself along, limping on the right edge of the column. A young Russian guard, holding his horse by the reins, walked not too far from me. It became more and more obvious that I couldn't continue much longer. My strength was diminishing by the minute, and my vision was increasingly blurred and hazy.

On the edge of the road and a few yards up ahead lay an empty gas mask canister. Everyone saw it. Everyone would have given anything to have it. A container with a well-fitting lid and shoulder belt could be filled with three or four liters of water each time we stopped to drink and then carried along for later.

As the young Russian passed the canister, he gave it a kick with his boot, and it rolled closer to the column of prisoners. No one dared bend over to pick it up. That might be considered a provocation. The Russian remained standing there near the can and, as I staggered past, he looked me directly in the eye and made a gesture with his head. Somehow I managed to pick up the canister and hang it over my shoulder. Within a few seconds a powerfully built German pushed himself next to me from the left, and another giant came from the back to my right side. They put my arms over their shoulders and carried me for the rest of that day and the next. We shared the water with the Berliner, who was still ahead of us. With a kick on a can, a young Russian soldier had taken pity on his prisoner and saved my life.

THE EVENTS AT BALTI

On the afternoon of the next day we reached an improvised camp where several hundred prisoners had already gathered. It was no more than an uncultivated field containing a few half-destroyed houses, enclosed by a barbed-wire fence. Machine guns pointed menacingly inward at the corners of the field, and mounted soldiers rode guard outside the perimeter.

Here, for the first time, the Russians gave us an official meal: kasha, or buckwheat cooked in water, with a few added pieces of cabbage and potato. I was grateful, not only to have something warm in my stomach, but even more for the reassurance that evidently they intended to treat us as human beings, to try to keep us alive.

Later I got into the long line of sick and wounded that had formed outside one of the buildings. After hours of waiting, I had my foot disinfected and bandaged. Since I was running a high temperature, I was given an old potato sack to hang around me. We slept on the bare ground out in the open, but, since it was only the beginning of September, it was still fairly warm.

During the days that followed, many more columns, each numbering several thousand prisoners, dragged into the camp. The dismal procession never varied: weary, dust-covered men, wounded and tattered, in barely recognizable German uniforms.

On the fourth day a group of Russian officers, including a female doctor, went through the camp and ordered the sick and wounded to stand in a designated area near the gate. Many who were not really sick at all sneaked themselves into this group, hoping for better treatment, but later the doctors returned to narrow down the selection. They ordered those of us who were chosen to wait outside the gate, explaining that we were to be taken to the train station. Supposedly from there a train would transport us to a hospital in the next town.

Soon thereafter we marched away, accompanied by a minimum of guards. Those who remained behind watched us go, their eyes filled with envy. The Berliner, who had also been selected, walked next to me through a pretty landscape that was slowly becoming autumnal. It was peaceful, with grazing cows and butterflies weaving lazy patterns in the air, seeming to declare that nothing had changed in their pastoral world.

In the afternoon we arrived at a small burned-out building near a railway track. A few hours passed during which absolutely nothing happened. No train went by; no people came to wait. Finally the guards informed us that the train wouldn't be coming after all. We would have to walk to the next station.

Weary and dull, the column began moving once more. My foot was hurting a great deal, and beads of perspiration stood on my forehead. The Berliner wasn't in much better shape. The prisoners straggled, and the column began stretching out in length. The guards no longer even attempted to keep the ragged line together. I neither wanted nor was able to go on.

Also, I had little faith that there was any more likelihood of a train being in the next station than in the one we had left behind.

"I think it's about time to make for the bushes again, don't you?" I said to the Berliner. "Are you coming along?"

"You're reading my thoughts. And I wouldn't mind at all biting into some of those plums and all that other fruit."

When there didn't seem to be any Russians in view, we simply wandered off into the high cornstalks. In the adjoining field we found a watermelon, ripped off a few ears of corn, and made ourselves comfortable in a pile of hay, not even caring to consider what might happen later.

I awakened the next morning to the sound of voices. Carefully I moved to the edge of the field, bent a few high stalks apart, and found myself facing only ten meters away a small blond boy, not more than six years old. He was dressed in a miniature Russian uniform, his gray military shirt with stand-up collar pulled together by a wide leather military belt. A little uniform cap with a red star was perched on his yellow curls.

Without a moment's hesitation, he began walking purposefully toward me while I nervously considered in what manner, preferably as silently as possible, I could kill him. In order to survive myself, I had to get him out of the way. I had to gain time until my foot was healed or else I would never be able to keep up with the column without falling back and being shot.

As the child came up to me and took hold of my jacket with his pudgy hand, I looked down at him . . . and did nothing at all. He began pulling me, and I followed without resisting. The Berliner, who had been a few yards farther back, remained in the field. My captor led me across autumn fields, past the working women whose voices I had heard, and past farmhouses in front of which men and women stood, calling out admiring comments to the proud youngster. Finally we arrived in the village, where the child handed me over to a few officers at the commandant's office.

So I was once again in the hands of the Russians, much sooner than planned. They locked me up in the windowless village jail, and around noon they brought a bowl full of food that they permitted me to eat outside, seated in front of the jailhouse door.

A few meters away, in a shady, open space between the adobe houses of the village, a dozen officers sat on benches around a long table. Three or four were women, and all were eating heartily. Cutlery, except for a large, crude knife, was nonexistent. The Russians tore the fried chickens apart by hand, stuffed the flesh into their mouths, and washed it down with wine or vodka. Watching them was fascinating, and this first view of the Russians away from the battlefield or the prisoner columns made a very strong impression on me.

The fried hunks of meat, torn pieces of tomatoes and cucumbers, and half-charcoaled potatoes were dipped into piles of coarse salt on the rustic tabletop. The juice ran over their faces and hands. The chicken bones and the unappealing parts of fruits or vegetables were simply thrown in an arc over their shoulders. Because of the heavy imbibing, the mood grew louder, but finally all were full and most lay down in the grass to rest.

One of the women, who seemed very young to be an officer, came over and examined my heel. She must have noticed me limping as I was brought in. At her order, one of the soldiers took me into a connecting house. The young lady officer was quite attractive, with Slavic features and dark hair. While attending to my foot she asked me, "What city do you come from?"

"From Vienna, in Austria," I said.

"Waltzes, Strauss, Danube," she said, smiling. And then all of a sudden she became excited. "Music! Can you fix a broken radio?"

"Of course," I bragged. "I'm a telegraphist."

I would have claimed with equal certainty that I could butcher a pig or repair a Venetian mirror. Anything to gain a few hours or days out of the great marching masses. For the moment, I seemed to be the only prisoner in the village, and that also gave me hope for better rations and care.

The young doctor led me to a house on the other side of the street and spoke to an officer. He took me inside and showed me the radio that sat on a table in a glassed-in veranda. It was a Braun portable, exactly the same model I had purchased in Vienna the year before I was drafted. At my request, the officer brought me a screwdriver and pliers. I unscrewed the back cover and peered into the tangle of wires, tubes, and condensers. One of the wires leading to the loudspeaker was loose. To repair it would be a simple matter and take a mere five minutes.

I turned to the officer standing at my shoulder and said solemnly, "I know this type. Given enough time, possibly I could repair it."

"Karascho," he answered.

He arranged for me to be brought a plate of food and a cup of wine, my second meal of the day. This struck me as an unexpectedly friendly gesture, and my hopes rose. Then he sent me back to the town jail for the night.

The next morning a soldier came for me and took me to the doctor. She disinfected my wound and made a new bandage. In her presence I suddenly felt, for the first time in what seemed like ages, that certain male/female feeling. It seemed like a forgotten wonder to me.

A few hours later, after a good breakfast and several appearances of the lady doctor and others, I permitted the radio to emit a loud crackling noise, which was interpreted as a good sign by those present in the next room. The second day I let the radio play music for a few seconds and was immediately rewarded with an especially large plate of food and a cup of wine. That same evening the radio played perfectly. Everyone danced and got tipsy to the program of a Russian military radio station. The doctor brought me two more glasses of wine, referring to it each time as medicine. It was close to midnight before they led me back to the jail.

I gained one more day of good rations for putting the radio back together, but the following day I was loaded into a horse wagon and driven ten kilometers back to the same camp from which I had marched away a week earlier.

The camp was now full to bursting. Twice a day, columns

of five hundred to a thousand prisoners marched off to unknown destinations. The third day after my return I was assigned to one of these columns. The landscape was now flat and treeless, and again we received only a few ears of corn for our daily rations. Once or twice a day we were permitted to drink from puddles or ponds.

The guards were very strict and unfriendly, especially following a few incidents. Once a German sprang out of the line toward a well. Bullets brought him down before he ever reached it. During the long nights many also tried to escape and were shot.

I had finally given up on the idea of escape. When my foot was so bad, I hadn't had any other choice, but by now it had become clear that I would never be able to make it all the way home. For now I was happy to have reached a point where I was no longer being shot at. If I could now come to terms with the fact that I was a prisoner, however long that might take, I might have a good chance of surviving.

I reasoned that if the Russians had intended to shoot us, they could have done that right at the start. If I tried to escape again, with the intention of making it home, I would only turn myself into a living target. Obviously I wouldn't be able to use any public or private transportation, and at any rate I had only the vaguest idea of what direction to take. Thus I would have to face a thousand barefoot kilometers without warm clothing, trying to survive on stolen food and chance finds of water, and all this with another Russian winter just around the corner.

A month had now passed since my original capture. The nights were becoming noticeably cooler, and more and more often it rained for a few hours. On those occasions we were soon covered with mud, and walking on the sodden track became more difficult. The advantage, however, was that we no longer had all that dust to swallow, and the rain provided additional puddles from which we were sometimes allowed to drink.

My strength began to flag once again, not least of all because of the contaminated water and the diarrhea that followed without fail. More and more of us, above all those with injuries, collapsed and didn't get up again. The Russians made short work of these. We heard the brief bursts from their machine guns more and more often. I had the feeling we were being urged to more speed than at the beginning. Some of the prisoners toyed with the idea of overcoming the guards. In my opinion, that could only have resulted in a monstrous bloodbath.

We began to realize that if this march didn't soon come to an end there would be very few survivors. Even those who were still relatively healthy couldn't endure much longer under the terrible conditions. On the sixth day we saw the silhouettes of watchtowers on the horizon. Until then, I would never have imagined that such a landmark could become a goal toward which I would strive with new hope, summoning my last remaining reserves of energy.

We finally arrived at Balti, an open field fencing in thousands of prisoners with barbed wire. No roof or shelter of any kind was to be seen. Machine-gun emplacements topped the wooden watchtowers. Mounted soldiers patrolled outside, their fingers on their triggers.

Our column was gobbled up into the gigantic mass of prisoners. I stretched out full length on the damp ground and felt relief simply at no longer having to walk. It was the beginning of a new stage, one that didn't seem to promise anything positive.

During the daytime the sun shone off and on, and the conditions were more or less bearable. We received one loaf of bread a day for twenty men, and its proportioning often led to arguments. When these developed into actual fights, the Russians simply came and took the bread away again. Twice a day we received a ladleful of buckwheat cooked in water. After waiting in the food line for hours, we held out pieces of wood or tin, a mess kit, or, lacking these, our empty hands. Then we gobbled the kasha down with our fingers. Nobody had a spoon.

The nights, however, were ghastly. My thin jacket and pants were no protection at all from the cold, wind, and rain. We had nothing soft or dry to lie on, nothing with which to cover ourselves, no corner into which we could crawl and curl up.

Three methods were developed for getting through the nights. One way was to keep in constant motion, especially important when it rained. We walked on beaten paths, with hundreds of others, in an enormous circle, always in the same tempo as those in front and behind. My eyes became accustomed to the dark, even in the rain, and soon I was familiar with all the obstacles, such as a small ditch or the large root of a bush. With our heads hanging down, half-asleep, we walked behind the others, next to the others. There was no talking.

The second method was to lie down at the end of a long row of prisoners who were lying on their sides, one body pressed spoonlike closely to the next, and hope that someone else would soon move in from behind so that you would be warmed from both sides and protected from the wind. The last man in the row always yelled loudly, making propaganda to enlist the next neighbor. Every half hour another loud call rang out, the signal for everyone to turn simultaneously to his other side. This turn command, a long, drawn-out "*hooruuuck*," droned throughout the night like an unending dirge.

Finally, there was the third method, the standing groups. Hundreds of men stood motionless, squeezed very tightly together into enormous blocks of humanity. Those on the outer edges also called out, soliciting others to join the block. In such groups you couldn't fall down, but it also was impossible to get out when you wanted or needed to. I was tempted by the promise of warmth, but the thought of having to stay inside until that entire mass of men dissolved itself at dawn was horrible to me. The standing blocks also stank abominably, since everyone had to answer the calls of nature standing up. I only tried this method once.

Usually I spent the first part of the night in the lying columns, using half a brick for a pillow. The rest of the hours I spent walking in the circle, catching what additional sleep I could during the next day.

One night while I was in the lying group, I heard the

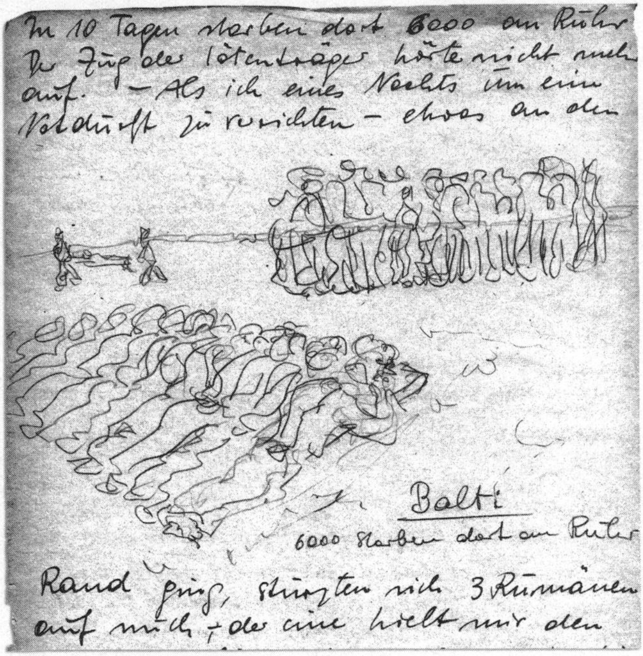

Sleeping methods at Balti, the first POW camp.

command to turn, and when I rolled over I noticed that the man pressed next to me on the left was cold and stiff. I spent the rest of the night sitting, my head on my knees, feeling sorry for myself.

The following morning we learned that dysentery had broken out in the camp. Very soon the lines of corpse carriers were unending. For an extra cup of kasha for each body, some of the prisoners carried or dragged the bodies outside the camp and threw them on a pile that was then splashed with petroleum and lit. Our nostrils were constantly filled with the smell of burning flesh. Inside the camp the Russians made their daily rounds, kicking any who were lying on the ground in order to discover the dead and have them carried away.

During one of those endless nights, as I was making my way in the dark to the area that served as latrine, three men jumped me. One held my mouth closed and pressed something sharp against my neck, while the others pulled off my pants and jacket. At dawn I stopped by the kitchen and begged for an old sack to cover my nakedness. Then I volunteered to carry a corpse. Before we threw him on the pile, I stripped off his clothing in order to have it for myself.

My strength ebbed daily. It cost me the greatest effort to get up to walk in the circle or to stand in line for our mush. It occurred to me that soon they could be carrying me out with the rest, and someone would earn an extra cup of kasha on my account. I thought of my mother. Had she survived the bombardment of Vienna? Was there still a human receiving station, one able to pick up the emergency signals?

Dear Mutti, Once again I've reached a low point in my life, a low that I wouldn't have believed possible. What a wretched thing it is when human beings go off to fight and kill their fellow men. Soldiers are sitting around me on the rain-softened ground, bent double from pain, sobbing. Young men are withering and fading away like cut flowers.

I already know how it feels to be coming close to the other side, how it is to be forced finally into a corner from which there no longer seems to be any exit. The countercurrent has become too strong. My brain no longer has any options at its disposal. Those three guardian angels you always said I had don't seem able to find me this time. That little bit extra, which gave me the advantage when everyone else was dying all around me, seems to have disappeared.

My hips are bloody from lying on the ground, my eyes have sunken deep in their sockets, and my cheeks are cavernous. My hair is encrusted with filth. When I go to the latrine, I check my excrement for blood, seeking the sign that I also finally have caught dysentery. Soon they will be carrying me out with the rest.

The soldiers who fell in battle were clean, with an insignificant little hole in the skull, a large spot of fresh blood on the jacket, but otherwise healthy, strong bodies. Sometimes they were even freshly shaven. Here we are stinking skeletons, covered with filth and excrement.

What a way to die. No women will run wailing through the village streets, no priest, not even a mournful dog. We don't know each other's names or the name of the closest town. If it gets to that point, if I never get out of here alive, you can imagine that I died from a shiny bullet flashing cleanly through my body. No one will be able to tell you any differently, because no one here knows or wants to know. If you are still there, live your life to the fullest, the way you promised when we said goodbye. I send you all my love and gratitude.

I lost all feeling for time. I became more and more immune to any kind of sensation. Thousands more were to die before the trucks finally came to take those of us who were left to the train station.

KIEV—PUSHKIN'S REQUEST

After what we had been through in the previous weeks, the experience of simply sitting in a moving train was an almost overwhelming novelty. Even though the cattle cars were stuffed with prisoners and locked from the outside, we were suspended in a kind of euphoria. It had required the strongest nerves and physical stamina to survive in that open camp at Balti, without even the most primitive human requirements, watching as every day hundreds more died. With each passing day it had seemed more and more likely that the Russians had decided this was the simplest way of eliminating us. No one believed any longer that our situation could or would change.

But now to be in a train, one that was actually moving, reawakened a hope that there might still be a chance for our survival after all. A moving train had to have a destination, however far that might be. Even if we were heading for Siberia, it would still be better than turning up our toes in an open field in the cold rain.

We sat close together on the dry plank floor of the cattle car. Some of us stood up to stretch for a while. Conversations began, and we started introducing ourselves to those seated nearby. Somehow we made room for the seriously ill so that they could lie a little more comfortably.

A piece of tin was nailed below one of the two sliding doors in such a way that it could be used as a primitive toilet, draining outside the car. For a few hours all went fairly well, and then it began to get dark.

When night finally fell, each man, overcome by exhaustion and weakness, started trying to stretch out. But there simply wasn't enough room. Sooner or later we toppled over and fell asleep wherever we were. Within a relatively brief time, bodies were layered on top of each other. Since no one wanted to be on the bottom, smothered by crisscrossing stinking bodies, we began rolling and tossing, and this activity didn't stop until dawn, when the first rays of light poked through the cracks between the boards in the walls and a few men began to rouse themselves.

At one of the many halts, the guards opened the doors and handed out loaves of bread, one loaf to twenty men. The already familiar distribution took place under the watchful eyes of the recipients. Nobody wanted to receive even a crumb less than his due. The same twenty men shared a bucket of water and a small bag of coarse salt.

We spent the third day stopped on the outskirts of a station and could hear the rain pelting the wooden roof. The next day the train was still standing in the same spot, but the sun was shining. The sky must have been cloudless, and it began to get hotter and hotter inside the cars. Each was crammed full with fifty men, and the ventilation was minimal. By noon we were all bathed in perspiration and having trouble breathing. We began to drum on the walls, and when this produced no reaction from the guards, we banged even louder. A rhythm began to build, and I suddenly heard wood splintering.

A burst from a submachine gun brought our protest to an abrupt halt. Voices of Russian soldiers rang out, and then, with a loud clatter, the sliding doors on one side of the train were opened. A battalion of soldiers was lined up parallel to the train, pointing weapons in our direction.

This is the end, I thought, expecting a salvo from the guns any second.

A loudly bellowing Russian officer appeared, and an interpreter called out the translation, "The doors will be shoved back again, but left open a handsbreadth. If anyone tries to open them wider or makes any noise at all, the soldiers have orders to shoot three men from each car!"

He had barely finished speaking when something completely unexpected occurred. The train made a sudden jerk, and all who were standing fell to the floor. After a second, lighter jolt, the train began to move. Away we chugged with wide-open doors, past the astonished soldiers with their guns still leveled, past the openmouthed officer who didn't seem to know how he should react.

Thanks to this lack of coordination between the officer and the locomotive engineers, we sat for an entire afternoon dangling our legs out the open doors and admiring the passing scene. Five more days transpired before our arrival in Kiev, during which time a few in my car died. We kept this fact from the guards so that our bread ration wouldn't be cut. During the night we squeezed the bodies through a narrow window below the roof.

We didn't get to see much of Kiev, the capital of the Ukraine. After leaving the train we dragged ourselves for two hours along the outskirts of the city until we reached an abandoned brick factory that was being used as a quarantine camp for prisoners.

Although many more died there during the following two weeks, it seemed like a paradise to those of us who survived. We had a roof over our heads, dry straw for a bed, and regular meals.

On the twelfth of November 1944, I left the quarantine camp in a column of six hundred. We marched all morning until we reached the bunker camp, which by now had been described to us many times.

This enormous camp was capable of sheltering several thousand prisoners of war. Except for some smaller administration buildings, the compound consisted primarily of numerous parallel, half-underground bunkers, with roofs of dirt hills overgrown with grass.

Inside each bunker stood two long rows of double-deck wooden bunks, separated down the middle by tables and benches nailed together from rough planks. A couple of heavily smoking petroleum lamps provided the only evening light.

Each of us received two threadbare military blankets and a bag stuffed with lumpy cotton for a pillow. As I lay down on the straw sack to which I had been assigned, I thought I was in heaven.

At 2:00 p.m. a camp policeman came into the bunker and yelled out in German, heavily accented with Polish, "Everybody fall in. On the double!"

We ran out to the large open area in front of the bunkers.

"Line up in columns of a hundred men each, four to a row, but fast!"

We stood shivering in our bare feet on muddy ground while we waited for the officers to appear.

"At ease. Dress ranks."

A small group of Russian officers strolled out of the building across from where we stood.

"Count off," yelled the camp policeman.

The man at the front right-hand corner of each column called out one, and we quickly continued through the rows until the last.

"Five hundred eighty men reporting for roll call," announced the policeman.

Thirty soldiers with submachine guns came marching up and positioned themselves just behind us. I waited, with sinking heart, to see what this new development could mean. The next command rang out.

"Remove all articles of clothing above the waist and raise your arms."

The soldiers went through the rows, inspecting our upper arms. When they were finished, they had ordered about twenty-five of the prisoners to step out of line. These were members of the Waffen-SS, troops who all had their blood types tattooed on their upper arms so that they could be given speedy transfusions on the battlefield. It had been one of their many special privileges. The twenty-five were executed that same day at dusk.

One of the well-dressed Russian officers said to the rest of us, in quite good German, "You will be taken next in small groups to the sauna, where you will receive clean clothing. Tomorrow we will begin taking down your personal data, and after that you will be assigned to various work groups.

"As long as you are here in camp, you will receive three warm meals a day, five hundred grams of bread, and coffee. You will give absolute obedience to every officer and camp guard. Any lack of discipline will be immediately and severely punished. Dismissed!"

When we were enrolled the following day, I stated my Austrian nationality, my training in mechanical drawing, and the fact of my Jewish blood. I was surprised to see so many non-Germans in the camp. The prisoner ranks included Hungarians, Czechs, Romanians, Poles, and even a Dutchman. One way or another, they all had fought for Germany, whether voluntarily or under coercion.

Although I had heavy diarrhea and was generally very run-down, I began to regain hope regarding my chances for survival. Everything seemed to be falling into an organized pattern. I was thankful for the roof over my head, for the warm soup, and for the chance to keep clean once again.

The biweekly bath in the sauna was one of our most welcome routines, though it also included certain drawbacks. During the all-too-brief minutes that we were allotted for washing off two weeks of grime, our uniforms were heated to just under burning temperature in order to kill any lice. The clothing was often returned to us in a slightly scorched condition, and once in a while it was so badly burned that we had to wait naked for hours until replacements could be obtained.

After leaving the sauna, we entered a small room where

the barbers were at work. Using a white liquid of unknown composition as a soap substitute, they shaved off all the hair on our heads and bodies.

I recall, in particular, the shaving of our pubic hair. The barber worked roughly and with great enthusiasm. This procedure was always fairly painful, but it was carried out in order to prevent an outbreak of yellow fever, an epidemic spread by lice nesting in the hair.

All of the camp police were German prisoners of war from the Polish-German border areas. Of course they all claimed Polish allegiance at this point. Because of their ability to understand Russian, a Slavic language similar to their own, and to speak it to some degree, they were relegated to the administrative jobs. That included the kitchen, food transport, and in-camp police. They also took over the role of officers in the work details and inside the bunkers.

As Poles, many of them had built up a certain amount of hatred for the Germans as the losers and gave vent to these feelings through general brutality. No Russian ever mishandled me, but once, when my diarrhea forced me to relieve myself in a place not designated as an official latrine, two of the Polish camp police kicked out two of my front teeth with their boots.

About mid-November a soldier came into our bunker and called out my name. When I stood up, he said, "You are expected in Captain Pushkin's office."

We walked to one of the administration buildings, where the officer in question awaited me with a friendly expression and offered me a chair. Captain Pushkin was about fifty years old, with a round Slavic face and gray hair starting to thin.

He said, in fluent German, "Prisoners here in camp who have worked in important German war industries have been called upon to provide as much exact information as possible about the factories: their locations, number of buildings, type of production, etc. The sketches they give us are usually poor and hastily drawn. With your background you should be able to work those rough sketches into more professional-looking drawings. As for all special tasks here in camp, you will receive double rations."

I began that same day. After I had completed my drawings, another prisoner in the office translated the German descriptions into Russian. The work was easy, the atmosphere in the office relaxed and pleasant. Captain Pushkin often brought potatoes from home that we sliced and fried over the little iron stove.

Two weeks later I arrived one day at work with bad stomach pains and feeling generally ill. The captain laid his hand on my forehead and said, "Come with me. I'm taking you to the infirmary."

At the rickety barracks that served as a hospital, the captain talked for a while with the Russian head doctor. Before he left he said, "I hope you will be well again soon. I'll visit you tomorrow and bring you something to read."

He left me with the feeling that it was important to him for me to recover. In the brief time we had spent together we had discovered many interests in common. His wife was a Viennese Jew, and he had visited Austria a few times before the war. We often talked about music and the museums in Vienna, as well as many other topics that had nothing to do with the war.

Pushkin was not a tall man, only about five feet five inches, but he made up in breadth what he lacked in height. His enormous chest was made to seem even larger by the overlarge epaulets worn by the Russian officers. His thick lips and small eyes, hidden behind round glasses, made him look very unmilitary. The general impression was much more that of a professor than of a career soldier.

Once he had brought a large cardboard folder filled with numerous etchings on yellowed paper. He spent some time studying each one painstakingly with a large magnifying glass.

During a pause I asked, "May I take a look at the prints?"

Pushkin nodded, saying, "Yes, but be careful. Some of them are very old."

I considered this a special privilege and enjoyed the wonderful feeling of being able to hold the delicate sheets in my roughened hands. Etchings and engravings had fascinated me ever since we had been taken as teenagers to the Albertina, the Viennese museum with the largest and richest collection of graphics in the world. I mentioned the museum to Captain Pushkin, and he answered rather dreamily, "Yes, I also spent many hours there."

After Pushkin left the hospital, an orderly led me past a few rooms overflowing with beds and patients to a small room containing only eight beds. Next door was a room where the German prison doctors made their examinations and also slept. After they had examined me, I heard the diagnosis that I had already suspected—dysentery.

It had finally caught up with me, after all. I had no idea whether my chance of survival was any better here in the infirmary than at Balti, where so many had died. My body wasn't in the best condition for withstanding a serious illness. I hadn't the slightest bit of fat under my skin, and my bones jutted out sharply all over. In any event, I didn't intend to give up easily, now that I was finally in an organized camp with no more shooting, where my only obligation was to survive until the time came to send me home!

The orderly took me back to the small room. The beds had iron frames. On these, three boards bent or sagging in different degrees and directions supported a thin and lumpy cotton mattress. The German orderly tried to find three boards curved more or less to the same degree for my bed. Then, to the general astonishment of the other patients, he laid two mattresses on top and gave me two relatively serviceable blankets. All the others lay two to a bed and shared one blanket. *It must help to know a captain,* I thought.

The other patients didn't speak to me, and the atmosphere was tense and strange. I felt so terrible that I really didn't care. I was dozing in my almost comfortable bed, when suddenly a man in a white apron appeared beside me. It was the cook from the camp kitchen. He looked down at me and asked, "What do you want to eat?"

"What is that supposed to mean?" I said. "Is it some kind of bad joke, or what?"

"I have orders to bring to you anything that is in the

kitchen, at any time of day, in any amount, prepared any way you wish."

That hit like a bomb. I glanced helplessly around the room, taking in all the amazed expressions. After a few seconds I recovered and said quietly, "Oatmeal with milk would be wonderful."

The cook didn't seem particularly happy about my exceptional position. He left abruptly, and half an hour later a different aproned person brought what I had requested. I ate it with a guilty conscience. The mood in the little room was very heavy and still. Then I fell asleep.

When I woke up I thought at first I must have dreamed it all. But there, next to me, stood the empty porridge bowl. Was this unusual treatment only because I had worked for two weeks for Captain Pushkin? I recalled our many conversations in his office.

Once he had asked me, "Why, with your Jewish blood, did you become a soldier in the German army?"

"I couldn't find any way out, any way of not becoming a soldier," I had replied. "A city boy, nineteen years old, with no money, where could I have gone?"

"Why didn't you come over to our side?"

"We were told that you took no prisoners, that all who surrendered would be shot."

"But you are now a prisoner, and we didn't shoot you."

"I didn't know that then."

Another time we had almost gotten into an argument because we disagreed about which museum contained a particular painting by Brueghel.

Perhaps he simply valued me as a person, regardless of my age, nationality, or status as the enemy, and that's why he was bringing his influence as a Russian officer to bear on my situation.

It had only cost him a few words, the three minutes he had spoken with the head doctor. I let it go at that and decided not to think about it anymore. An old Jewish saying came to mind: "If you are offered something, then take it. If something is taken from you, then yell!"

The days passed, and my condition remained the same, with fever, pain, and dark blood in my stool. I could barely get down a spoonful of what I ordered to eat, so the doctor prescribed a large daily injection of glucose and vitamin pills. All of these special medications originated in the United States of America, as well as a hypodermic syringe with cracked glass. It had only one needle, which had to be boiled over and over again.

I became accustomed to my preferential treatment, and the other patients cautiously began including me in their conversations. They ate their cabbage soup, millet gruel, and gluey black bread while I continued to receive my light and special diet, the only one in the entire camp to the best of my knowledge.

When I began to feel somewhat better, I ordered considerably more than I was able to eat myself and shared it with the others in the room. They thought I was a distant relation of the captain's Austrian wife, and I neither corrected nor confirmed that impression. On the twenty-fourth of December, the orderlies brought in a little pine tree and set it up near the door leading to the doctors' room. They decorated it with pieces of colored paper and attached a few of the empty glass glucose ampoules. These, filled with sunflower oil and lit, took the place of the traditional candles.

When evening fell the candles were lit, and a group of prisoners strolled from room to room singing German Christmas carols. I felt my throat tighten, pulled my blankets over my head, and sobbed into my pillow. Would I ever be able to spend another Christmas at home?

Why was Christmas such a special day for me? No one in my family went to church or to a synagogue. Not even my grandmother had been a practicing Jew, as far as I knew. We observed neither the Christian nor the Jewish holidays. But in spite of that, the twenty-fourth of December had been the day that we all looked forward to from earliest childhood.

Was it because of the presents? Or was it all the mysterious goings-on until, at dusk, our parents finally led us into the parlor that had been locked all day long and we stood, wide-eyed, singing "Silent Night" in front of the enormous fir tree blazing with two hundred real candles? It was certainly the day when families got together if at all possible, a family celebration.

Even though my mother did not attend any church, she wasn't an unbeliever. She believed in something that she could define only for herself, for which there existed no dogma, no rituals in church or synagogue. She studied many theological books and was fascinated by the great physicists such as Werner Heisenberg and Max Planck who, with their findings, seemed to come so close to the connection between science and religion.

Now, in my wobbly bed in Russia, I would have given a great deal to have one of those books that she had always recommended to me but I had never read. I had preferred going out to paint another tree or invent a still more complicated alarm system. I thought all this over while the voices of the carolers became fainter as they moved on to more distant rooms.

A few days after Christmas I was provided with rather different reading material when Captain Pushkin brought me some books by Lenin, Marx, and Engels, as well as a few issues of the German newspaper printed in Russia, *Freies Deutschland*.

"How are you feeling now?" he asked. "You look as though the worst is already behind you."

"I still feel very weak," I answered, "but I am much better. The fever and the pains are both gone."

"Do you feel strong enough to come to my office tomorrow?"

"I'll try."

"Good," he said. "I'll send a soldier over for you tomorrow morning at ten."

The soldier arrived punctually the next day and accompanied me to where the captain and two other high-ranking officers were waiting. One of them told me to sit down, and he began reading from a piece of paper while Captain Pushkin translated for me.

"Your name is Georg Rauch? You are an Austrian of Jewish descent and twenty years old?"

"Jawohl, Herr Oberst."

"During your basic training you worked for a few months at the automobile factory in Chemnitz?"

"Jawohl, Herr Oberst."

"According to the information I have received concerning you, I believe that you are qualified to work for Russia, to help us end the war as soon as possible. This is an offer, and you have two days to think it over. If you decide to accept, we shall see to it that you become well again as soon as possible and then we will send you home.

"We will inform you at a later date what you can do for us when you are back in Vienna. Primarily it will concern certain information that we need in order to coordinate our activities. We will expect your answer the day after tomorrow, at the same hour. That is all for today."

Captain Pushkin smiled at me kindly, and I returned to my bed to do some heavy thinking. Spies are people who betray their fatherland, who are eventually caught and shot. That much I knew from German books and movies. I had never thought much about it, but my intuition told me that everything to do with espionage was nasty, dangerous, deceitful, and generally unpleasant! What's more, I had the impression that once one had become mixed up in such things, it was impossible ever to get out again.

Suddenly it became all too clear to me why I had received such very special treatment. My services were required. The only thing I couldn't understand was why me in particular, the only one in thousands? But was I the only one? At any rate, I didn't know any others who received diet on demand or glucose injections. I was flattered, but very uncertain whether I really wanted this honor.

By now I had been able to observe that most of the sick men in the hospital didn't ever recover. Most of them died after a few weeks, especially those who developed bloody stools or spit up blood when they coughed.

I didn't have to be a doctor to see that most of the patients simply starved to death. They could no more digest the sticky, sour black bread than they could the coarse cabbage soup. They got nutritional edema, water in the legs, which slowly ascended higher in their bodies until it finally filled their chests and squeezed their hearts. I could hear them rattling in the night.

Extra medicine didn't seem available for anyone else, either. Not that I thought they would let me die on purpose, but after all, Russia had a war to win and needed medicine for her own people, especially if they had so little that they had to get the most basic medicines, and even vitamin pills, from the United States.

There had obviously been plans to recruit me as a spy for some time. Captain Pushkin was the one who had provided higher officials with the details. From the moment I was delivered to the hospital, I had been allotted special treatment—the double mattresses and blankets, the special diet, medicines, the books and newspapers.

What if I refused the offer? All of the special treatment surely would be discontinued immediately, and in a few weeks I would kick the bucket, just like all the rest. But what if I said yes? The newspapers I was reading were full of the continuing Russian victories and the successful advances of the Allied invasion. How much longer could the war go on? How long would it be until the Germans were crushed in their own country by the hard-pressing superior forces?

By the time I could be brought back to health, had completed something like basic spy training, and had been smuggled behind the German lines, surely it would all be over anyway. And I would be alive. To say no obviously meant to be dead. What's more, I didn't want the Germans to win the war anyway.

I thought of the Jews in the attic and of what my mother would say when her son returned as a spy. That is, if she were still alive after all those devastating bomb attacks. I remembered again the banner slogan, "Might comes before Right," that had made my mother so angry. What was right must always come before anything else, she had said. In this sense it wasn't even a disgrace to help out as a spy in order to bring an end to the National Socialistic system as soon as possible.

Two days later, on December 30, I told the secret service officer that I had decided to accept the offer.

"Karascho," he replied, as though he had never expected that I would decide otherwise. Then he continued, "For the time being you will remain lying in the same room, and your first mission, if you want to interpret it that way, will be to find out which of the other patients in your room were members of the Nazi Party. Your cover will be 'Flussman.' In a little while—let's say two weeks—when someone comes up and addresses you by that name, you will tell him what you have discovered. Nothing in writing, please. You may go now."

ENCOUNTER WITH A SPOON

New Year's Day we had to walk across the icy courtyard from the hospital to the sauna. We wrapped our blankets around our shoulders but were barefoot. The following day I was running a fever again, and the day after that it hurt to breathe. The doctor informed me that I had pneumonia. An hour later I overheard from the adjoining room a loud discussion between him and Captain Pushkin. "Why wasn't he given shoes before going to the sauna?" Pushkin demanded. "Why is his room so cold?"

Within the hour orderlies brought extra coal and heated up the little oven until it glowed. The next day I was taken by car to the main prisoner-of-war hospital in Kiev. It was a three-story building with real windows and large tile stoves in each room.

Captain Pushkin came the same day, bringing with him a white-haired civilian. Dr. Petrovsky was an internist who gave me an examination, complete with all possible tapping, thumping, pressing, and listening. The Russian head doctor from the hospital and two German doctors stood next to my bed while the nineteen other patients watched, astonished at all the excitement and fuss being made over the health of one prisoner.

Dr. Petrovsky prescribed *banki*, and a Russian nurse brought these shortly after everyone else had left. On a tray next to a

Bunsen burner lay fifteen hollow balls made of thick glass, about the size of small apples. Each had an opening approximately one and a half inches in diameter.

I was told to lie on my stomach. The nurse held each glass ball for a few seconds over the flame of the burner until the air inside became hot. Then she pressed it against my back, holding it there until the air inside had cooled somewhat, making a vacuum and sucking my skin inside. Blood was drawn to the surface for a supposedly therapeutic effect. It was a painful procedure.

After fifteen minutes the balls were pulled off, and this was no less painful as the air filled the vacuum with a smacking sound. I was covered with blue and purple splotches, plus blisters wherever the edges of the glasses had been a few degrees too hot when they made contact with my skin. The whole procedure was repeated each afternoon for ten days.

Evidently a report of my unusual status had traveled with me to the new hospital, for soon after my arrival the cook came asking what he could do for me in the kitchen. Again, the others in the room were struck dumb, but this time I was in such bad shape with fever and pain that I only took note of such minor details at the periphery of my general misery.

The mood in the room was very oppressive, above all because most of the men were seriously ill. Every day one or two of them died. Some of the patients moaned and complained unceasingly. Others whimpered quietly. A few drank water by the liter, and when water wasn't available, they drank their own urine in order to still the burning thirst produced by the dysentery and their inflamed intestines.

Physically, I wasn't one bit better off than the others. The mere act of breathing led to stabbing pains in my chest. I was too weak to attend to the calls of nature without help, and the flies crawled shamelessly over my face and into my mouth when I opened it. I was delirious for long periods, had no appetite and could barely eat, and still suffered heavy diarrhea. The glucose injections provided my main nourishment.

Perhaps it was my periodic fever fantasies that led to the idea of trying to make my mind the object of an experiment in self-distraction. With my eyes closed, in order to shut out the noise of the others, I went "inside."

Since my childhood I had possessed this wonderful place of escape to which I could retreat whenever I found my surroundings or a particular situation unsatisfying. Now, in Russia, I retreated to that special place in order to find out whether it could provide me with distraction and alleviation of my pains. With the nonphysical part of me, I left my poor miserable body and went, like a guest, to visit myself. The importance and happiness of this state came from the realization that no one, absolutely no one, could follow me there. In my place of retreat I was not subservient to any rules. No one could give me orders or attempt to influence my thoughts—a wonderful thing when one considers that in my life up until then, I had always been expected to carry out the commands of others.

As a child my complete obedience had been expected as a matter of course. Later, in addition to my parents' expectations, I had those of the school, where there was the eternal threat of having to repeat a year. This was followed by military service and new, more radical demands, including the demand to kill other human beings. And in the prison camp, my last little scrap of independence and freedom had been taken away. I was now reduced to a pitiful bundle of humanity, in a bed of pain, without the slightest physical or mental freedom. Or, perhaps not?

When I gazed inward, I usually could perceive a room. In the room I envisioned myself as a completely healthy being. Directly in front of me was a light-colored wall upon which I could project a relatively clear image of a particular landscape or some person or thing. I could build complicated pieces of machinery in my mind, let them run, and then correct their mistakes. Once, as a five-year-old, after hours of such mental fantasizing, I had marched to my Matador building set and proceeded to build an automat that popped out a sugar cube when a small coin was inserted. My mental constructions usually functioned perfectly.

By analyzing, I discovered that the light in my imaginary room always came from above. It was as though the ceiling consisted of milky glass through which the light streamed. There were no walls to the left and right, but rather slightly darkened areas in which abstract cupboards containing all that I had hitherto experienced in my life were located. Whenever necessary, I could draw from there whatever constructive thoughts I needed regarding experiences, data, and feelings. The most important implements seemed always to come from the left side of the room, and for this reason I regarded the right side as the darker one.

Additional rooms under me related to my past life. They seemed to build a tower of dark walls, with one room placed on top of the next but no connecting stairways. In the same manner, I sensed a room above, but I had no idea what it was like or when I would be able to move up. That I would eventually get there, however, seemed a certainty. Up there, in my mental room, there was no pain and seldom a disappointment. In those dark days of my need and weakness, I was able to create a certain small amount of strength just by ascending into my little room to observe with great interest my own emaciated body. "Just how long will that poor devil down there be able to hold out?" was a favorite question, one without the slightest feeling of fear that suddenly the poor devil's heart might stop beating and everything would be all over.

During one of his visits, Dr. Petrovsky established the fact that I also had pleurisy. The fever continued to rise. I had excruciating chest pains and more and more difficulty breathing. The complete loss of appetite and the diarrhea had weakened me to such a degree that I was no longer able to sit up in bed without help. The orderlies had to lift me onto a bedpan several times a day.

One day during this period the doctors pierced my back in the lung area with a very long needle in order to find out whether my pleurisy was dry or wet—whatever that was supposed to indicate. The verdict was dry, but once the needle entered my body, I fell over unconscious from the shock.

I lost all sense for the passage of hours, days, for time in general, and didn't even notice at first when they stopped administering the glucose injections. *Well, once again it's come to that point,* I thought. *The end seems to be almost here.*

But this time it was different. I didn't feel driven into a

corner, with the need to mobilize all my capacities like a good chess player seeking the right move to avoid the final checkmate. To the contrary, I lay peacefully in bed, running the events of my life past me like a pleasant movie: my childhood, Vienna, the glorious Austrian mountains, my parents . . .

Russia, sometime toward the end

Dear Mutti,

My thoughts aren't very clear today. A short time ago a priest sat for a few minutes on the edge of my bed. He said I was on my way to another kingdom where everything would be beautiful, where I wouldn't have to fight anymore, and where I would finally see all my loved ones again.

It seems to me as though I'm dying like an old person, where all is being reduced in equal amounts—the physical and mental strength, the will to live, and the creative spirit. Even the pain and fever are becoming less, as well as any resistance to my evidently unavoidable end. You are so close to me in my thoughts, soft and warm, as though I could reach out and touch you. It is getting darker fast; it must be evening. Your son embraces you . . .

It seemed as though I sailed soundlessly into a dark and friendly tunnel. All was completely still around me, soft and dark. I sailed away into eternity.

The orderly's report on my case, justifying the hospital's actions, must have read more or less as follows:

> On January 12, 1945, the head physician left on vacation, taking with her the keys to the medicine cabinet by mistake. It became impossible, therefore, to administer the patient's daily glucose injections.
>
> Dr. Petrovsky was also out of town for a week and unable to attend to the patient, whose condition worsened by the hour. The doctors and nurses knew from experience that the patient was close to death. The suspension of the injections, as well as Dr. Petrovsky's nonappearance, were taken to mean that all were in agreement that the patient could no longer be saved.
>
> On the afternoon of January 15, the German field chaplain arrived, a man who also recognized the correct moment for a final prayer and a few words of comfort. He administered the last rites to the patient.
>
> That same evening forty new patients were delivered. I tried to find patient Rauch's pulse, and when I could discover none, I had him transferred to the morgue so that I could make his bed up fresh.
>
> The next day Dr. Petrovsky arrived and asked for the patient. I informed him that he had died the previous day, whereupon he asked to see the

body. Since I knew that it hadn't been picked up yet, I took Dr. Petrovsky to the morgue.

Shortly afterward Dr. Petrovsky yelled something, and all the other doctors came running. They carried the patient to the examining room, and what took place there is unknown to me, but later a bed was found for him in a different room, where another patient had died the night before.

I am not concerned with exactly why my flight into eternity was interrupted. The only thing that really matters to me is that I left this world for an indefinite period of time and returned as someone considerably different. However long or short that period was, it initiated the end of one life and the beginning of a new one.

When my interior lights were turned back on and I started to be aware of myself once more, I tried to open just one eye in order to see this world to which I had returned. After straining for some time, I finally succeeded in the effort, and the first thing I saw was the wooden spoon next to my bed, the spoon with which I had been eating my soups and gruels for the past months.

With great difficulty I stretched out my right hand and picked up the spoon—more a ladle, actually—and brought it closer to my eyes. What a personality it had! The bowl was whittled rather roughly, but it had been polished smooth through use. The handle, somewhat longer than normal, had a little knob at the end with facets like a diamond. There were small notches at regular intervals along the handle, so that the dark reddish wood could be held securely between the fingers.

How many people had already filled their stomachs with the help of this spoon? Who had felled the tree and provided the wood from which someone else had so carefully and lovingly carved this utensil? How many thousands of years had it taken to develop such a practical form, so perfectly adapted to the size and shape of the human mouth?

Everything around me appeared in a vastly different light from before. Each thing I saw or feeling I perceived provided sufficient material for contented hours of thought. It seemed to me as though part of my personality had been left behind somewhere and replaced by something new and excitingly different. My relationship to the idea of life and death had altered drastically, and I determined that I would enjoy to the fullest, using all my senses, this indefinite but additional span of time that had been granted me.

I remained on the critical list for the next few weeks. Dr. Petrovsky seemed to have taken on my recovery as his personal goal. He was a good doctor of the old school, a wise man with little or no apparatus at his disposal but with all the more experience and concern for humanity.

Slowly my appetite returned, and the doctor told me that my eyes had a brighter shine. After another week I began playing a game of chess now and then, or reading a chapter or two in those books by Lenin and Marx. Then, in order to help reduce my diarrhea, I was given an oak bark tea that was brewed too strong, and as a result my fever soared again for a few days. Oak bark contains tannin, which is a diuretic, but too much of a good thing acted as a poison on my overweakened system, and my recovery was set back considerably.

Meanwhile, the other patients in the room had become accustomed to my special status. I ordered enormous amounts of food and gave it to them. To show their gratitude, each one spoiled me in his own fashion. Some brought me the bedpan when there were no orderlies nearby. One man tore off a piece of sheet and embroidered two very artistic napkins. Another made me a gift of a knife with a beautifully hand-carved handle.

As prisoners we weren't supposed to possess anything other than eating tools, a cup, German money—worthless to the Russians—family photos, and a piece of fabric that served as handkerchief, hand towel, and napkin. I, however, was permitted a sack that I kept hanging at the head of my bed and in which I gathered together all sorts of things: the borrowed books, a bright orange butter can, a little cloth sack filled with sugar, a glass, and an aluminum set of folding knife, fork, and spoon.

In spite of the prohibition on personal possessions, many of the others also had things that they had smuggled in for their own use or to trade for other items. They hid these items under their mattresses or somewhere in the building, for example, under the water container in the toilet or in the roof spouts outside the window. Once a month we received a handful of *machorka*, a coarse tobacco that could be rolled in newspaper into long, thin cigarettes. Heavy smokers, often with tuberculosis, traded their food for this tobacco. For many it was one last pleasure before they died.

It must have been February when I sat up in bed for the first time and let my legs dangle over the side. I immediately lost consciousness. After a few more attempts, I finally succeeded, and looking out from my third-floor window I was able to see the snow-covered roofs of the destroyed city. Another patient pointed out to me the bombed-out factories where they allegedly took the bodies of those who died in the hospital and walled them up. No records were kept of these deaths, no lists of names.

My body was now just skin and bones, and my muscles had disappeared completely. Making a circle with the thumb and forefinger on one hand, I could run it all the way up and down the other arm. Skin detached itself everywhere in large dry scales. I also had many painful sores on my back and sides from lying for so long on the hard bed.

Captain Pushkin appeared on one of the first days of March, bringing me two red apples. "Well, it looks as though you are back among the living. Dr. Petrovsksy thinks the worst is behind you now, and you are on the way to recovery. Tomorrow you will be transferred to a camp infirmary near the woods, on the outskirts of the city. The air is better there, and pretty soon you'll be able to lie outside. How does that sound to you?"

"It sounds wonderful," I said. "Anything that will get me back up on my feet is fine with me!"

The woods hospital was a barracks surrounded by trees and meadows, similar to the one in the bunker camp. A few steps away, behind a wire fence, was the part of the POW camp from which columns of prisoners went out daily to work in the nearby dairy farms, nurseries, and forests.

I was placed in a room with twelve others. At first my fellow patients gave me the usual cold shoulder when they noticed my preferential treatment. Nobody asked why I was receiving all the special privileges. But I had learned by now how to thaw the most stubborn blocks of ice with presents of food. In this way a pleasant atmosphere soon reigned in the room, and that was more important to me now, since I hardly slept anymore during the day. Contact with the other prisoners helped a great deal to pass the time.

Each of my roommates had an interesting story to tell. I asked unusual questions about their professions, and I was a good listener. In this way I found out, from a delicatessen store owner, that one can keep large wheels of cheese freshly stored if they are wrapped from time to time in towels dipped in vinegar. Another told me how to look for and prepare the different kinds of wood required to build a cuckoo clock.

One morning an orderly appeared and said, "They just put a countryman of yours in the next room, a Viennese."

"From Vienna? What's wrong with him?" I asked.

"Just a broken arm. It was a woodcutting accident."

"Well, give him my regards," I said. "Maybe he can visit me soon."

He came the next morning, an educated-looking man in his fifties, wearing a white cotton shirt with the corresponding regulation long white underwear.

"*Grüss Gott,*" he said, with a light Viennese accent. "My

name is Oskar Fuchs." He stretched out his hand in greeting.

"Georg Rauch. It's nice to see someone from back home. How are you doing?"

"Oh, it's not much. The bone was just splintered," he answered, pointing to his arm. "It shouldn't take long. And how about you? Have you been here a while?"

After half an hour's conversation we knew the general outlines of each other's life histories, and his contained quite a surprise for me. He had been a cello professor at the conservatory in Vienna. As a young music student he had come into Vienna daily by train from the suburbs. In the evenings he often played chamber music with friends, and it was in this way that he had met my mother, who was twenty years old at the time and studying piano.

My grandfather was a very well-to-do man and a great music lover. It was not unusual for the musical evenings at his home to include up to twenty instruments, and hardly a mealtime went by without guests, often from other countries. Many of the young musicians who were "at home" in my grandparents' house went on to become conductors of the Vienna Philharmonic or famous soloists. Oskar told me that he often stayed overnight at my mother's when it became too late for him to catch the last train home. What an incredible coincidence!

Oskar was in much better physical condition than I was, since he had never been forced to take part in any of the long starvation marches, nor had he been in camps with outbreaks of dysentery and other similar epidemics.

He spent a great deal of time with me during the following days, and when a bed was vacated in my room, I asked the head doctor for permission to move Oskar in.

Although he must have noticed my unusual status very quickly, during the first few days Oskar said nothing concerning my special care, books, and vitamin pills. Once when I ordered an extra bowl of soup and gave it to him, he finally posed the question that had never been asked before. "How is it that you can get food on demand, and all the other things?"

I couldn't tell him the truth, so I gave him the answer I had already prepared much earlier. "Before I became ill, I worked as a draftsman for a friendly Russian captain. Evidently he took a shine to me, and when I got sick he arranged all of this. Now and then he comes to visit. He's married to a Viennese Jew."

"Not bad. One just has to be lucky. 'A Viennese doesn't go under.'"

"Without him I would have gone under, underground, a long time ago," I said.

A little later Oskar asked, "Is it possible for you to order butter or oil?"

"Why? There's some butter in the can in my sack hanging there."

"Your skin is so dry. I could massage it with the butter."

With this began a daily routine that continued for the following weeks and demonstrated to me what a disciplined and caring person Oskar was. Every day he spent at least an hour systematically massaging one part of my body after the other with butter. He spent another hour bending my joints and having me press my arms and feet against the palms of his hands. I soon felt my skin becoming softer and more elastic, and sitting also became less of an effort.

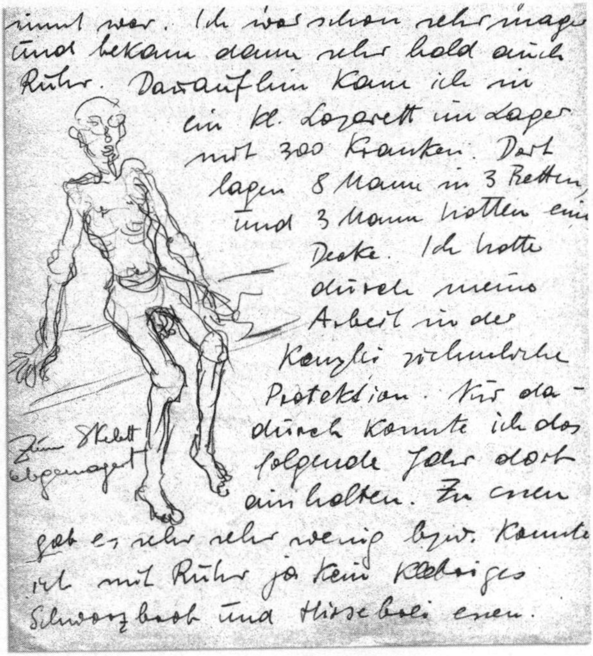

Self-portrait. Reduced to a skeleton in the camps.

Next he made plans for my diet. He told me to order two loaves of bread and extra butter. When they arrived he disappeared with them. He also took the wine bottle half full of vodka that I had in my cloth bag. Weeks earlier someone had come up with the crazy idea that two tablespoons of vodka per day would be good for my digestion and would also stimulate my appetite. I accepted the vodka, but when the nurse left I always poured it out of the cup into my bottle. The only time I had tried it, it burned my tongue and I had been unable to swallow it.

When Oskar returned a couple of hours later, he brought two plates, one with lightly browned fresh fish, sliced new potatoes, and a fresh green salad. The second was filled with beautiful red strawberries, partially covered with cream.

When I saw all this, I thought I had to be hallucinating. I, the poor fellow with no appetite, felt my mouth watering for the first time in months.

"Where did you get all this?" I asked.

"I traded the bread and butter at the fence with workers coming home. If someone has had nothing but fish all day long, he dreams of bread and butter. The same for those coming from the nursery and dairy farm. All of them steal something and smuggle it into camp. I found out that there's always heavy trading every evening at the fence."

"But who prepared it so beautifully?"

"Oh, that overstuffed cook will do anything for a little extra vodka." Oskar laughed.

Everyone in my room ate well. Thanks to Oskar, I ate particularly well. A large part of Oskar's day was occupied with my exercises and obtaining special foods. Often when I ordered shamelessly large amounts of food, I would think I had surely overstepped my limits, but nothing happened. Promptly, and without further ado, I received whatever I had requested.

By mid-April I had made such progress that I was able to walk up and down the room, and I began visiting the large barrel out in the hall a few times a day. Two men could sit on it at one time, and all that were able to get out of bed used this primitive toilet facility. Quarrels often broke out if the barrel was occupied and someone was in a particular hurry. After so many months, with no reason or occasion for laughter, it struck me as really funny to see my fellow skeletons, their white pants halfway down, fighting to decide who would sit on the barrel first. On one such occasion the half-full barrel was tipped over, and the skinny squabblers lay exhausted in the brew.

Once again, the world was beginning to bloom, and I obtained permission to lie outside on a mattress in the shade. Supported by Oskar, I would walk back and forth for several minutes a few times per day. I began to enjoy ever more fully the reality that I was still alive.

Spring also had its less pleasant aspects, however. When it rained the water came through the roof, and the orderlies pushed our beds into a chaotic arrangement so that we wouldn't get wet. The flies also returned with the warmer weather and crawled around on us endlessly. After a while we gave up shooing them away, because they were everywhere, by the hundreds.

Bedbugs also fell down on us from the ceiling to suck our blood during the night. At dawn they crept past our beds on their way back up the walls to the ceiling, where they disappeared into the cracks for their hard-earned rest. When they passed my bed within reach on their way up the wall, I squashed them, trying to produce an interesting design at the same time.

One afternoon, as I was lying under a tree in the meadow, Captain Pushkin came and sat down beside me.

"How are you feeling?" he asked.

"I'm doing much better, thanks to my compatriot, Oskar Fuchs. He has been massaging me with such patience and persistence. I'll miss him when he is well and has to go back to work." I imagined I was being subtle.

"Herr Fuchs has been well enough to return to work for some time now. We know that. But don't worry, he'll stay."

"Hmmm," I murmured, reddening a little from embarrassment.

"We also know all that you have been ordering from the kitchen . . . and receiving."

I smiled somewhat guiltily. The captain also smiled, so everything seemed to be all right.

"Do you remember the task we assigned you?"

"I remember," I answered.

"We haven't pressed you during the past months, because you were in such poor physical condition. Now you should start thinking about your assignment again."

"I'll do that," I replied.

After a few more polite phrases the captain made his departure. I knew I definitely wouldn't be alive at that moment if I had decided differently in Captain Pushkin's office back in November. But now it was all too clear that the day of reckoning had finally arrived. I would now be obliged to deliver, to pay for all those good things I had managed to squeeze out of them since I had agreed to spy for Russia.

THE RELUCTANT SPY

While hoping to figure out a way to evade my mission, I began analyzing the various individuals in my sickroom. One of them was a Romanian, another a Pole. They could be omitted as suspect Nazis right from the beginning. Foreigners hadn't been party members; the Nazi party had been purely a German affair.

Another prisoner, a German, lay near death and probably wouldn't survive the following day. The man in the bed across the way from me was a farmer who had a little farm high up in the Bavarian Mountains near the Austrian border. I didn't believe he could be considered as a party member, especially remembering the stories about how he and his brother had smeared their faces with black shoe polish and smuggled bicycle parts across the border into Austria before the Anschluss.

The fellow in the bed next to me owned a delicatessen and had told us not too long ago of all the tricks he had employed in trying to stay out of the army, including some sort of injections that faked a liver problem. He surely wasn't a Nazi. The boy in the bed to the right of the farmer had just turned seventeen, so he wasn't a likely candidate either.

In the next row of beds lay an accountant who had worked at a *Lebkuchen* factory in Nuremberg. He was a father of five who had entertained us enormously with his stories of trading sugar stolen from the factory for butter, potatoes, and bacon that the farmers had in abundance. Also not your typical party member.

Farther down the row was a seriously ill man in his midthirties. He had only one arm, and his face was twisted and contorted from the many shell splinters that had entered when he was hit. He had hardly spoken since his arrival, but I seemed to recall that he had been a dentist before the war. "I'll simply leave him out," I decided. "He's already suffered enough, shot up the way he is, and there's little enough chance that he'll still make it home anyway."

The patient in the far corner of the room was an engineer. He was somewhat older than the rest and obviously in the advanced stages of lung tuberculosis—coughing, spitting, and still smoking. Going by his general type, he might have been a Nazi, but it was very unlikely that he would survive the coming week.

That left only the gabby storeroom superintendent from the Dresden opera who, in his simplicity, had told us more about his uninteresting life than anyone cared to know. He was absolutely not a party member.

And that was everyone except for Oskar and me. And he—Oskar? Recently he had told me proudly about his two sons. They held high ranks in the Hitler Youth, and one of them had received a medal for exceptional leadership of his group at premilitary exercises on skis in the Austrian Alps. It also occurred to me that he had once made a remark that the still-awaited German wonder weapons would certainly play a role in the final outcome of the war.

Now that I really considered him, yes, he could very likely

be a Nazi. Because he had been a guest of my Jewish grandmother thirty years ago and now massaged my legs, I must have become deaf and blind to any evidence of his political convictions. But I still couldn't be certain.

"Oskar," I said, "how long have you been a soldier?"

"Since October 1941."

"They overlooked you during the first two years of the war?"

"I was director of a music school in Berlin. That seemed to be more important to them. Why do you ask?"

"No reason. It just seemed to me from your stories that you hadn't been in the war from the beginning."

In order to be the director of a school during Hitler's thousand-year reign, one had to be a member of the National Socialist German Workers Party. Such a position, with influence over young people, wouldn't have been handed over to someone whose political views were not incontestably clear and pro-Hitler. Oskar was a party member.

Would he have voted to let my grandmother disappear, if she had still been alive? I couldn't understand how a man so obviously intelligent and highly cultivated, in addition to being a sensitive artist, could be a Nazi. How could he justify simply occupying European countries in order to push down their throats the German idea of pure and impure races?

I recalled a recent conversation during which I had said, "Our countryman Hitler certainly did some heavy speculating with this war."

"Just wait a while," Oskar had answered. "Everything could

still turn out differently. The Allies can't just spread around large pieces of German-speaking countries, giving them away to the winners the way they did last time in the Treaty of Versailles, without those countries eventually wanting to be reunited. It's just a matter of time."

At that point I still wasn't strong enough to carry on an involved political discussion. I was also aware of a number of factors that could have been considered in Hitler's favor at the time of his takeover, factors that partially explained the general enthusiasm for him. It wouldn't have been a crime to reunite all the German-speaking territories, had he attempted to achieve this through negotiation and a good foreign policy. To lead a country out of a depression like that of the thirties, basically just through hard work—by building the autobahns and numerous new factories and by encouraging everyone to believe that they had a right to a Volkswagen and a radio—wasn't necessarily bad either.

Of course, as it turned out, the autobahns had been built for military-strategic purposes and the factories were intended for producing the biggest stockpile of weapons in Europe. The radio for everyone had provided the perfect means of continually showering the entire German nation with previously unknown levels of propaganda. No, all of that hadn't looked or sounded so good after all. At that point, many who had leaned toward the idea of being Nazis turned away, but Oskar, evidently, had not been one of those.

I began to feel a horror of my duties as a spy. I felt miserable. When I had been given this first task, I had secretly hoped that I would never discover a party member. And now

I was faced with the decision of whether to turn in the one prisoner who had done the most for me.

What if I didn't turn him in but they found out later by themselves? Or perhaps they already knew he was with the party and had put him in close contact with me on purpose, to test me. His injury had never really been serious at all.

I didn't want to think about it anymore. My pulse was very high, as it often had been recently. I could feel it in my neck and in my feet. If I really paid attention, I could actually feel it in my whole body. Now that my general condition had improved, I had begun to detect all the "little" pains and problems. For instance, when blowing my nose, I could blow right through my left ear. That was from the time when a grenade had exploded so close to me.

There were certain light twinges in my chest whenever I took a deep breath or turned over in bed. At night, when I wasn't well covered, I also felt pains in my lower back, in the general region of my kidneys.

"But I'm alive," I said to myself, "with or without high pulse and whatever else may turn up." With that I decided to fall asleep in order not to have to think anymore about Oskar or the mysterious man who would someday turn up and address me as Flussman.

At the beginning of May, Captain Pushkin came and sat down with me under the tree. I had just finished my two rounds of the barracks, without having to lean on Oskar or a cane.

"The colonel would like to have a report from you concerning your political views," he said. "Could you have it ready in a week?"

"How should I do that?" I asked

"Sorry, I can't help you there," he replied. "You'll just have to figure that out for yourself," and after a few more words about my improving state of health, he left. I sat there, completely at a loss, with a blank sheet of paper that he had handed me.

At two o'clock that same afternoon, a wild racket of shooting and yelling broke out in the area where the Russian guards were quartered. The noise kept building higher and higher to an unbelievable pitch. I couldn't imagine what might be happening until an orderly called over from inside the building, "The war is over! Capitulation of the Germans."

"Thank God," I said out loud to myself. I rolled from my mattress onto the ground and buried my face in the juicy spring grass. I filled my lungs with the wonderful smell of damp earth and young plants, stretched my arms and legs out wide, and gave myself up to a deep feeling of thankfulness. If everyone at home had managed to survive the bombs and the Gestapo, perhaps we could be together again in peace after all.

I'd been told a joke in Vienna during the first years of the war and had carried it around inside of me ever since. The recollection had helped me many times to hang in there just a little bit longer:

Two well-known Austrian folk figures, Count Rudy and Count Bobby, are standing in front of a globe, and Rudy asks, "What are all these pink spots?"

Bobby replies, "Those are England with all her colonies."

"And what about the purple spots?"

"Those are France and her colonies."

"Well, then," Rudy asks, "what is that great big green area over there?"

"Oh, that's the United States of America."

"And how about the enormous orange one?"

"That's Russia."

"Do you happen to know what this little, teeny-tiny brown spot is?"

"That's Germany."

At this point Rudy becomes quite pensive, and then very quietly he asks the question of the century, "Do you think Hitler knows that?"

On May 7, 1945, I thought, *Finally, he has learned it!*

The next morning, just before sunrise and without any prior notification, a great number of military vehicles arrived and began to load and drive away the prisoners from the connecting camp. Immediately the rumors began to circulate.

"The prisoners are being taken to the train station and sent home."

"No, they are being taken to a different camp."

"I heard they are being sent to Siberia."

By afternoon it was the turn of the hospital inmates. A few of the sick men became hysterical with joyful anticipation. By the time they came for me the word was official. This camp, including the hospital, was being dissolved and the inmates distributed to other camps in the Kiev area.

Some of us were loaded into an open truck and taken back to the main hospital, where I had been so ill the previous winter. Oskar was in a different car. I didn't even have a chance to say goodbye.

THE GERMAN PLOT

I spent my first week in the main Kiev hospital in a hall, on a long row of mattresses, pressed closely together with many other prisoners. My diet was identical to everyone else's, and no one seemed to be aware of the special treatment I had been given during my last visit. I said nothing, asked for nothing unusual.

Perhaps the whole espionage business had burst overnight, like a soap bubble. *The war is over,* I thought, *so what do they still need spies for?* And if they no longer needed me as a spy, it was also clear they no longer needed to keep me in better health than anyone else.

I tried to be as inconspicuous as possible. The only suspicious item was my cloth bag, which I hid under the mattress. Finally I was assigned a bed, and life fell into a routine. My physical condition didn't seem to change any longer. My pulse remained just under a high 120, my legs continued to be weak and swollen, and I had pains in various parts of my body, but since I didn't suffer a relapse or worsen drastically, I was more or less content.

About the end of June, the head doctor came into my room. When she saw me, she seemed at first surprised, but then she smiled and greeted me. "Rauch, how are you coming along?"

"Thanks, I'm doing all right."

"Do you want to work? The dentist needs an assistant."

"Of course, if I'm strong enough."

"Come with me, then."

We went up to the third floor and entered a room where a blond and robust Russian woman was just in the process of drilling a prisoner's tooth. She was using a foot-powered machine that would have been considered an antique in Vienna thirty years earlier.

The head doctor spoke awhile with the dentist and then said to me, "You may begin here tomorrow morning at ten. I will arrange for you to receive double rations."

I thanked her and left. This new arrangement seemed further proof that I no longer had to worry about my job as a spy. After all, the head doctor knew about my previous status. She obviously also remembered that I had almost died because she had taken the key to the medicine chest with her on holiday. Evidently it was her slightly guilty conscience that was prompting her to do me this special favor. She had offered me the easiest job in the entire hospital for which one could receive double rations.

Nobody will ever approach me now and address me as Flussman, and Oskar, wherever he is, can continue to live in peace, I thought.

The job with the dentist brought about an additional small change in my status that would later have much greater ramifications. Bureaucracy in the camps was minimal, and one possible reason was simply a lack of paper. Whatever was written in camp by doctors or officials, whether medical reports, official notices, or memos, usually consisted of dark purple scribbles on old newspapers.

But there was one bureaucratic detail to which the Russians

strictly adhered. Each prisoner was assigned two classification numbers. The first was based on his ability to work. A *0* signified that one was completely unfit for work, a *1* denoted an ability to do light tasks, and a *3* indicated that the man was completely able-bodied.

The second classification number dealt with the undernourishment/dystrophy factor: the number *1* represented the lightest degree of infirmity, and *3* the highest. I had originally been assigned fitness-for-work number *0* and dystrophy number *3* until I received the job with the dentist. That change automatically promoted me to work group *1* without any further physical examinations or particular improvement in my overall condition.

The job with the dentist was easy enough, requiring only four hours a day, four days a week. In the morning I had to dust the drilling machine and the two wooden cupboards where the pliers and drill bits were kept. Then I called in the patients one by one and handed the dentist her tools as she worked.

The most indispensable ingredient for our work was vodka. The pliers were first dipped in vodka to be cleaned, and then they were held over the burner (also filled with vodka) to be disinfected. The dentist dunked the cotton balls in vodka before rubbing the patients' teeth or gums, and now and then she took a hefty swig herself.

One afternoon she said, "Take this bottle and come with me."

We left the building and crossed the courtyard to the ground floor of another building, which was functioning as a warehouse. The supervisor came to meet us and greeted the dentist in a friendly fashion. We entered a huge room where piles of military blankets, uniforms, and underwear (the type worn by all the hospital prisoners) were stacked onto shelves, and mountains of mattresses and collapsible iron beds leaned against the walls. The warehouse supervisor went over to one corner and filled the two bottles we had brought from enormous glass containers of vodka. Then he and the dentist disappeared and left me waiting for an hour. I had a pretty good idea what they were doing during that time, and the manner in which they later took leave of each other confirmed my suspicions.

The following week it was quite cold when we left at the same hour for another visit to the warehouse, so I borrowed an overcoat and fitted my own two glass containers inside. When I was left to cool my heels once again, I had plenty of time in which to fill my private bottles. Thus a pleasant routine developed that lasted all summer. They had their stolen hour together, and I my stolen vodka that I was able to exchange in the kitchen for fried fish, hard-cooked eggs, and bacon.

The summer passed. My pulse remained high, and the pains in my kidneys returned whenever I didn't keep my back at a steady temperature. Except for this, no further complications developed.

The hope that we would be sent home as soon as the war ended had been in vain. Once, when we were standing for our daily count and the number didn't come out correctly, the Russian officer in charge became very upset. Then he yelled,

"You will learn to do this right, and if you think we are taking care of you here so that you can be returned to Germany fat and happy, you couldn't be more wrong! You will remain here for years, until you have built up again all that you destroyed!" That sentence made the rounds very quickly and produced a heavy depression among the prisoners.

All the Germans and Poles who were not patients but employed in some fashion in the hospital as kitchen help, doctors, clergy, administrators, and so on, slept in small rooms on the top floor of the building. One day a one-handed German, who spoke Russian well and was employed as an interpreter, came to my bed and said, "I noticed that you play chess. Would you like to try a game with me?"

"Why not?" I replied.

"If you wish, we can go upstairs to the room where I sleep. It is quieter there and better for concentration."

I would later sit for hours with this intelligent partner, playing many exciting games of chess—we were about equal in our ability—and engaging in numerous interesting conversations.

There were six beds in my chess partner's room, but his roommates were seldom present. They got used to me, and in time I also became accustomed to the manner in which these unusual prisoners lived. Once, as I entered the room, a door was closed very quickly, but not before I had caught a glimpse of one of them fooling around with one of the Russian nurses.

Then there was the matter of how the upper-floor prisoners dressed. It was obvious that some who slept in this room at night went into the city by day to pick up supplies for the hospital. They went accompanied by their Russian girlfriends and were guarded, of course, by soldiers with submachine guns who probably received a portion of the bartered-away foodstuffs or their equivalent in rubles.

Thanks to their connections to the civilian population and their financial resources, a number of the top-floor prisoners had been able to order tailor-made uniforms and boots. They were of the finest materials but so exaggerated in design that they turned their wearers into comical caricatures. Most of these men had been simple soldiers; in this manner, they seemed to be promoting themselves to officers.

The jodhpur pants were widened at the thighs, bulging to twice their normal width. The epaulettes were also 50 percent too large, with an overabundance of gold or silver thread. Topping it all off were small caps, which were so narrow that they resembled tiny canoes, almost lost on top of the bald-shaven heads.

I decided that my chess partner must not be a member of this group, since he often made disparaging remarks about the others and was dressed in a fairly shabby lieutenant's uniform.

One day, around the middle of September, I was involved in a good chess game with my partner when a chess figure fell on the floor. I crawled under one of the beds to pick it up, and there, pushed back near the wall, were three wooden suitcases fitted with metal bands, all the same size and color. That wouldn't have been so unusual in itself, if I hadn't noticed a bundle of German bank notes caught in the lid of one of them.

Strange, I thought, but I said nothing.

We finished the game and I went back downstairs to my room, the money still in my thoughts. All Germans at the front had had German money with them. There had been few opportunities to spend it, but some had played cards and won or lost their pay that way. Others had made bets, and those who were able to go on leave had made good use of their winnings, I'm certain. Some, like myself, had sent most of their money home. After I was taken prisoner, we were all searched innumerable times, and everything was taken. First the Russians relieved us of our watches and any other valuables, then our boots. All that finally remained, being of no use to our captors, were family photos and German money. The prisoners were usually also permitted to keep their wedding rings, probably because it was too much trouble to get them off their fingers.

Still thinking of those mysterious trunks, I began to ask myself what became of the money after a prisoner was brought to the hospital. It was taken when we handed in our uniforms. A few of us still had a photo or two, but no one had any money.

The next time I went upstairs to play chess, I decided to get another look at those suitcases. My partner was still in the next room when I opened the box of chessmen so clumsily that they all fell on the floor and I had to crawl under the bed again to pick them up. I lifted the lid of the suitcase where the money was peeking out. Incredible! It was filled from top to bottom with German bills. I gathered the chess figures together, but before I crawled out from under the bed, I lifted the lid of the next suitcase. The contents were the same, plus a paper sack filled with gold dental fillings and wedding rings.

That afternoon I wasn't able to win even one chess game. I kept thinking of the man, or men, who had collected all that money. What could they have in mind to do with it? I knew it was still legal tender in Germany.

Two weeks passed. On October 4, a group of Russian officers, including a few doctors, visited the hospital. They went from room to room examining all who had been assigned to work group *0* and dystrophy group *3*. Only non-Germans were examined: Romanians, Hungarians, Czechs, Poles, and Austrians. I wasn't included, of course, even though I was skinnicr and wcakcr than many who had been chosen and placed on the mysterious list. I was no longer a member of work group *0* because of my job with the dentist.

When the officers left, the speculations began. Those who were on the list would receive better rations, would be sent home, would be transferred to another hospital, et cetera.

Two days later, on October 6, the excitement intensified when two orderlies came across the courtyard from the warehouse, staggering under piles of old uniforms: jackets and pants, coats, caps, and shoes, as well as mess kits and bread bags. The official news began blazing through the hospital like a brushfire: "Tomorrow a westbound train is leaving with 1,000 non-Germans. The transport will be carrying only sick prisoners—280 from our hospital, everyone who is on the list!"

Now, wherever you looked you saw either ecstatic faces or very sad ones. The chosen ones, those with enough strength, tried on different pieces of clothing and shoes. They were delighted if they were able to put together a uniform that more or less fit. Some on the list were too weak for this game and had to be content with whatever the orderlies laid on their beds. I was convinced that a number of them would never survive the trip.

October 7, 1945. Everyone was dressed, shoes on feet, caps on heads, cloth bags with mess kit, cup, and spoon over each shoulder. But the order to leave never came. They waited all day long, but nothing happened. Evening brought the explanation; there was no locomotive.

October 8. The uniforms were laid once more on the beds, but no train arrived that day. Everyone put on his white hospital shirt and long white pants again. I played chess, went for vodka with the dentist, and waited while she enjoyed her weekly meeting with the warehouse supervisor. I also tried to squelch the rising and ignoble wave of gloating I felt because the locomotive hadn't arrived.

October 9. No news. October 10 and 11. The same. On October 12, I went upstairs to play chess. When we were about to begin my partner was called downstairs, and he asked me to wait for him. I leafed through a book for a few minutes. Then, from the neighboring room, through the slightly open door, I heard voices. Two men were arguing. I began to pay attention when I heard the words "the German money."

Although they suddenly lowered their voices, I could still make out most of the conversation.

"We'll only report one of the three who have died."

"But how?"

"Alfred and I will take our places in the other column. We'll be counted twice."

"And?"

"Well, since we are the thinnest, we will have the best chance of slipping in without being noticed. We'll carry as much as possible of the money and gold with us to Germany. You'll get your share later, of course."

At this moment my chess partner returned. I lost the game, making a headache the excuse for my poor playing.

I passed a sleepless night, and the next day a statement was issued that those on the list would be brought to the train station the following morning.

As I went about my duties with the dentist that day, my mind was elsewhere. Without wanting to, I had uncovered a plot that didn't please me one bit. Two of those upstairs prisoners, healthy, overfed, and with brand-new German uniforms and Russian girlfriends, were planning to smuggle themselves in place of two dead prisoners into the group of those leaving in the first transport. What's more, they would arrive in Germany as rich men, having plundered their dead comrades of everything, down to the fillings in their teeth.

With each passing hour and the growing excitement of those about to leave the next day, I could feel the fury building inside me. Two of the 280 would not be sick men sent home by the Russians so that the death toll wouldn't be so high when the International Red Cross arrived for their inspection. No, those two would be Germans with Polish accents, their pockets stuffed with money and gold.

At 5:00 p.m. I went to the head physician and spoke with her a few minutes. She became very excited and upset.

At 6:00 p.m. she watched from the second floor while the afternoon count was being taken in the courtyard. She saw how two men were counted twice each.

At 6:15 she went up to the top floor, accompanied by an officer and four guards, the latter carrying submachine guns with the safety catches released. Three suitcases full of German money and an unspecified quantity of gold were brought out of the room.

At 6:25 all the German administrative and kitchen personnel were shoved into trucks and driven away.

That evening there was nothing to eat in the hospital. I had lost my appetite anyway. The next morning, as the uniformed prisoners began going down to line up in the courtyard for their departure, the head doctor came into my room with an orderly. He was carrying parts of uniforms and shoes in his arms.

The doctor glanced around the room and pointed, seemingly indiscriminately, to a fellow sitting on a bed and said, "You there, and you (pointing at me), get dressed and get down to the courtyard right away. I'm adding your names to the list!" Without another word, she turned and left.

The other man was the only German among the first thousand to leave. Many months were to pass before any more Germans were released from the Russian camps. I doubt whether he ever found out why his fate so suddenly changed for the better.

PART 3

Marching west

HOMEWARD

With forty others I sat on clean, dry straw in a cattle car and waited. My heart hammered even more rapidly than usual in recent months. Outside an official was yelling something unintelligible. A whistle blew; the train gave a jerk. That was the only thing that counted, the moment the train actually began to move in the direction of home. No one could now come and say, "You're on this train by mistake. Get down. You belong to work group number *1*."

The train rumbled over the switches of the suburban station, and one of the soldiers began a song. All those pale creatures with the sunken eyes—old men, many of whom hadn't yet reached their twenty-fifth birthdays—joined in. It seemed I heard the words "home," "homeland," "far away," and "I'll see you again" in every stanza. A few who were still standing began to hug each other and to dance around in circles until the train rattled over another switch, and everyone fell to the floor. One man kept repeating over and over, "I can't believe it. It can't be true."

I rolled myself together like an embryo in one corner of the car, pulled the collar of my coat over my head, and attempted to digest in solitude the importance and implications of the situation. I would have preferred just falling asleep and waking up again in Vienna.

Before the train pulled out, one of the soldiers had figured out that we were about 1,000 kilometers away from home and should be able to make it easily in three days, because 330 kilometers a day wasn't that much for even a slow train to accomplish. In spite of those calculations, I was reassured to catch sight of a car with a goulash cannon (field kitchen) and another, supposedly filled with food, at the end of the train next to the guards' passenger coach.

On this trip the sliding doors were no longer locked. Depending on the time of day and the weather, we were able to leave a portion open and look out at the passing landscape. God knows there wasn't much worth seeing, only burned-out villages and plains with already harvested fields, everything veiled in a late autumnal gray. Yet it all seemed wonderful to me, since I was already busy imagining how soon I would wander through nature, in sunshine or rain, as a free man. I would stop when and where I wished for as long as it pleased me. I would bend down to look at a flower, stretch out in a meadow, or stand on my head, and nobody in the whole world would be able to command me to do otherwise.

The clothing I was wearing was already a foretaste of my new freedom. Though shabby and oversized, it belonged to me, and in a few more days I would be able to do whatever I wanted with it. It was no longer the standard-issue hospital white underwear, from which I hadn't even been permitted to cut the sleeves. After fourteen months of that apparel, I now had real articles of clothing on my body.

The laced boots were about four centimeters too long. Instead of shoelaces, pieces of hemp had been strung back and forth between the eyelets. I was dressed in a pair of yellowish-green military pants with knee patches, a shirt of an indefinable shade of green, and a German infantry jacket still in fairly good condition, with a sewn-on eagle and swastika. Over all that I wore a Russian military overcoat that was so long the hem dragged on the floor. It was belted around the waist with a piece of rope, and since it no longer boasted even a single button, I had pulled it together by inserting short lengths of wire through the buttonholes.

The German cap was also much too large for me, and I wore it pushed far back on my head so it wouldn't slip over my eyes. A string over my shoulder supported the half of a potato sack in which I carried a dented and scratched tin cup, an equally battered mess kit, and an aluminum spoon. A field canteen without its original felt cover dangled from another string. The canteen cap was a gnawed-off corncob.

The first afternoon, the train stopped on a sidetrack. One of the guards walked along the train and yelled, "Four men from each car to bring the food." We were all pretty hungry by this time, and the question of whether or when we would be given something to eat again was never far from our minds. A free man doesn't have to think about these things as long as there is a bowl of soup and a hunk of bread nearby. The soldier, and much more so the prisoner, is always dependent on the hope that someone else will bring him something to eat, and bring it often enough for the body to continue to function properly. Again and again I had heard the soldiers swearing the same oath: "If I ever get out of this and make it home alive, I swear I'll never be hungry again!"

The volunteers returned with a bucket full of kasha,

another bucket of sweetened tea, and two loaves of bread. Chunks of meat floated in the kasha, and everyone in the car even received a good-sized portion of tobacco.

Rations continued to be plentiful the second day. The train wasn't progressing very rapidly, since there was only one set of tracks, and we often had to wait for hours for trains coming from the other direction or to let trains more important than ours pass us from the rear.

On the third day there was no longer any meat in the kasha, and on the fourth day around sunset, we were pushed onto a sidetrack. The locomotive disappeared, and the guards took off in the direction of the little town nearby. Our car remained stationary for the next four days, and never again did we receive anything from the food car. We also received nothing to drink. The Russians had bartered all the accompanying supplies, and in the days to come, whenever we saw the guards, they were always drunk. Once one of the prisoners called out "drunken pigs" as the Russians staggered past, and one of them turned and emptied the entire magazine of his submachine gun into the side of the train, fortunately without inflicting any serious harm.

Some of us who were strong enough went out into the cold, foggy October fields to dig out cabbage stems or, if we were lucky, a potato that had been overlooked in the harvest. We dipped water from the rain puddles and cooked the cabbage-stem soup over little fires that we made from pieces of coal gathered along the tracks. We starved.

I had to distribute my energy very carefully, because my heart began beating wildly after even the slightest physical effort. Out of a feeling of solidarity, we shared whatever edible things we produced with those who were too sick to care for themselves. One of those in my car had already died; another wouldn't be able to hold out much longer.

On the fifth day a train filled with Russian soldiers stopped on a parallel track and stayed for a few hours. Obviously on their way home, the soldiers were all in the best of spirits, singing and drinking. They began throwing us bread, half-eaten apples, and bacon rinds and had great sport watching to see how we gobbled up their leftovers or cooked them over our little fires. They relished the role of the victors, throwing their gnawed bones to the starving dogs on the losing side of the battle.

On the sixth day I was awakened at dawn by a jolt from the train as it finally began rolling again. The following week passed very, very slowly. We kept advancing short distances, but usually the train stood still. It rained most of the time, so at least we had no problems with drinking water, but the search in the fields became that much more exhausting. It wasn't easy at all, burrowing around in the cold and muddy earth, trying to discover something edible. Above all, we didn't dare go too far from the train, since we never knew when it might decide to depart. A state of general languor set in, and more and more of us were simply unable to go out searching for food any longer.

During the twelfth night I was awakened by a kick on the knee. "Wake up, fast!"

"What's going on?" I grumbled, still half-asleep.

"There is a whole train filled with potatoes on a sidetrack. One of us is already on top and he's throwing them down."

Instantly wide-awake, I let myself down from the car onto the gravel embankment. It was very far down, and for a moment I worried about how I would manage to get back up again. Three of us pushed another prisoner up into the high, open car, and he immediately began throwing down scores of potatoes. The train's locomotive was only four cars away, and even though the continuously escaping steam made a considerable amount of noise, we still had to be careful not to be discovered.

The night wasn't very dark; there must have been a fairly full moon behind the clouds. We moved like phantoms, bending and gathering the potatoes into our sacks. Suddenly we heard the short blast of a whistle, and the train jolted. The two who were up top had quite a time of it, falling rather than climbing to make it down and off the car before the train picked up too much speed.

The next day someone discovered a fast and easy way of making the potatoes edible. A friendly stoker offered to hang the potatoes, strung on a length of wire, in the locomotive fire for a few minutes. When he threw them down to us, they were burned to a crisp but at least cooked through.

At long last we reached Marmarossziget, the border city between Hungary and Russia. Soldiers in Hungarian uniforms and women with Red Cross bands on their arms were waiting on the platform. When they realized in what poor condition many of us were, they brought stretchers and carried the weakest to the front of the train station. From there they transported us in trucks to a school. We were duly marveled at by the local populace, and we learned that ours was the first transport of eastern prisoners of war to come through that point. The locals became almost hysterical when they found out that there were at least fifty Hungarians in our shipment, men who couldn't be officially released, however, until they got to Budapest.

That evening we ate an incredibly good-tasting pea soup with bacon pieces and white bread with milk. I hadn't tasted milk for fifteen months. We slept on clean straw sacks, and the next morning, after being served bread and milk once more, we were taken back to the train station and loaded into a train with passenger coaches, the kind with compartments and upholstered seats. It was an experience, just using real flush toilets again after such a long time. As the train began moving and we sat on those upholstered seats with our skinny legs dangling down, most of us wished we were back on the straw in the cattle car, where we could stretch out and sleep. We were so weak that normal sitting was in itself too much of an effort.

After a while someone magically produced a razor with a dull blade and scraped off his three-week-old beard, using the bathroom mirror. It was a rather bloody business, especially without shaving cream. Others came and sharpened the tired blade on the inside of a water glass. I was amazed to see how important it was for many to arrive home freshly shaven. Without beards, the white skin of their sunken cheeks and the skeletal form of their heads could be seen much more clearly.

My parents, if they still exist, wouldn't even notice the condition of my beard, I thought. And if they no longer existed? What would I do then? Where would I go? I had seen soldiers at the front who were happy to return to battle when their furloughs were over because, instead of their family homes, they had found only an enormous pile of rubble. The closer I came to the Austrian border, the more I worried that I might have survived the war while the rest of my family had been reduced to nothing in a giant bomb crater. After all, our house stood not far from a train station, and I had heard many times that the air attacks were especially concentrated on industrial areas and railway centers.

On our way through Hungary we passed many pretty villages and small cities that seemed not to have suffered from the events of the war. People in colorful costumes were working in the fields. Suddenly the train stopped in the station of a small town. When we leaned out the windows, we saw an almost surrealistic picture: a railway platform decorated with flags and colored paper, and hundreds of men, women, and children in their Sunday best. Bread, sausage, cheese, and sweet rolls were arranged on long tables. There were large kettles full of soup and goulash, bottles of wine, and schnapps. It was all for us. Someone had found out that the first prisoner transport from Russia was coming through the town, and that there were also Hungarians on board.

The men staggered out of the coaches and began stuffing themselves with these wonders, washing everything down with wine. It was a real festival, and there was even a group of Gypsy musicians. But when the train took off again, it soon became very obvious that the nice people of the village hadn't done the home-comers such a good turn after all. It wasn't long until one after the other leaned out the window to regurgitate everything he had consumed. Their stomachs were no longer able to handle such large amounts of food, especially the fat and alcohol. I had eaten only a little bit of soup with some white bread and had stuck a biscuit in my pocket to nibble on in the hours to come. Thus, I was spared the ill effects of the fiesta.

We reached Budapest during the night, and there the Hungarians and Czechs were separated from the rest of us. A train with just two cars brought the little group of Austrians to Marchegg, the Austrian border station. It was about 2:00 a.m. Three faint lamps swung in the wind and rain, barely illuminating the tracks and the two little station buildings.

A train official in a rubber raincoat with a red-white-red band around his arm came to where we stood next to the coaches and said, in heavy Austrian dialect, "I am a representative of the Austrian government, and I welcome you in its name. I have been given the privilege of bringing you to Vienna, and I hope we will be able to put a special train together tonight. Meanwhile will you please go over to that building, and I'll call you when everything is ready."

After years in foreign lands, these were the first words I heard spoken by a free countryman. I felt my throat tighten.

At 5:00 a.m. we reached Vienna. In a house next to the bombed-out North Station, each of the forty-five homecoming soldiers received a piece of paper, as small and almost as thin as a cigarette paper, with a few faint words in Russian, our name in Cyrillic letters, and a rubber stamp. It was our discharge paper from the Russian war imprisonment. Each of us could now go wherever he wished. We were free.

VIENNA

I stood shivering in front of the ruins of the train station on that dark morning in late October. A few electric streetlamps faintly illuminated the giant piles of rubble around me. Those heaps of bricks and cement had once been five-story houses, typical Viennese apartment buildings constructed at the turn of the nineteenth century. A few of the houses, or parts of them, were still standing, enough to give a general idea of where the streets used to run. Shadows wrapped in old winter coats hurried past me with rapid footsteps.

I turned down a path trodden between the ruins toward a corner where a streetlamp glowed and sat there on a block of granite while I attempted to order my thoughts. From now on I was completely responsible for myself. To reach our home on the Landstrasse—presuming it was still standing—I would have to cover a distance of six or seven kilometers, as nearly as I could judge. That had still been my parents' address on the last letter I had received before being captured, but that was more than fifteen months previous.

When I looked around me at the devastated lunar landscape near the North Station and thought of how our home lay only five blocks from the South Station, I felt a heavy, fearful chill. Could I even cover that distance on foot? I wasn't certain. After all, I was just a hundred-pound bag of bones with a heart that beat much too quickly, and I had next to no energy in reserve.

Daylight was breaking now. After questioning a man about the general direction of the Danube Canal, I set off. I pulled a piece of wood from the rubble and used it as a cane to give me a little more support. People approaching on the street regarded me with a mixture of curiosity and horror. A group of women, made brave by their numbers, stopped and asked from where I had come. When I told them "from Russia," one of the women pulled a photograph of a young soldier in German uniform from her bag and asked whether by chance I might ever have seen him.

Half an hour later I reached the Danube Canal, and as I stepped onto a temporary bridge, I saw a company of Russian soldiers marching toward me. For a panicky moment I thought I would have to jump over the side into the water so as not to be taken prisoner again. *The war is over. It's past.* I had to keep repeating that to myself. *For six months my country has been at peace. The shooting is over, and never again can I be taken prisoner.*

Back in May, when the news of the German surrender had reached us, all of the Russians had gotten drunk. But for the rest of us, nothing whatsoever had changed. We were and remained prisoners. Now, for the first time, the fact that the war was truly over began to have meaning for me. People would begin to rebuild the ruined cities. Families could live together in peace once more without the man, the father, being taken away to die in a uniform and be buried on foreign soil.

Those citizens scurrying past me, thin and pale, carrying bundles or pulling a three-wheeled baby carriage full of ancient household belongings, why weren't they singing and dancing for joy? If I should find my family again, safe and unhurt, I was certain that that's the way I would act.

As I crossed through the city park, I stopped to rest under a chestnut tree with a few remaining brown leaves. Soon an old man came and sat down next to me. He offered me a piece of his black bread and asked me where I had come from, and as we ate he enlightened me concerning the current political situation.

At the end of the war, Austria had been divided into four zones that were occupied by the four Allied powers: Russia, the United States, France, and Great Britain. The capital, Vienna, was also divided into four zones and was likewise under the administration of the four powers.

The Russians had become famous for dismantling everything possible and taking all they could carry back to Russia as prizes of war, whereas the Americans had introduced the Marshall Plan and brought with them every kind of help, including foodstuffs. The economic situation in the eastern portion of Austria, occupied by the Russians, was very bad, while the part of the country farther to the west, held by the Americans, was considerably better off.

I thanked the old man and continued on my way. The closer I came to the Landstrasse, following the tracks of the tramway, the worse was the devastation. Whole blocks of houses lay in ruins. My hopes of finding our house still standing were rapidly disappearing. I reached the Landstrasse, but, since it curved slightly, I still couldn't see down the last kilometer to the place where our building should have stood. Whether because of my physical exhaustion or the tension produced by the uncertainty of what lay ahead, everything began to go around in circles, and I had to sit down in the street. I leaned against a wall, and for a short time everything went black. When I regained consciousness, a woman was kneeling next to me, trying to pour some warm tea from a thermos bottle into my mouth. Shortly thereafter, I pulled myself together in order to complete the last stretch.

I had already figured out that I should be able to see our house by the time I reached the shot-up sign of a certain shoe store. When I reached the store, I stopped and took in the wonderful sight. Our house and a few before it and beyond seemed to be whole.

I hurried forward as fast as my legs could carry me. Large holes became visible in some of the walls. The overhead trolley wires were hanging down crazily across the street, and a group of people were shoveling dirt into a bomb crater not far away. Nevertheless, our building stood there with walls and roof intact. I was almost in front of it when I first saw the marks of rifle bullets in the wall and a large hole where a window should have been.

Opening the wrought-iron gate of the fence, I crossed the forecourt, and as I climbed the steps to the entrance hall, I saw the Russian guard sitting on the old wooden trunk that had always stood on that particular spot. He got up and asked, in an unfriendly tone, "What do you want?"

In Russian, I answered, "This is the house where my family lives, or used to live, on the top floor."

Pointing to a sign fastened to the wall next to the mailbox, the guard said, "This house is now the headquarters of the Twelfth Infantry Regiment of the Russian army. I know nothing about your family."

I turned around and went back out to the street. A light rain had begun falling. Across the way from our house stood a former cloister that had served as a hospital since the war's beginning. I hesitated. The mere act of making a decision was strange and almost intoxicating, it having been so long since I had entered a building as a free man to ask for information. Should I go to that building or another farther up the street?

Shyly I opened the door and entered the cloister. In the hall I encountered a brisk coming and going of nuns in nursing habits and orderlies carrying patients on stretchers. All along one wall people leaned, waiting for an empty chair. A nun who seemed to be a receptionist sat behind a desk.

Approaching her, I removed my cap and said, "Excuse me, could you please tell me whether the telephones are functioning in this city?"

She looked up, examining me from my bald-shaven head down to the overlarge, mud-encrusted shoes. In that moment I felt, for the first time, something akin to shame because of my appearance. The floor on which I stood was shiny marble, the nuns' habits a pure and snowy white. I began to realize that it would have been much better to go to a junk store to make my inquiries, rather than a hospital full of sick people. After all, I was full of lice and bacteria.

"The phones are functioning only in a few zones of the city, mostly in the immediate surroundings. Do you have the number?"

"No, but they are in the telephone book."

She smiled sympathetically. "We have no telephone books, and it will take a long time until they are available again."

"Well, perhaps I can call information?" I asked, with a final hope. She simply shook her head. Thanking her, I turned away to consider what I should attempt next.

The nun had stood up from her desk and came after me, taking me by the arm. "Why don't you sit down over there?" she said. "I'll bring you something to eat. You look as though you could use it."

While greedily gulping down the plate of potato goulash, I decided not to search any longer in this devastated city, but to try, somehow, to get to Mondsee, a village near Salzburg. I knew from my last correspondence with my parents that my sister had rented an upper floor in a farmhouse there to ensure her family's safety.

The nurse told me that to the best of her knowledge, at least one train was leaving daily from the West Station. She advised me to try to catch it at Hütteldorf, on the edge of the city, since all was complete chaos at the West Station itself. What's more, she told me, if I continued to wander around Vienna looking as I did, the authorities would most likely pick me up and put me into quarantine for at least a week. I thanked her and left, feeling much better with something in my stomach.

After a twenty-minute walk, I reached the Stadtbahn and had to wait for almost half an hour at the barrier gate until a woman gave me the twenty *Pfennige* for a tram ticket. During the trip the other passengers told me that the authorities were picking up soldiers in Hütteldorf also, confining them in quarantine for one or two weeks. From all parts of Europe the soldiers were returning, either from camps or from wherever they had found themselves when the war ended. They had been trickling slowly back to Vienna for some time now. But so far, no one had heard of any soldiers returning from Russia. As the first, I made a definite sensation, and various people wanted to squeeze all sorts of information out of me, many offering something to eat in return.

I arrived at the station in Hütteldorf around noon and decided to try reaching the train platform by taking a considerable detour through the freight yards, hoping in that way to avoid the officials. I crept through long rows of freight cars, and when finally I could see the platform not far away, I climbed up into a passenger coach and made myself comfortable for the night. My fellow Stadtbahn passengers had informed me that my train wouldn't be leaving until morning, so I fell asleep immediately on the upholstered seat.

A few hundred people were already assembled when I got up and went over to the platform the following morning. I sat down on a wooden baggage cart to wait for the train, which arrived punctually at eight. When it groaned to a stop, several hundred prospective passengers were on hand, but the cars were already stuffed to overflowing. The determined would-be travelers yanked the doors open and tried to squeeze themselves in by force, but only a few were successful with this method. I knew I hadn't a chance and didn't even get up to try.

Some men who had been sitting near me earlier and knew

my story tried forcing their way in, and one of them succeeded. Suddenly something completely unexpected happened. A man waved from the open bathroom window in one of the cars, at which two men who were still sitting next to me on the baggage cart stood up and seized me, one under each arm, and ran with me to the train. They lifted me up to the window while from inside others reached out to grab me and pull me through. The man who had originally been my neighbor on the baggage cart now stood next to me in the train bathroom, waving goodbye to his friends who remained behind.

END OF THE ODYSSEY

For the next hour the five of us in the bathroom took turns sitting on the toilet until enough people had left the train to create some space. Then, one by one, we found seats in the cars.

The travelers were all under way with a common purpose: to root out and buy food at the farms in the countryside. Most carried empty suitcases and backpacks. The food rations in the city were so scant that those with no opportunity to uncover something extra were always hungry.

For the farmers, money wasn't necessarily the most desirable exchange, since there was hardly anything to purchase, so the city dwellers traded every imaginable kind of valuable for butter, bacon, potatoes, smoked meats, and flour. It was rumored that a piano was worth only one or two kilos of butter and that the farmers acquired incredible riches in this manner.

A few hours passed. I had obtained a comfortable seat, and my fellow passengers pumped me regarding my wheres and hows. After about 150 kilometers, the train halted.

"*Enns!* Everybody out. End of the line." We had reached the demarcation line between the Russian sector and the American, and by now I had covered about a third of my journey to Mondsee.

The station at Enns was practically out of commission, and

only a few cars in working condition stood on the many parallel running tracks. Entire trains consisting of burned-out skeletons lay twisted into grotesque shapes, and bomb craters yawned everywhere. I asked an official about the schedule for the westbound trains.

"There is no schedule," he said. "Now and then the Russians let a food train through from the American side. Once in a while an empty train also returns, but no passengers are allowed."

The sun was shining quite warmly for a late autumn day, and being utterly exhausted from the day's exertions, I sat down on a grass-covered slope and dozed. I might have remained sitting there until evening, or even through the night, if I hadn't noticed an old steam engine with two freight cars that kept chugging back and forth in front of me.

At first I simply watched, because it was pleasant to look at, but after a while I realized that a train was forming a few tracks away. The locomotive continued to bring more and more cars, and a train official coupled them together. The large sliding doors of the freight cars were open on both sides.

Nothing further took place for about an hour, and I had almost lost interest, when suddenly the locomotive returned and was coupled to the west end of the train. That electrified me! From my slightly elevated position on the slope, I could see that just a little distance away, all those parallel tracks eventually were reduced to just two rails, running in a straight line directly to the bridge! The river under that bridge represented the border within my own country that I must somehow conquer.

I pulled myself together and, grabbing my sack, my canteen, and the makeshift cane that had proved so helpful, hobbled as fast as I could over to the freight cars. Pushing a handcart close to the doors of one of the cars, I used it to work my way up inside. Then, patient and hopeful, I sat down in a dim corner to wait.

Mine wasn't the waiting of a person who has made a definite plan for his day, who knows that when evening comes he will find himself in a particular place where supper and a clean bed will be waiting. My bed was wherever I happened to be when night fell, my supper a piece of bread given me by a fellow traveler and a few gulps of water from my canteen.

I knew I didn't possess that special document that I must have in order to cross over from the Russian zone to the American, but that fact didn't have any particular meaning for me. I was determined to get to Mondsee, no matter how many people or bureaucrats stood in my way. Even if prior to that I should be yelled at, handled roughly, or locked up in the town jail, in the end they would have to let me go.

The train started up. It hadn't traveled a hundred meters when two women and three men with bags and backpacks jumped up and crept wordlessly into the remaining corners. The train continued to move very slowly, inching forward, until it had finally covered the distance to the bridge, where it stopped once again.

Up front I could hear Russians yelling and a general racket breaking out. They came closer. No one in our car uttered a word. Suddenly a Russian soldier with a submachine gun sprang up into our car. Yelling and swearing, he stomped from corner to corner, herding out the others. He pushed them toward the door with the barrel of his gun, and they all jumped down. Then he came to me. For a moment he stood motionless, examining me, then he asked in Russian, "What are you doing here?"

Obviously, because of my clothing and shaven head, he had taken me for a Russian. In his own tongue, which I more or less commanded, I answered, "I was released yesterday in Vienna from the Russian prisoner-of-war camp. My sister lives near Salzburg, and she is the only one who knows where my parents are." I pulled out my discharge paper and gave it to him.

"Where have you come from?" he asked.

When I answered, "Kiev," his eyes lit up. "Kiev? How does it look now? I lived there as a child."

Even though I had seen next to nothing of the city, I said, "It's a beautiful city."

"Was it heavily damaged?"

"Not so badly that it can't be rebuilt. It will always be beautiful."

He rubbed his hand over his forehead for a second, as though debating with himself, returned my discharge paper without further words, and jumped down from the car.

Shortly thereafter the train began moving once more, and a few hours later I reached Wels, another hundred kilometers closer to my destination. Wels, a charming little town in Upper Austria, was much cleaner, the people better dressed and fed than any I had seen since my discharge. The train station was intact, the tracks free of burned-out cars, and everywhere people were carrying away the remaining rubble and applying fresh paint.

We had arrived in the American zone now, and there was no mistaking the difference. The platform was cleanly swept, and the official answered me politely that the first train west would not be departing until the following morning. I sat down on a bench, deciding to wait until the next day.

Looking through the window of the station restaurant, I could see people sitting at tables with white tablecloths, dining with forks and knives. After a few minutes, a waitress in a white apron came out and asked whether I was hungry. She led me inside and maneuvered me to a table decorated with a bouquet of purple asters. Then she brought the food for which I obviously wasn't able to pay.

There must still be good and generous people alive, I thought, *people who aren't concerned only with their personal well-being.* It was incredible to think that anyone would politely bid a filthy, lousy, ragged, and obviously ill creature to a decent table and serve him a three-course meal, including a glass of beer, without any hope of payment. And that the waitress, a girl about my age in a typical Austrian dirndl, would even sit down and join me for a few minutes—it was all too much for my tear ducts.

I told her about my trip from Kiev and my fervent hope of finding my parents still alive. I wiped my eyes dry on the edge of the tablecloth and was ashamed of my dirty hands. This was the first time I had eaten a normal Austrian three-course meal since those lovely days in Braila, almost exactly one and a half years ago. Before I had finished eating, the waitress returned and presented me with twenty-five German marks.

"I collected that for you from the other guests. You'll need it," she said in a shy, almost guilty voice, as though she wasn't certain how I would react. I took the money and buried my face in my hands to hide my tears.

What was the matter with me, anyway? I, the hardened warrior, who had been rolled over by tanks, who had killed and stolen, who had survived the worst snowstorms for days without food or a roof over my head, had finally returned to my own country and couldn't refrain from blubbering at the slightest opportunity. I knew it was partially due to my physical weakness, but I was ashamed nonetheless.

The waitress explained to me that just three hundred meters away was a spot where all the trucks stopped to pick up hitchhikers. Still blushing with embarrassment, I thanked my benefactors, who sat watching sympathetically. Then I stumbled down the steep road to where hopeful hitchhikers were gathering. Trucks stopped every few minutes, and the drivers called out their destinations. Any who wanted to go in that direction paid a small amount and got in. Soon a truck arrived that was heading my way.

When one of the others said, "He's just returning home from Russia," the driver wouldn't take any money, and I was helped up into the cab.

I got out fifty kilometers later in Vöcklabruck. Dusk was gathering as I sat down on the steps of the town fountain in the little medieval city. The farther west I made it, the more drastic became the difference between my clothing and that worn by the rest of the people in the streets. More and more people stopped to stare or quiz me. When I told one of those who sat down next to me that I wanted to get to Mondsee, he jumped up, saying, "That's Lugerbauer's truck over there, the mover from Mondsee. He's just leaving!" He ran across the square, and after speaking a few words with the driver, who was just getting into his vehicle, he waved me over.

For two hours we drove over a narrow, curving road through a night brilliant with stars. I perched in back on top of a mountain of sailcloth tarpaulins and tried to think about what might lie ahead. Would I find my sister in Mondsee? I didn't know where she lived or even whether she was still in that town. It would be dark. Should I sleep first and wait for morning to begin my search? And what if she weren't there? If no one knew anything about her? In fact, what would I do now in general? Tomorrow? In a month, a year?

I was twenty-one and a half years old and felt like an ancient and decrepit grandfather. Weak and run-down as I was, it would be some time before I would be able to do even light work in order to earn my living. In case I couldn't find any of my family, might there be some sort of government organization for men like me, a place where I could be cared for until I had recovered my strength?

And how would I earn my living in the future? As a technical draftsman, the only thing I had any training for? Or as an artist, a painter, doing that which had always given me so much pleasure as a child? An image of the hand-carved spoon that had welcomed me back from the dead came to me. I turned the spoon around in my mind, again examining it from all sides. A pity I had had to leave it behind.

The next thing I knew the driver was tugging at my leg. "We've arrived. End of the line, everybody out," he said jokingly.

The tiny village square was quite dark. A few lights twinkled from the windows of the surrounding houses. "By any chance, do you know the Baroness von Krüdener?" I asked the driver.

"Oh yes, she lives up on the mountain on the Pichlerbauer farm. Take the road toward Zeller See for one and a half kilometers, and then go right on the little path with the apple trees on each side. It's the big farmhouse. You can't miss it."

I thanked him, walked to the edge of town, and sat down on the ground, leaning against the trunk of a tree. The idea of having to climb a mountain seemed overwhelming. I was feeling dizzy more and more often, as though not enough blood was getting to my brain.

In front of me, on both sides of the street, I could see the silhouettes of large pear trees. I knew the kind of pears they produced—hard and sour—and the wonderful cider the farmers pressed from them. I sat and speculated for a while longer, wondering whether the wisest thing wouldn't be to wait until dawn and then go up when I was fresher. I counted the shadows of five pear trees. Maybe I could make it after all by going past five trees and then resting, five more, and so on. After almost three years, I was so close.

Deciding to make the effort, I pulled myself up, leaning

more heavily than ever on my cane. Five trees up the hill. Then five more. A long rest, and another five. Slowly I came up to where the road disappeared in front of me into the pale sky, evidently because it led down into a depression. It was as though the closeness of my destination gave me strength.

I don't know when I reached the place where the path branched off to the right, only that my heart was thumping as though it would explode, and I could see zigzagging lines in front of my eyes. The narrow, stony path between the apple trees was too steep for me to walk. I ended by crawling up most of it on all fours.

It must have been about ten o'clock when I arrived in front of a fine, imposing farmhouse. For a few moments I sat down on the edge of the wooden well trough. Clear, cold well water was running continuously through a wooden pipe, and I scooped some of it up in my hand. Lights were glowing behind the little windows on the ground floor of the house as well as upstairs. I could hear the snuffling and murmuring of the cows in the stable nearby.

I walked to the heavy, hand-carved door of the farmhouse and knocked. A light went on inside. The door opened just a crack and I caught a brief glimpse of a young girl, who slammed the door again immediately, a frightened expression on her face.

I knocked a second time, and after a couple of minutes the farmer's wife asked through the closed door, "Who are you? What do you want, in the middle of the night?"

"Is this the house of the Pichlerbauer?"

"Yes, it is," she answered.

"I'm Baroness von Krüdener's brother. Is she here? I've just come back from Russia."

The door slowly opened, and the farmer's wife, with the girl peeping from behind her shoulder, said only, "Oh dear, oh my goodness."

She gestured at me to come in. Wordlessly we climbed the wooden stairs to the second floor. She knocked on a door and said, "Frau Baronin, there's someone here who wants to see you."

"Yes," I heard my sister's voice answer.

The door opened upon a large but cozy room. At the sight of me, my sister's eyes widened, and she backed up a few steps involuntarily. Somewhat behind her, near the blue-tiled stove, stood my mother. For a few seconds no one moved or said a word, then both of them started rushing toward me to embrace me. I held up my hands to ward them off, pointing to my clothing. None of us could speak. They must have understood, because, still silently, they lifted off the heavy Russian coat and spread it on the floor. Then they threw one piece of clothing after the other on top of it, until I was standing naked in front of them.

Still without saying a word, my mother dragged over a large wooden tub full of water and began to wash my bony body from top to bottom with soap and warm water. As overcome as I was by emotion and exhaustion, I was still shocked to see how old my mother had become in just three years. My sister meanwhile took the bundle of my clothing back down the stairs and burned it outside.

Then they pulled a long white linen nightshirt over my

head, laid me on a large, soft bed, and covered me with an eiderdown comforter. Everything was white and soft and clean, and I was shaking uncontrollably. My mother fed me warm farina pudding with a spoon while the tears rolled down my cheeks. I pulled the quilt over my head and sobbed like a little child.

AUTHOR'S NOTE
GLOSSARY
ABOUT THE TRANSLATOR

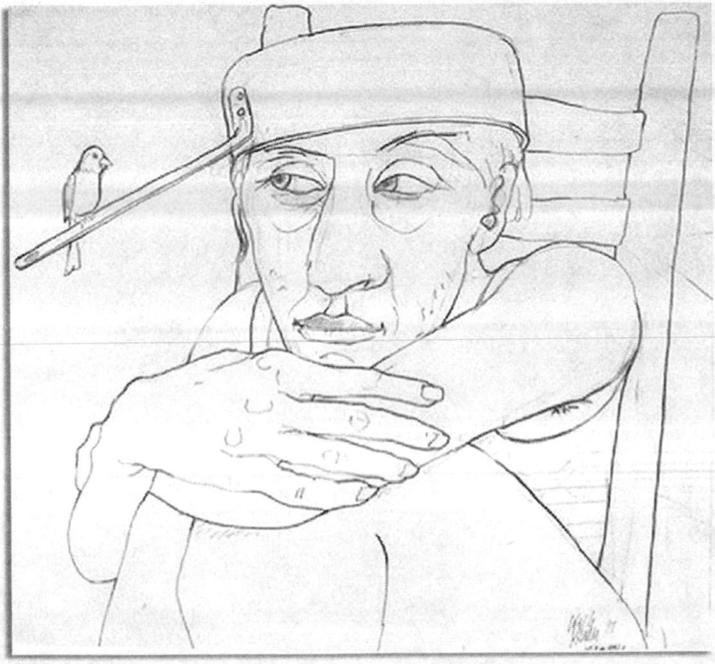

Man with bird, 1989

AUTHOR'S NOTE

My mother carefully saved and numbered each letter and note I sent from the trenches of the Eastern Front. Many of these were scribbled in pencil on tiny salvaged scraps of paper. In the chaos of the war, when often all that remained was our rifles and the clothes on our backs, it was impossible to preserve her letters to me.

After returning home, and following a two-year stay in a tuberculosis sanatorium, I began to paint, and eventually became a professional artist. I left Europe in 1966, moving to New York and California before settling for the past thirty years in Mexico. The letters from Russia always accompanied me. Though I sometimes shared humorous or exciting events from the war years, the letters themselves were never reopened or read. I was certain I would only be embarrassed by the ramblings and complaints of a frightened nineteen-year-old.

One afternoon in February 1984, my wife, Phyllis, and I were discussing that evening's activity. Each month a group got together and read from their latest literary efforts. Phyllis said she had nothing prepared, but that it didn't really matter. I suddenly realized that the date was almost exactly forty years after those terrible frozen days of my first Russian winter.

I looked up and read what I had written on three days in February 1944. Phyllis quickly translated the letters, and we took the versions in both languages to the party. When it was our turn, I began to read a letter in the original German and then faded into the background while Phyllis took over, reading the English translation. We felt the strong impact our presentation had made on those present, mostly artists and retirees living in beautiful, balmy Mexico, people who were free to follow their passions and whims every day of the year. The contrast was powerful.

Next, I reread all of my letters for the first time and found they were quite different from what I had imagined. Surprised at the humor and the honesty, I began to imagine a book about my war experiences that could set the record straight. Mine would be a very different story from those in the movies. I had always complained about war films, with their phony uniforms and backward swastikas. Worst of all, they told a tale that was very different from anything I had experienced. An antiwar book featuring a nonhero might even be helpful for upcoming generations of young men faced with other wars.

When I began writing, long-forgotten events, including the minutest details, poured out from a deeply buried source. I stopped painting and did nothing but write until the book was completed. In the process I recognized that my true reason for writing had been to heal myself. Even after ten years of painting sad-faced men and harlequins, I still hadn't completely dealt with the guilt and shame of the war years. Writing this book gave me much-needed clarity and helped me to deal with emotions I had never permitted myself to feel.

During the writing of this book, another Austrian artist told me that his experience was similar to mine, since he also had a Jewish grandmother. As far as I knew we were perhaps the only two one-quarter Jews who had been drafted. During the war I met no other soldiers of Jewish extraction, though I never hid my own background.

It wasn't until the recent publication of Bryan Mark Rigg's heavily researched book *Hitler's Jewish Soldiers* that I learned that there were many thousands of full, one-half, and one-quarter Jews in the German Wehrmacht. I'm sure that of those who survived, each must have had a unique and moving tale to tell. I have encountered no other autobiography, however, by one of these soldiers.

My mother's anti-Hitler involvement was terribly dangerous, and I worried about her after I went to the front. Obviously there was no way she could either comfort me or keep me informed, if she was to preserve her safety. After I was captured and all letters stopped, I wasn't to know for a long time if she had even survived.

After the war, I was to learn very little from my mother regarding the Jews in our attic and how that story concluded. She never wanted to talk about it, and the few times I asked her directly, she started to cry. I did know that Haday hadn't made it, since I never saw her again, and she had been a family friend.

A few others obviously hadn't gotten away, because a number of valuable art objects belonging to them remained in our apartment and were never reclaimed. Some did make it successfully to England or America and sent my mother word. These had no desire ever to return to Vienna, preferring that this period of their lives be permanently erased from memory.

In one of the postwar years, a nearby coal merchant delivered a load of heating materials sufficient to heat our apartment for the entire winter. He said someone outside the country who preferred to remain anonymous had paid for it. I was happy to believe the coal was a gift from another Jewish couple who had successfully escaped.

My parents divorced after the war, and I remained particularly close to my mother. She did achieve that full and happy life that she had assured me she would enjoy, even were I not to return from Russia. She would have loved being an artist herself, but the circumstances of her life, including two world wars, weren't to permit this. Probably that's why she especially enjoyed being in the company of the young artists who were around our apartment after the war.

When Russian tanks occupied Hungary in 1956, thousands of Hungarians came streaming over the Austrian border with no more than the clothing on their backs. Many slept on the streets of Vienna the first few nights, but my mother was soon again in her element. She sprang into action, mobilizing family and friends to take in as many refugees as possible.

Beatrix Rauch died at eighty-one in 1970, and up until her death she continued to study important books by physicists, poets, and philosophers. She was a fine pianist, and music always remained a major pleasure in her life.

GLOSSARY OF GERMAN WORDS

Anschluss	annexation of Austria to Germany, in 1938
Bussis	kisses
Cremeschnitten	Napoleon-type pastry
Freies Deutschland	"Free Germany," German newspaper published in Russia
Funkeigenheiten	abbreviations of wireless operators' names
Funker	telegraphist
Grüss Gott	"Greet God," typical Austrian greeting
Hauptmann	captain
Jawohl	affirmative, yes
Komissbrot	rye bread
Lebkuchen	hard gingerbread, a Christmas favorite
Mensch	"person" or "man," used as a slang term of address
Mischlinge	Hitler's term for persons one-quarter or one-half Jewish
Mutti, Mui	mother
Naschmarkt	famous street market in Vienna
Obergefreiter	lance corporal
Oberleutnant	lieutenant
Oberstleutnant	lieutenant colonel
Papi, Papschi	father
Pfennige	smallest German coins
Pioniere	Army Corps of Engineers

Rollbahn . . . . wide military road
Schnapps . . . . brandy
Schnitzel . . . . thin, breaded cutlet, normally of veal
Schütz . . . . private
SS . . . . *Schutzstaffel* (protective squadron); paramilitary organization that was a major component of the Nazi party
Tante . . . . aunt
Unteroffizier . . . . . . sergeant
Vaterland . . . . fatherland
Volk . . . . people, nation
Waffen-SS . . . . elite police and military units of the *Schutzstaffel*
Wehrmacht . . . . army

GLOSSARY OF RUSSIAN/UKRAINIAN WORDS

arestant	prisoner
banki	glass jars used in a medical procedure that draws blood to surface of skin for therapeutic purposes
Boche moi	Oh my God!
Gospodi	O Lord!
karascho	good
kasha	buckwheat groats cooked in water
kolchos	barn
machorka	crude tobacco substitute
Ponimaesch?	Do you understand?

ABOUT THE TRANSLATOR

Phyllis Rauch grew up in Ohio and received her bachelor's degree in English at Bowling Green State University and her master's degree in library science at the University of Michigan at Ann Arbor. She studied German at the Goethe Institute in Rothenburg ob der Tauber and then worked at German libraries, including the Internationale Kinderbibliothek in Munich and the Amerika Gedenkbibliothek in Berlin. She met Georg Rauch in Vienna in 1965 and they were married the following year.

Fluent in Spanish as well as German, Phyllis has written extensively in Mexico for English-language magazines, newspapers, and Web sites and has also worked as a Spanish-to-English translator. As an innkeeper in central Mexico, she welcomes visitors to her home and to Georg's art studio (www.losdosmexico.com and www.georgrauch.com).

Unlikely Warrior, Phyllis's first book-length translation, has been a labor of love.